ASCENT
CENTER FOR TECHNICAL KNOWLEDGE

CATIA V5-6R2017:
Generative Drafting (ANSI)

Learning Guide
1ˢᵗ Edition

ASCENT - Center for Technical Knowledge®
CATIA V5-6R2017: Generative Drafting (ANSI)
1st Edition

Prepared and produced by:

ASCENT Center for Technical Knowledge
630 Peter Jefferson Parkway, Suite 175
Charlottesville, VA 22911

866-527-2368
www.ASCENTed.com

Lead Contributor: Scott Hendren

ASCENT - Center for Technical Knowledge is a division of Rand Worldwide, Inc., providing custom developed knowledge products and services for leading engineering software applications. ASCENT is focused on specializing in the creation of education programs that incorporate the best of classroom learning and technology-based training offerings.

We welcome any comments you may have regarding this learning guide, or any of our products. To contact us please email: feedback@ASCENTed.com.

Contents

Preface

The *CATIA V5-6R2017: Generative Drafting* learning guide enables you to use the generative capabilities of CATIA V5 to create an ANSI drawing from a 3D solid Part. This course is appropriate for new CATIA V5 users.

Topics Covered:

- Start a generative drawing

- Define the main views

- Define section views and cuts

- Define secondary views: detail, clipping, broken, breakout, auxiliary, isometric and unfolded views

- Edit a view and sheet properties

- Add sheets to a drawing

- Reposition views

- Modify section, detail and auxiliary profiles

- Modify section, detail and auxiliary graphical definitions

- Modify section hatching representations

- Create generative dimensions and tolerances

- Generate assembly drawings

- Create annotations and drawing tables

- Create balloons

- Check links to a solid 3D part and update a drawing

- Add a title block

- Print the drawing

- Set drafting options

Note on Software Setup

This learning guide assumes a standard installation of the software using the default preferences during installation. Lectures and practices use the standard software templates and default options for the Content Libraries.

This guide was developed against CATIA V5-6R2017, Service Pack 1.

Lead Contributor: Scott Hendren

Scott Hendren has been a trainer and curriculum developer in the PLM industry for over 20 years, with experience on multiple CAD systems, including Pro/ENGINEER, Creo Parametric, and CATIA. Trained in Instructional Design, Scott uses his skills to develop instructor-led and web-based training products.

Scott has held training and development positions with several high profile PLM companies, and has been with the Ascent team since 2013.

Scott holds a Bachelor of Mechanical Engineering Degree as well as a Bachelor of Science in Mathematics from Dalhousie University, Nova Scotia, Canada.

Scott Hendren has been the Lead Contributor for *CATIA: Generative Drafting (ANSI)* since 2013.

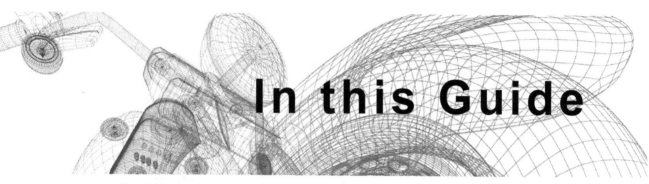

In this Guide

The following images highlight some of the features that can be found in this Learning Guide.

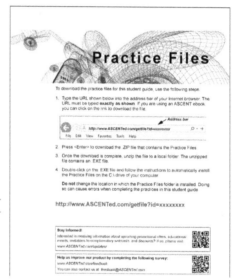

Practice Files

The Practice Files page tells you how to download and install the practice files that are provided with this learning guide.

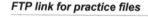
FTP link for practice files

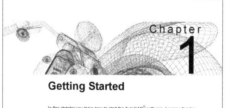

Chapters

Each chapter begins with a brief introduction and a list of the chapter's Learning Objectives.

Learning Objectives for the chapter

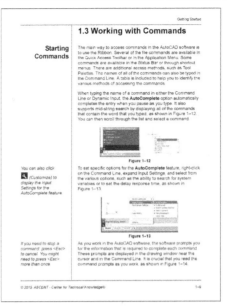

Instructional Content

Each chapter is split into a series of sections of instructional content on specific topics. These lectures include the descriptions, step-by-step procedures, figures, hints, and information you need to achieve the chapter's Learning Objectives.

Side notes

Side notes are hints or additional information for the current topic.

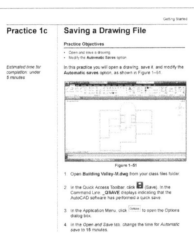

Practice Objectives

Practices

Practices enable you to use the software to perform a hands-on review of a topic.

Some practices require you to use prepared practice files, which can be downloaded from the link found on the Practice Files page.

Practice Files

To download the practice files for this learning guide, use the following steps:

1. Type the URL shown below into the address bar of your Internet browser. The URL must be typed **exactly as shown**. If you are using an ASCENT ebook, you can click on the link to download the file.

Address bar

http://www.ASCENTed.com/getfile?id=melopsittacus

File   Edit   View   Favorites   Tools   Help

2. Press <Enter> to download the .ZIP file that contains the Practice Files.

3. Once the download is complete, unzip the file to a local folder. The unzipped file contains an .EXE file.

4. Double-click on the .EXE file and follow the instructions to automatically install the Practice Files on the C:\ drive of your computer.

   Do not change the location in which the Practice Files folder is installed. Doing so can cause errors when completing the practices in this learning guide.

http://www.ASCENTed.com/getfile?id=melopsittacus

Stay Informed!

Interested in receiving information about upcoming promotional offers, educational events, invitations to complimentary webcasts, and discounts? If so, please visit:

www.ASCENTed.com/updates/

Help us improve our product by completing the following survey:

www.ASCENTed.com/feedback

You can also contact us at: *feedback@ASCENTed.com*

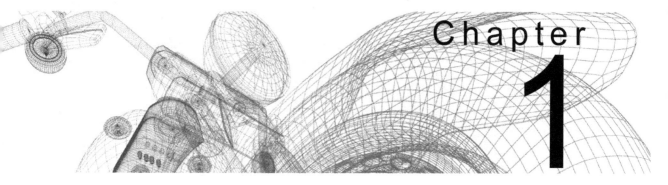

Generative Drafting Workbench

The Generative Drafting workbench is used to create 2D drawings from 3D models that are created in the Part Design and Assembly Design workbenches. This chapter introduces the workbench interface and outlines the process that can be used to create simple and complex drawings.

Learning Objectives in this Chapter

- Understand the Generative Drafting process.
- Learn how to create a drawing.
- Recognize elements of the Generative Drafting user interface.
- Use the various view types.
- Create Section Views/Cuts.
- Create a manual view.
- Use the View Creation wizard.
- Add additional sheets to a drawing.
- Understand file associations.

1.1 Generative Drafting Process

To complete a production drawing, several steps must be performed as shown in Figure 1–1.

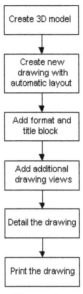

Figure 1–1

The creation of the 3D model is covered in the *Introduction to Modeling*, *Advanced Part Design,* and *Advanced Assembly Design & Management* courses. This course assumes that you are either familiar with the creation of 3D geometry or are not responsible for its creation.

In the Generative Drafting workbench, the geometry of each view is linked to the 3D model. This permits changes to the 3D model to drive the drawing and ensures that you are always working with the latest version of the 3D geometry.

With the 3D geometry in session, you are ready to move to the next step of creating a new drawing.

1.2 Create a Drawing

You can access the Generative Drafting workbench by opening an existing drawing file (*.CATDrawing) or creating a new drawing.

General Steps

Use the following steps to create a new drawing:

1. Open the 3D model.
2. Initiate drawing creation.
3. Modify parameters of the drawing.

Step 1 - Open the 3D model.

You should always create the 3D model before beginning any 2D work when working in the Generative Drafting environment. The part or assembly model should be open in CATIA, as shown in Figure 1–2, in preparation for drawing creation.

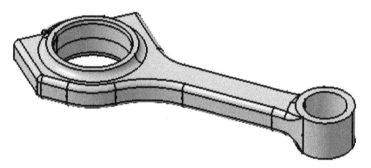

Figure 1–2

Step 2 - Initiate drawing creation.

Enter the Drafting workbench by selecting **Start>Mechanical Design>Drafting** with the model active. The New Drawing Creation dialog box opens as shown in Figure 1–3.

*A new drawing can also be created by selecting **File>New>Drawing**. However, this method does not permit you to select an automatic layout.*

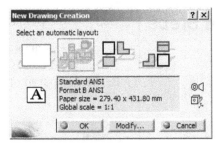

Figure 1–3

Select the predefined layout that applies. The **Automatic Layout** options are described as follows:

Option	Description
(Empty Sheet)	No views are added to the drawing. The new drawing consists of an empty sheet.
(All Views)	Seven views are automatically added to the drawing: Front, Back, Top, Bottom, Right, Left, and Isometric.
(Front, Bottom, and Right)	Three views are automatically added to the drawing: Front, Bottom, and Right.
(Front, Top, and Left)	Three views are automatically added to the drawing: Front, Top, and Left.

Step 3 - Modify parameters of the drawing.

The default settings for the drawing parameters are listed at the bottom of the New Drawing Creation dialog box, as shown in Figure 1–4.

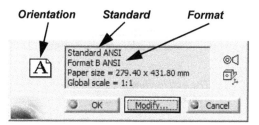

Figure 1–4

How To: Change These Parameters

1. Click **Modify** to change the settings. The New Drawing dialog box opens as shown in Figure 1–5.

Figure 1–5

2. Select the drawing standard (e.g., ANSI, ISO, JIS, etc.).
3. Select the drawing sheet style and orientation (as required).
4. Click **OK** in the New Drawing dialog box to complete the modifications.

Once you are ready to create the drawing, click **OK** in the New Drawing Creation dialog box. The drawing displays as shown in Figure 1–6. The active view displays with a red border.

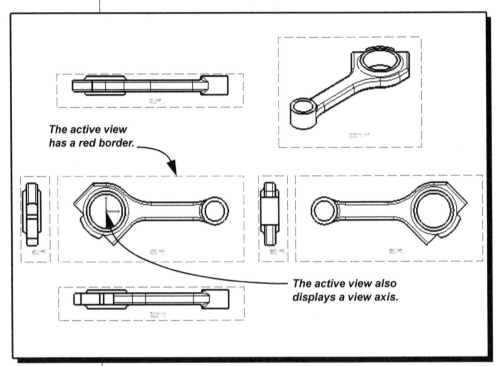

The active view has a red border.

The active view also displays a view axis.

Figure 1–6

1.3 User Interface

The user interface of the Generative Drafting workbench displays as shown in Figure 1–7.

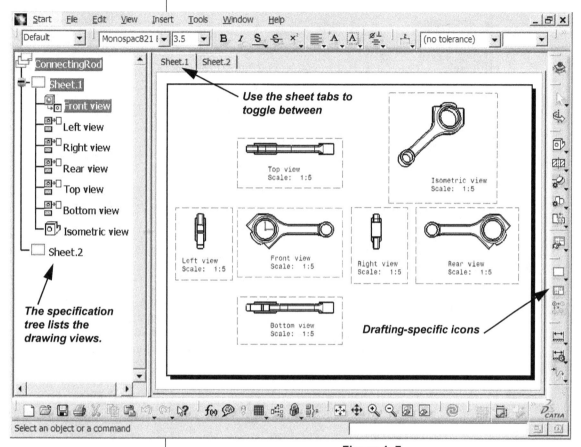

Figure 1–7

Active View

All actions are performed in the Active view. For example, the view geometry is projected from the Active view when a Projection view is created.

The Active view is highlighted in the specification tree and also indicated by the color of its view border, as shown in Figure 1–8. The Active view has a red border, while all other views have a blue border. To set the Active view, double-click on the view border or the view name in the specification tree.

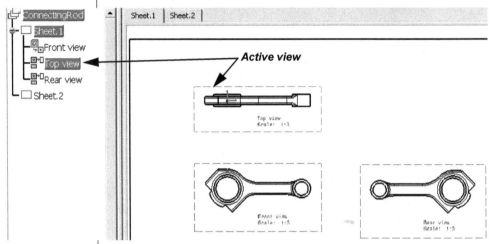

Figure 1–8

Toolbars

The Generative Drafting workbench has a unique set of Drafting-specific toolbar icons, as shown in Figure 1–7. The toolbars can be divided into three different areas of functionality: View Creation, Dimensioning, and Annotation. These toolbars are shown in Figure 1–9 and discussed below.

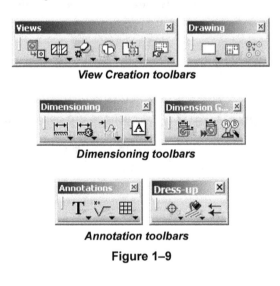

View Creation toolbars

Dimensioning toolbars

Annotation toolbars

Figure 1–9

Toolbar	Features Provided
Views	Create front, projection, isometric, section, detail, clipping, and broken view types. Open the View Creation Wizard.
Drawing	Create new sheets, views, and 2D components.
Dimensioning	Create dimensions and datum features and re-route dimensions manually.
Dimension G...	Create dimensions and balloons automatically and semi-automatically.
Annotations	Insert text, symbols, and tables.
Dress-up	Create drafting features, such as center lines, axis lines, area fills, and arrows.

Tile Horizontally

The geometry of a generative drafting file is always driven from the 3D geometry of the model. You need to switch between the drawing and model window frequently to locate views and build your drawing. Horizontally tiling the windows enables you to quickly access either window at the same time. You can also use <Ctrl> + <Tab> to toggle between the drawing and 3D model.

Select **Window>Tile Horizontally** to horizontally tile your windows. The drawing and model windows display as shown in Figure 1–10. Maximize the drawing window to switch back to a full view of the drawing.

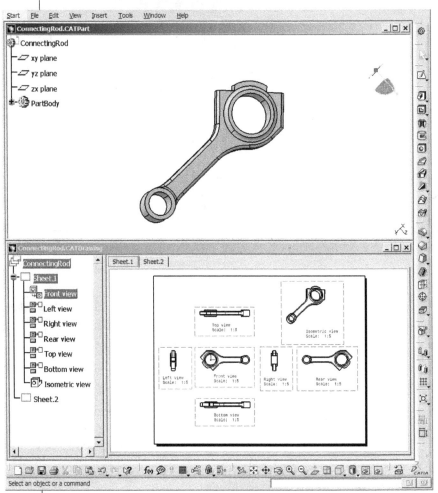

Figure 1–10

1.4 View Types

The Views toolbar enables you to create a variety of different types of drawing views. The Views toolbar is shown in Figure 1–11.

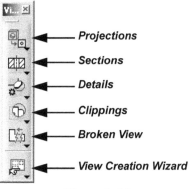

Figure 1–11

Projections

Use the Projection View toolbar to create a view of the model based on its projection from a parent view. The types of views that can be created using the Projection View toolbar are shown in Figure 1–12.

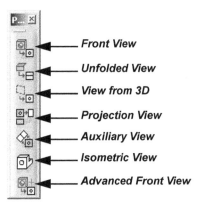

Figure 1–12

Front View

The Front view is also known as the main view, as shown in Figure 1–13. It is the parent to any related projection, auxiliary, and detail views that reference it.

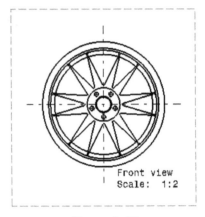

Front view
Scale: 1:2

Figure 1–13

Unfolded View

The Unfolded view displays the flat pattern of a sheet metal model. The drawing view automatically displays the bend axes and bend limits of the sheet metal part, as shown in Figure 1–14.

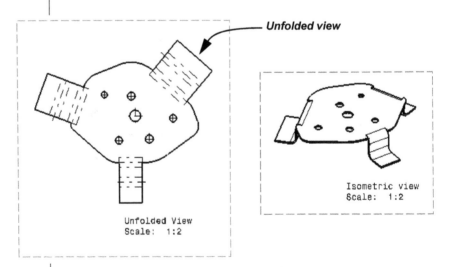

Unfolded view

Unfolded View
Scale: 1:2

Isometric view
Scale: 1:2

Figure 1–14

View from 3D

The View from 3D view displays a saved view from a model that was generated using the Functional Tolerancing and Annotation workbench. CATIA creates a view based on the selected annotation plane. All geometric dimensions and tolerances added to the annotation plane are automatically displayed in the new view.

Projection View

The Projection view projects a view from the active view. This creates views, such as top, right, left, and bottom. It is placed by selecting a location on the screen. The system applies the correct view name based on its position to the Front view. A Projection view maintains the same scale value as its parent view, as shown in Figure 1–15.

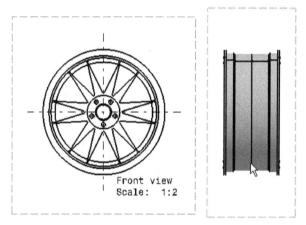

Front view
Scale: 1:2

Figure 1–15

Auxiliary View

An Auxiliary view projects a view normal to a reference plane, edge, or axis of the active view, as shown in Figure 1–16. Auxiliary views can be created by referencing a reference plane, edge, or axis from the active view.

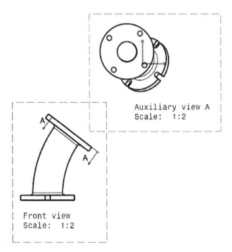

Auxiliary view A
Scale: 1:2

Front view
Scale: 1:2

Figure 1–16

Isometric View

An Isometric view is used as a reference view, as shown in Figure 1–17, and is typically set at a smaller scale. CATIA creates the view based on the current model orientation when the reference face is selected from the 3D model.

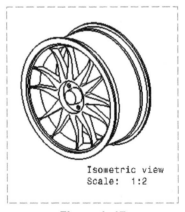

Isometric view
Scale: 1:2

Figure 1–17

Advanced Front View

The Advanced Front view is the same as the Front view and also enables you to specify the name and scale, as shown in Figure 1–18.

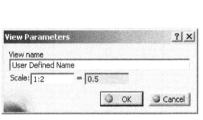

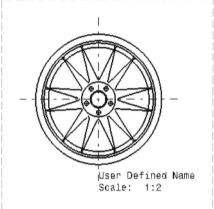

Figure 1–18

Sections

Once a view of the model is created using the Projections toolbar, you can begin to create new views to display specific sections of the model. Section views must be created as separate views. An existing view cannot be modified to become a section view.

Use the icons in the Sections toolbar to create section views, as shown in Figure 1–19.

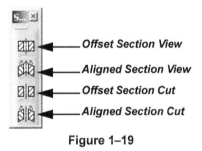

Offset Section View

Aligned Section View

Offset Section Cut

Aligned Section Cut

Figure 1–19

Offset Section View

The Offset section view creates a section and displays all of the edges that are behind the cutting plane. You can create this view as planar (as shown in Figure 1–20) or as a sketched cutting plane (as shown in Figure 1–21).

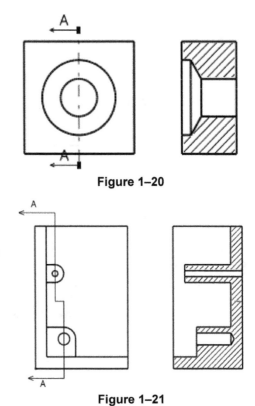

Figure 1–20

Figure 1–21

Aligned Section View

The Aligned section view unfolds the view until it is parallel to the screen, as shown in Figure 1–22.

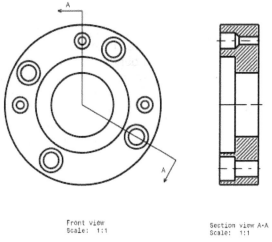

Front view
Scale: 1:1

Section view A·A
Scale: 1:1

Figure 1–22

Offset Section Cut View

The Offset Section Cut view creates a section that only displays the material in the cutting plane, as shown in Figure 1–23. Edges behind the cutting plane are hidden.

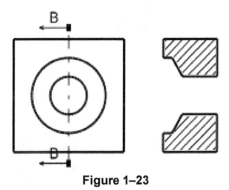

Figure 1–23

Aligned Section Cut View

The Aligned Section Cut view unfolds the view until it is parallel to the screen, but only displays material that is in the cutting plane. Edges behind the cutting plane are hidden.

Details

The Detail view creates a scaled view that focuses on a specific area of an existing view. The Detail view is created by defining a boundary on an existing view that encloses the geometry to be represented and selecting a location in which to place the view. The system automatically assigns a label identifying the scale value and view name of the Detail view. The orientation of this view corresponds to its parent view. The types of views that can be created using the Details toolbar are shown in Figure 1–24.

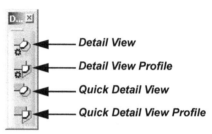

Figure 1–24

Detail View

Define the boundary of the Detail view by sketching a circle in the parent view. The view is generated by calculating a boolean cut from the 3D model geometry. An example of a Detail view is shown in Figure 1–25.

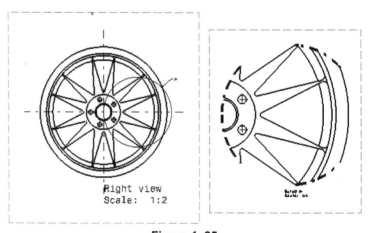

Right view
Scale: 1:2

Figure 1–25

Detail View Profile

Define the boundary of the Detail view profile by sketching a closed chain of lines in the parent view. This enables the view to remove any unwanted geometry from the parent view by sketching around it. An example of a Detail view profile is shown in Figure 1–26.

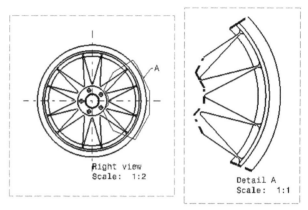

Figure 1–26

Quick Detail View/Quick Detail View Profile

These views are identical to the Detail View and Detail View Profile except that the view is generated from the 2D geometry of the parent view rather than the 3D model. This enables a view that is still associative to the 3D model to be generated quickly. The display properties of the view are different. For example, the line display of the view cannot be altered.

Clipping View

A Clipping view simplifies an existing view. It displays a focused area by removing the geometry outside the circle or profile boundary. You must sketch the boundary in the active view. The types of views that can be created using the Clippings toolbar are shown in Figure 1–27.

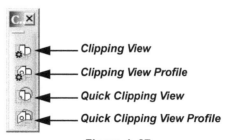

Figure 1–27

A clipping view is different from a detail view in that a new view is not created. The clipping view modifies an existing view by removing geometry from the view.

Similar to a Detail view, a Clipping view defines the view boundary using a sketched circle, while the Clipping View Profile defines the view boundary using a closed chain of lines. Figure 1–28 shows a Front Projection view that has been clipped using a circular boundary.

A Clipped view can be restored to a regular view by right-clicking on the view and selecting ＊object>Unclip, where ＊ is the view name.

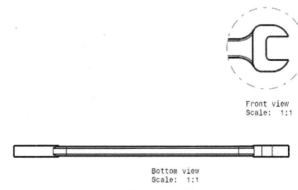

```
Front view
Scale:  1:1
```

```
Bottom view
Scale:  1:1
```

Figure 1–28

Break Views

The Break view toolbar enables you to remove view geometry from within a sketched area on an existing view. The types of view breaks that can be created using the Break view toolbar are displayed in Figure 1–29.

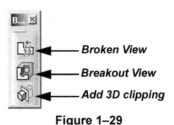

Broken View
Breakout View
Add 3D clipping

Figure 1–29

Broken View

A Broken view removes the view geometry between two break lines and only displays the important features of a model, as shown in Figure 1–30.

A Broken view can be restored to a regular view by right-clicking on the view and selecting * view object>Unbreak, where * is the view name.

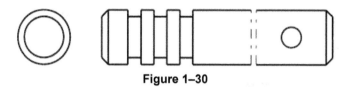

Figure 1–30

Breakout

The Breakout view displays a section in a sketched area. The system automatically adds the rough edges to your sketched area, as shown in Figure 1–31.

A Breakout view can be restored to a regular view by right-clicking on the view and selecting * view object>Remove Breakout, where * is the view name.

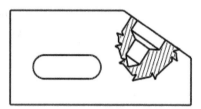

Figure 1–31

1.5 Section Views/Cuts

The three methods used to create section views are as follows:

- Create a Section view/cut

- Create a Profile in 3D

- Use Planes

Create a Section View/Cut

The Section view/cut method involves sketching the section profile on the parent drawing view.

How To: Create a Section View

1. Activate the parent view and click 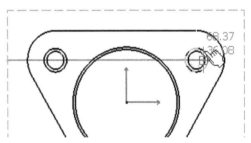 (Offset Section View).
2. Define the starting point of the profile.
3. Create the profile. While creating your profile, you can snap to existing geometry in the view. For example, to place a section through the center of a hole, select its edge, as shown in Figure 1–32.

Figure 1–32

Additionally, you can use the Tools Palette toolbar. You can specify four types of constraints, as shown in Figure 1–33.

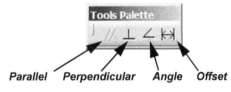

Parallel   Perpendicular   Angle   Offset

Figure 1–33

For example, to keep the profile perpendicular to one of the edges of the model, click ⊥ (Perpendicular). Then select the edge in the view, as shown in Figure 1–34.

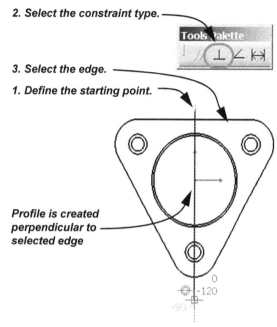

2. Select the constraint type.

3. Select the edge.

1. Define the starting point.

Profile is created perpendicular to selected edge

Figure 1–34

4. To finish the profile creation, double-click at the end of your profile. Then place the view in an appropriate location on the drawing.

Create a Profile in 3D

Positioned sketches are considered a best practice. They ensure more robust models with predictable results.

How To: Create a Section View/Cut Using the Profile in 3D Method

1. Create a sketch in the 3D part.
2. Draw the approximate shape of the required cutting line in Sketcher.
3. Constrain the profile to the geometry through which the section must cut, as shown in Figure 1–35.

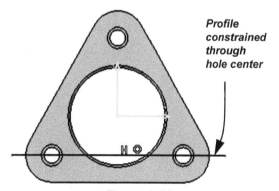

Profile constrained through hole center

Figure 1–35

4. Exit the sketch.
5. Activate the drawing.
6. Ensure that the parent view for the section is activated.
7. In the Sections toolbar, click the appropriate icon. For

   example, click (Offset Section View) to create an offset section view.
8. Activate the 3D model and select the sketch.
9. Activate the drawing and select a location for the view. The section profile is now linked to the 3D geometry and changes if the cutting sketch is changed.

You can only select 3D profiles that are appropriate for the type of view selected.

Use Planes

Reference planes can also be selected from the 3D model to define a section view. When this is done, the position of the reference plane determines the cut location on the part. Modifications to the reference plane update in the section view.

To use a plane to define a section cut, select the appropriate icon in the Sections toolbar. Activate the 3D model and select the reference plane in the model or specification tree.

1.6 Create a Manual View

The creation of drawing views is the first step in creating a drawing. View creation takes a 2D view from the 3D model and displays it on the drawing. You can use the following two methods of view creation when using the Generative Drafting workbench: Manual view creation or View Wizard.

Drawing views can be created once a 3D model has been opened and a new drawing document has been created.

General Steps

Use the following general steps to manually create drawing views:

1. Create a Front view.
2. Orient the view.
3. Create additional views.

Step 1 - Create a Front view.

Click ⬚ (Front View) to create a Front view.

Step 2 - Orient the view.

Activate the 3D model window and select a planar reference, as shown in Figure 1–36. A preview of the drawing view displays in the bottom, right corner of the window.

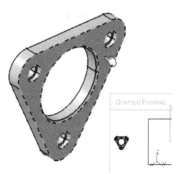

Figure 1–36

The view orientation compass enables you to rotate and flip the Front view until the required orientation has been achieved, as shown in Figure 1–37.

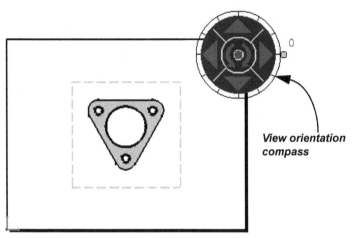

View orientation compass

Figure 1–37

The view compass functionality is shown in Figure 1–38.

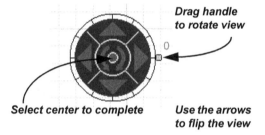

Drag handle to rotate view

Select center to complete

Use the arrows to flip the view

Figure 1–38

Use the shortcut menu to change the compass properties, as shown in Figure 1–39 (right-click on the green rotate handle).

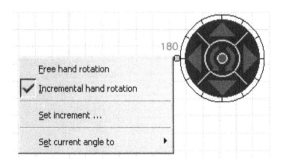

Figure 1–39

Orient the view using the compass. When you reach the required view orientation, select the center of the compass or select anywhere on the drawing sheet to complete the view definition. The completed view definition displays as shown in Figure 1–40.

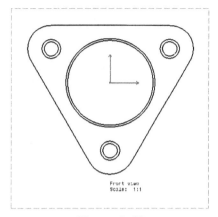

Figure 1–40

Step 3 - Create additional views.

Use the View toolbar to create additional views as required. The View toolbar is shown in Figure 1–41.

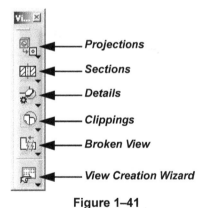

Figure 1–41

1.7 View Creation Wizard

The View Creation Wizard can be used to quickly customize the view layout.

To access the View Creation Wizard, ensure that the 3D model is open in a CATIA window and click 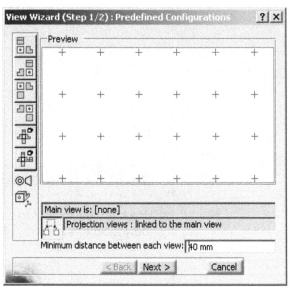 (View Creation Wizard) in the Views toolbar. The View Wizard dialog box opens as shown in Figure 1–42.

Figure 1–42

1.8 Use the View Creation Wizard

General Steps

Use the following steps to customize the view layout using the View Creation Wizard:

1. Select a predefined configuration.
2. Arrange the configuration.
3. Orient the drawing views.
4. Generate the views.

Step 1 - Select a predefined configuration.

Select the required view layout from the icons on the left side of the dialog box. Drag the layout to a location on the sheet, as shown in Figure 1–43.

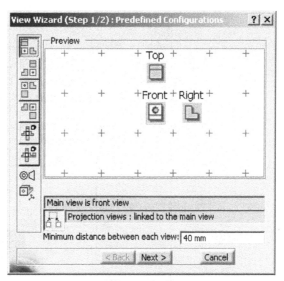

Figure 1–43

Toggle ⌞⌝ (Views Link) to unlink the views, if required. Keeping a link with projection views is recommended. It ensures that any linked views are moved to the new location if the parent view is moved. Click **Next** to proceed to the next step.

Step 2 - Arrange the configuration.

Select the icons on the left side of the dialog box to add
additional views to the drawing, as shown in Figure 1–44.

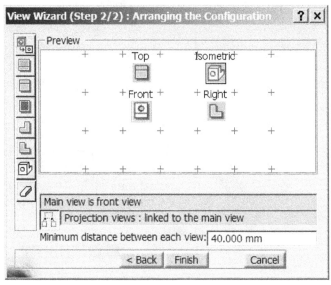

Figure 1–44

Delete unwanted views by right-clicking on a view and selecting
Delete, as shown in Figure 1–45.

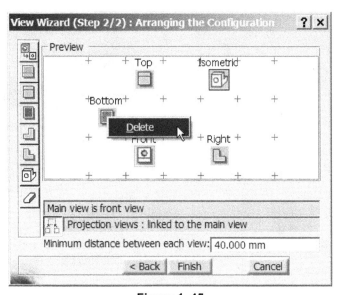

Figure 1–45

Enter the minimum distance between views in the field at the bottom of the dialog box. Note that the main view is specified as the Front view in the View Wizard dialog box. Click **Finish** to complete the operation.

Step 3 - Orient the drawing views.

As the model is already open in a second window, select **Window>Tile Horizontally** to display both the drawing and the model at the same time. Activate the model window and select a surface on the model to determine the orientation of the Front view, as shown in Figure 1–46.

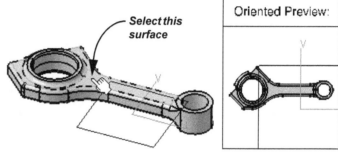

Figure 1–46

Step 4 - Generate the views.

Reorient the views as required using the compass, as shown in Figure 1–47.

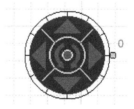

Figure 1–47

Generate the views by selecting anywhere on the sheet.

1.9 Adding an Additional Sheet

A CATDrawing file can contain more than one sheet. The sheets are displayed in the specification tree and along the top of the drawing window as tabs. To switch between sheets, either double-click on the sheet in the tree or select the tab.

Use one of the following methods to add a new sheet:

- Click 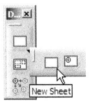 (New Sheet) in the Drawing toolbar, as shown in Figure 1–48.

- Select **Insert>Drawing>Sheets>New Sheet**.

Figure 1–48

Sheet Properties

To display the sheet properties, right-click on the sheet name in the specification tree and select **Properties**. The Properties dialog box opens as shown in Figure 1–49.

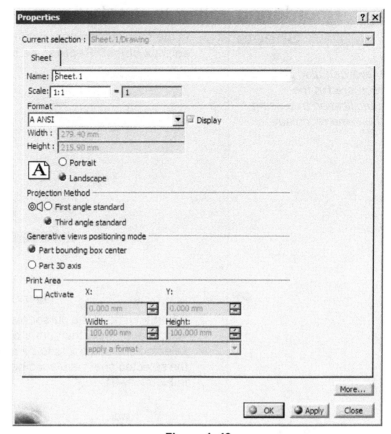

Figure 1–49

The following sheet properties can be modified:

- Sheet name and scale

- Sheet size and orientation

- Projection method (first or third angle)

- View positioning in the frame (geometric center or part axis)

- Print area

Reordering Sheets

Views can also be reordered in the specification tree using the same technique.

How To: Reorder Sheets

1. In the specification tree, right-click on the sheet name and select **x object>Reorder**, as shown in Figure 1–50.

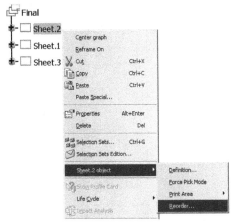

Figure 1–50

2. When you move the cursor over the sheets in the specification tree, the cursor changes to indicate where the selected sheet is going to be placed in the tree. By default, the selected sheet is placed below the target sheet, as shown in Figure 1–51.

Press and hold <Ctrl> to place the selected sheets above the target sheet. The cursor changes to  .

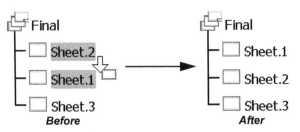

Figure 1–51

Limitations

Reordering has the following limitations:

- Sheets and views cannot be reordered at the same time.

- Sheets can only be reordered under their parent drawing.

- Views can only be reordered under their parent sheet.

- Detail sheets can only be placed after regular sheets.

1.10 File Associations

Since the views of a drawing depend on the 3D model geometry, a link is established between the model and drawing when drawing views are created. CATIA must be able to load the 3D geometry from the associated CATPart or CATProduct file for the drawing views to update.

The associated model must be moved with the drawing if it is moved. Similarly, the associated model must be saved when the drawing is saved. A warning box opens if a drawing is saved and the linked model is not saved with it, as shown in Figure 1–52. Select **File>Save Management** to ensure that all associated models are saved with the drawing file.

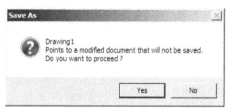

Figure 1–52

Restoring Links

The specification tree displays with a broken link icon when a drawing is opened without its linked document, as shown in Figure 1–53. The symbols indicate that the links to the referenced document are broken.

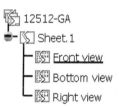

Figure 1–53

At this point, the views of the drawing are displayed and you can modify the properties of the views. However, you cannot add new views or add detail to existing views until the link to the model has been re-established.

You can verify the links for a drawing by selecting **Edit>Links**. The Links dialog box opens, as shown in Figure 1–54.

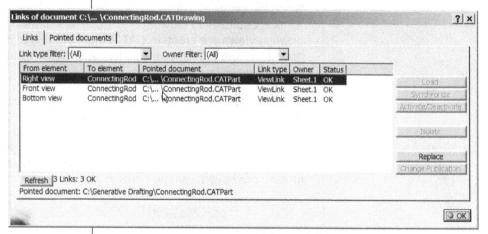

Figure 1–54

The *Links* tab displays a status for each view on the drawing. Use the *Pointed documents* tab to locate or replace the missing linked documents and bring them into session to update the drawing geometry. The *Pointed documents* tab is shown in Figure 1–55.

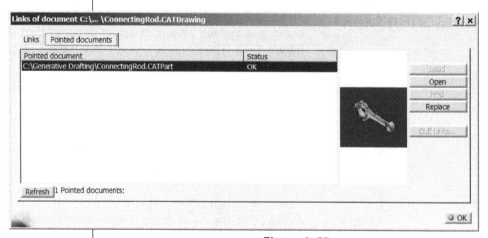

Figure 1–55

Practice 1a

Create a Part Drawing

Practice Objectives

- Create a part drawing.
- Create Front, Projection, Detail, and Isometric views.
- Modify page properties and drawing options.

In this practice, you will create a part drawing for **ExhaustFlange.CATPart**.

Task 1 - Open a part file.

1. Select **File>Open** and select **ExhaustFlange.CATPart** in the *Exhaust Manifold* directory. The 3D model displays as shown in Figure 1–56.

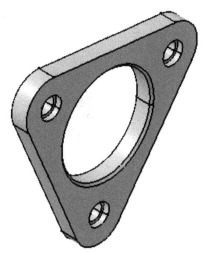

Figure 1–56

Task 2 - Create a drawing.

1. Select **File>New**. In the New dialog box, in the List of Types, select **Drawing**.

2. Click **OK**. The New Drawing dialog box opens.

3. For the *Standard*, enter **ANSI** and for the *Sheet Style*, select **C ANSI**, as shown in Figure 1–57.

Figure 1–57

4. Click **OK**. An empty sheet displays.

Task 3 - Create a Front view.

1. In the Projections toolbar, click ⬛ (Front View).

2. Select a planar surface to orient the view by selecting **Window>ExhaustFlange.CATPart** and then selecting the surface shown in Figure 1–58.

Note the preview in the bottom right corner of the display.

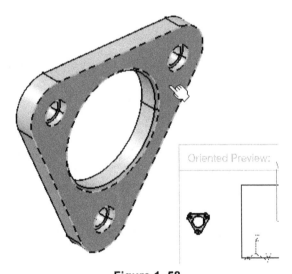

Figure 1–58

The drawing window becomes active, and the view preview and the compass display, as shown in Figure 1–59.

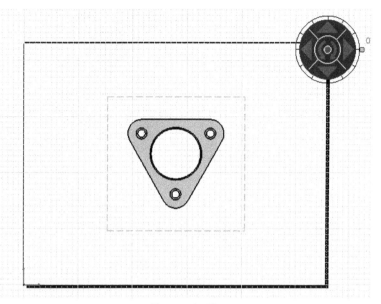

Figure 1–59

3. Select anywhere in the display to complete the creation of the Front view, as shown in Figure 1–60.

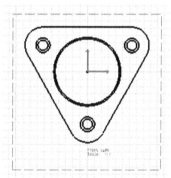

Figure 1–60

Task 4 - Modify properties of a view.

1. In the specification tree, right-click on the Front view and select **Properties**, as shown in Figure 1–61. The Properties dialog box opens.

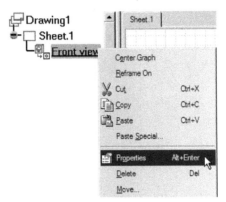

Figure 1–61

2. Select the *View* tab. For the *Scale* value, enter **1:2**, as shown in Figure 1–62.

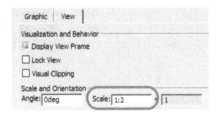

Figure 1–62

3. Click **OK** to complete the change. The view updates with the new scale value.

4. Move the view to the location shown in Figure 1–63 by selecting the view frame and dragging it to the new location.

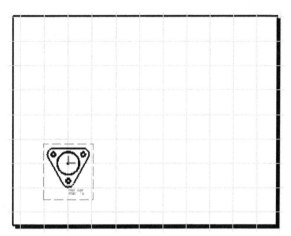

Figure 1–63

Task 5 - Modify the sheet size.

1. Select **File>Page Setup**. The Page Setup dialog box opens. Expand the Sheet Style drop-down list and select **B ANSI**, as shown in Figure 1–64.

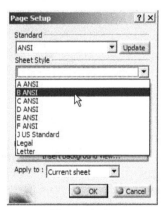

Figure 1–64

2. Click **OK**. The sheet size updates as shown in Figure 1–65.

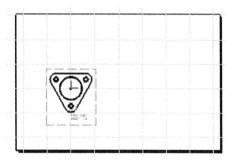

Figure 1–65

Task 6 - Set the drafting options.

1. Select **Tools>Options**. In the left side of the dialog box, select **Mechanical Design>Drafting**. Select the *General* tab.

2. In the *Grid* area, clear the **Display** and **Snap to point** options, as shown in Figure 1–66.

*You can also disable the **Sketcher Grid** option in the Visualization toolbar and the **Snap to Point** option in the Tools toolbar.*

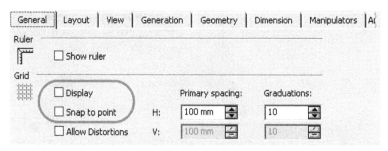

Figure 1–66

3. Click **OK**.

Task 7 - Create a section view.

Section views can only be created from the active view. Ensure that the view you are cutting has a red border.

1. Zoom in on the Front view, as shown in Figure 1–67. In the Sections toolbar, click ⊡ (Offset Section View).

2. Position the cursor so that a witness line displays at the center of the hole, as shown in Figure 1–67. Select the location with the left mouse button.

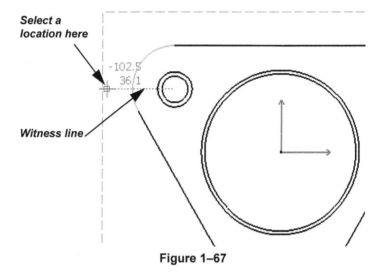

Figure 1–67

3. Move the cursor to the right of the view, as shown in Figure 1–68. Ensure that the line is blue (this indicates that the line is horizontal). Double-click on the end point of the line to finish defining the location of the cross-section.

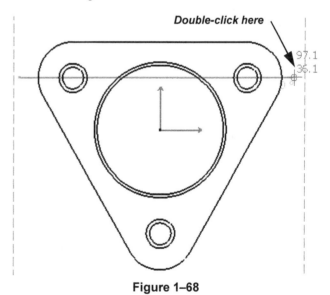

Figure 1–68

4. Place the cursor above the Front view, as shown in Figure 1–69, and click the left mouse button to place the view.

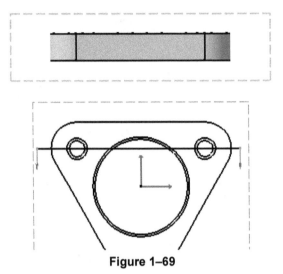

Figure 1–69

The section view displays as shown in Figure 1–70.

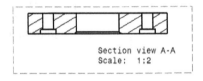

Section view A-A
Scale: 1:2

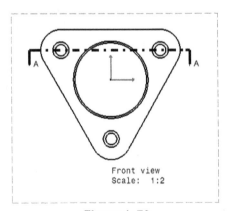

Front view
Scale: 1:2

Figure 1–70

Task 8 - Create a projection view.

1. In the Projections toolbar, click ⬚ (Projection View) and place the projected view in the location shown in Figure 1–71.

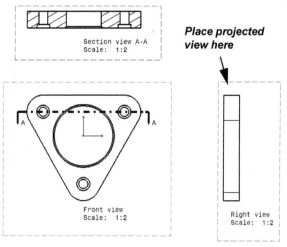

Figure 1–71

Task 9 - Activate and modify a view.

1. Double-click on the view frame of the projected view created in Task 8 (Right view) to activate the view. The view frame of an active view is displayed in red.

   Open the Properties dialog box of the active view.

   In the *Dress-up* area, select the **Hidden Lines** and **3D spec** options and clear the remaining options, as shown in Figure 1–72.

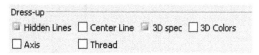

Figure 1–72

2. Click **OK**. The projection view displays as shown in Figure 1–73.

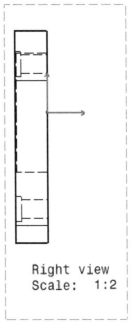

Figure 1–73

Task 10 - Create a detail view.

1. In the Details toolbar, click 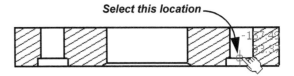 (Detail View).

2. Select a location on the section view, as shown in Figure 1–74.

Select this location

Section view A-A
Scale: 1:2

Figure 1–74

3. Draw the circle callout with the cursor, as shown in Figure 1–75, and click the left mouse button.

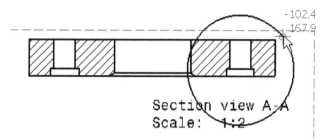

Figure 1–75

4. An error message box opens as shown in Figure 1–76, indicating that a Detail view definition does not intersect with the active view. Click **OK** to close the dialog box.

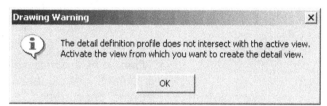

Figure 1–76

5. Click 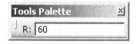 (Detail View) to deactivate it.

6. Activate the section view and create the Detail view shown in Figure 1–77.

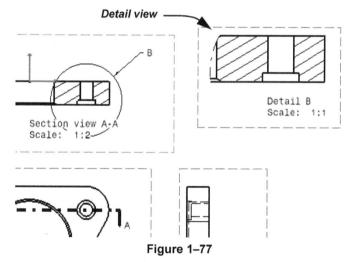

Figure 1–77

The radius for the detail callout can be entered in the Tools Palette.

Tools Palette
R: 60

Task 11 - Create an isometric view.

1. Click 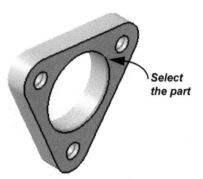 (Isometric View).

2. Activate the **ExhaustFlange.CATPart** window and select the part, as shown in Figure 1–78.

*Select
the part*

Figure 1–78

When creating an Isometric view, you select the part to orient it, rather than a planar surface. The drawing view displays the result of the current orientation of the model and is not necessarily a true isometric orientation.

3. Place the isometric view in the location shown in Figure 1–79.

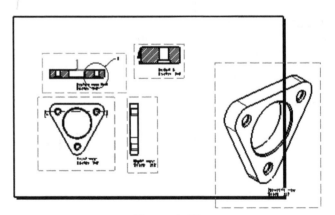

Figure 1–79

4. Rescale the *isometric view* to **1:3** and move it to the location shown in Figure 1–80.

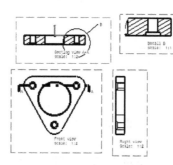

Figure 1–80

5. Move the view names of each view so that they display as shown in Figure 1–81. Relocate the Detail view to the bottom right corner of the page.

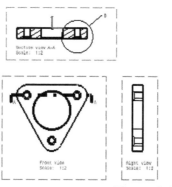

Figure 1–81

6. Open the Properties dialog box for the isometric view and enter **Reference View** in the Prefix field, as shown in Figure 1–82.

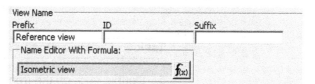

Figure 1–82

7. Save the drawing in the *Exhaust Manifold* directory of the training files. For the *drawing name*, enter **ExhaustFlange**.

8. Close all files.

Practice 1b | Create a Sectional View

Practice Objectives

*   Create a cross-section view.
*   Create a cross-section view from 3D.

In this practice, you will create a sectional view in a drawing and on the model.

Task 1 - Open the drawing.

1. Open **Bracket.CATDrawing**. The model displays as shown in Figure 1–83.

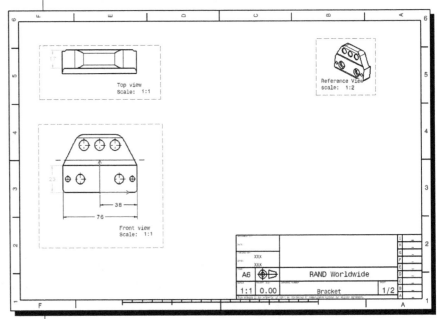

Figure 1–83

Task 2 - Create a cross-section view.

1. Double-click on the front view to make it active.

2. Click (Offset Section View).

3. Sketch the cross-section profile shown in Figure 1–84. Ensure that the section intersects the two holes at their centers. Double-click on the sketch to complete it.

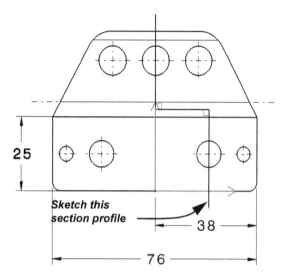

Front view
Scale: 1:1

Figure 1–84

4. Move the cursor to the right of the front view. Position the section preview and click the left mouse button to place the view on the drawing.

Task 3 - Modify the part.

1. Open **Bracket.CATPart**. The model displays as shown in Figure 1–85.

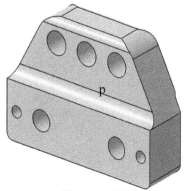

Figure 1–85

2. In the specification tree, locate and double-click on the **Pad.1** feature.

3. Double-click on the **38mm** dimension. For the *new dimension value*, enter **44mm** and click **OK**.

The standard Windows shortcut keys, <Ctrl> + <Tab>, can also be used to toggle display windows.

4. Select **Window>Bracket.CATDrawing** to switch to the drawing view.

5. Update the drawing by clicking 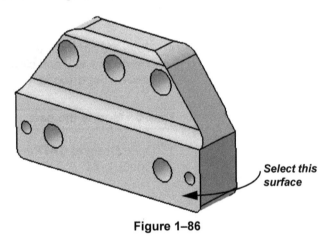 (Update current sheet). The drawing views update to display the modified part geometry.

6. Note that Section view A-A, created in Task 2, no longer intersects the counterbored holes at their centers, as originally intended. This type of cross-section profile sketch is not constrained to the geometry of the model.

Task 4 - Create a sketch in the 3D model.

1. Switch back to the part file window and select the front face shown in Figure 1–86.

Select this surface

Figure 1–86

2. Delete the Section A-A view.

3. Click (Positioned Sketch) to start the creation of a positioned sketch.

4. At the bottom of the Sketch Positioning dialog box, select **Swap**.

5. At the bottom of the Sketch Positioning dialog box, select **Reverse V**, as shown in Figure 1–87.

Figure 1–87

6. Click **OK** to close the dialog box and enter the Sketcher workbench.

7. Sketch the cross-section profile shown in Figure 1–88. Constrain the left vertical line of sketch to the vertical axis, and the right vertical line to the center of the hole. This can be done by selecting the vertical line and the inside surface of the hole (which automatically selects the implicit axis of the hole), and applying a coincidence constraint. Exit the Sketcher workbench when the sketch is complete.

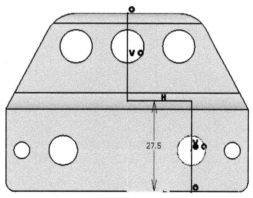

Figure 1–88

8. In the specification tree, locate and double-click on the **Pad.1** feature. Revert the *44mm dimension* to **38mm**.

Task 5 - Create a 3D-linked section view.

1. Activate the drawing window and update the drawing.

2. Click ⬚ (Offset Section View) to create a new section view.

3. Without sketching any cross-section lines, switch to the part window and select the newly created sketch feature.

4. The display automatically reverts to the drawing window. Move the cursor to the right of the front view. Position and place the section view.

5. Switch to the part window and change the *38mm Pad.1* dimension to **44mm**.

6. Activate the drawing window and update the drawing. Note the positioning of the cross-section profile. The intent of the drawing has been captured using a positioned sketch.

7. Save and close all of the files.

Practice 1c

Create a Part Drawing

Practice Objectives

- Create a projection view.
- Create a broken view.
- Create a clipping plane.
- Modify view properties.

In this practice, you will create the drawing that includes multiple view types.

Task 1 - Create a drawing.

1. Select **File>New**. In the New dialog box, in the List of Types, select **Drawing**.

2. For the *Standard*, specify **ANSI** and for the *Sheet Style*, select **C ANSI** as shown in Figure 1–89.

Figure 1–89

3. Click **OK**. An empty sheet displays.

Task 2 - Open a part file.

1. Open **SteeringColumn.CATPart**. The model displays as shown in Figure 1–90.

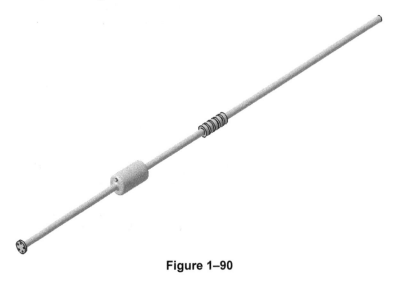

Figure 1–90

Task 3 - Create a Front view.

1. Activate the drawing window.

2. In the Projections toolbar, click (Front View).

3. Activate the **SteeringColumn.CATPart** window. Orient the part and select the surface shown in Figure 1–91.

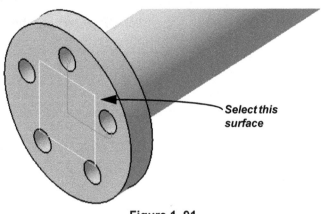

Select this surface

Figure 1–91

4. Orient the view using the view definition compass, as shown in Figure 1–92. Select anywhere on the sheet to complete the view.

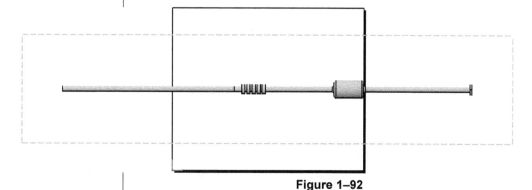

Figure 1–92

Task 4 - Create a Broken view.

1. Click 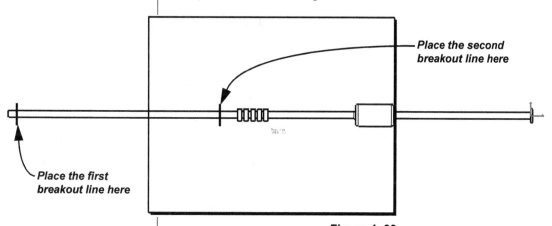 (Broken View).

2. To specify the first breaking line, select the front view at the position shown in Figure 1–93.

Place the second
breakout line here

Place the first
breakout line here

Figure 1–93

3. A dashed green line perpendicular to the column shaft displays. Select the dashed line so that it becomes solid. It defines the orientation of the breakout lines, which can be horizontal or vertical.

4. Select the position of the second vertical breakout line as shown in Figure 1–93.

5. Select on the sheet to complete the view. The broken front view displays as shown in Figure 1–94.

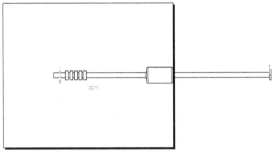

Figure 1–94

6. Create a second broken view on the right side of the column shaft, as shown in Figure 1–95. Note that a dotted line does not display during the placement of the first breakout line because the orientation of the breakout has already been defined for this view.

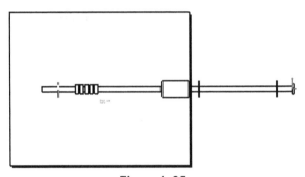

Figure 1–95

7. Click and drag the view text to move it under the Front view.

8. Position the completed view, as shown in Figure 1–96.

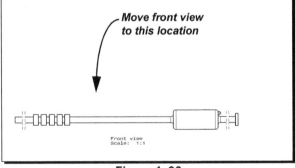

Figure 1–96

Task 5 - Create a Projection view.

1. In the Projections toolbar, click 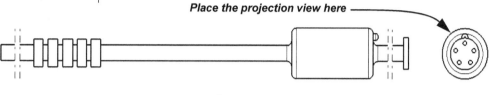 (Projection View). Place the projected view at the location shown in Figure 1–97.

Place the projection view here

```
Front view                                    Right view
Scale:  1:1                                    Scale:  1:1
```

Figure 1–97

Task 6 - Create an Isometric view.

1. Click 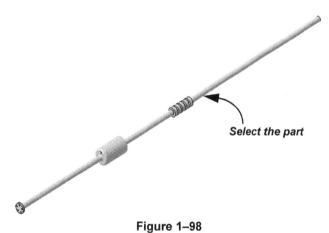 (Isometric View).

2. Activate the **SteeringColumn.CATPart** window.

3. Click (Isometric View) and select the part, as shown in Figure 1–98.

Select the part

Figure 1–98

4. Place the isometric view. Rescale the *view* to **1:4** and move it to the location shown in Figure 1–99.

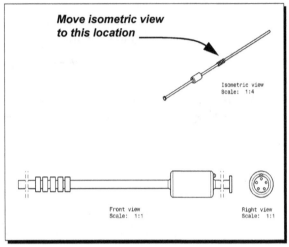

Figure 1–99

Task 7 - Create a Clipping view.

1. Create a new isometric view anywhere on the sheet. Do not rescale it.

2. Ensure that the new isometric view is active.

3. Click (Quick Clipping View). Zoom in on the newly created isometric view and define the center of the clipping circle, as shown in Figure 1–100.

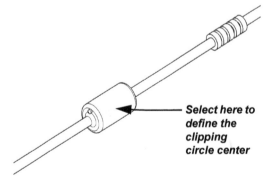

Figure 1–100

4. Expand the clipping circle so that it extends past the steering column spindle. Left-click on the circle to complete the view.

5. Move the clipped view to the location shown in Figure 1–101.

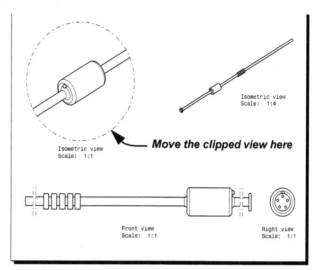

Figure 1–101

Task 8 - Display hidden lines in the clipped isometric view.

1. In the specification tree, right-click on the second Isometric view and select **Properties**. In the *View* tab, in the *Dress-up* area, select **Hidden Lines** to enable it, as shown in Figure 1–102.

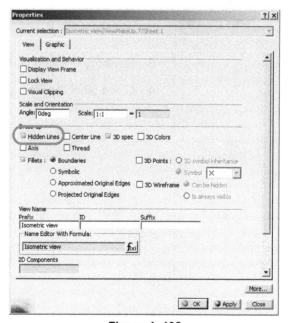

Figure 1–102

2. Click **OK** to close the Properties dialog box. The completed drawing displays as shown in Figure 1–103.

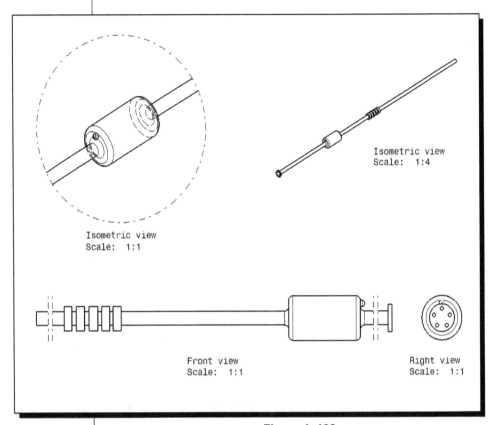

Figure 1–103

3. Save the drawing as **ExhaustFlange**.

4. Close all of the files.

Practice 1d | Create a Product Drawing

Practice Objectives

- Create a product drawing.
- Create drawing views using the View Wizard.
- Create an Auxiliary view.

In this practice, you create a product drawing for **ExhaustManifold.CATProduct**.

Task 1 - Retrieve a product file.

1. Open **ExhaustManifold.CATProduct** from the *Exhaust Manifold* directory. The assembly displays as shown in Figure 1–104.

Figure 1–104

Task 2 - Create a new drawing.

1. Create a new drawing file using an **ANSI** Standard and an **E ANSI** sheet size.

Task 3 - Set the global scale value.

1. In the specification tree, right-click on **Sheet.1** and select **Properties**.

2. Enter a *Scale* value of **1:3**. This controls the default scale for any new view that is added to the sheet. The Properties dialog box opens as shown in Figure 1–105.

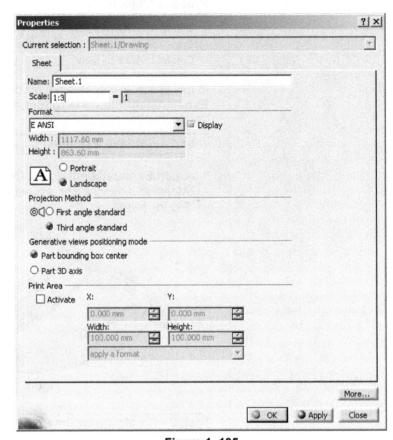

Figure 1–105

3. Click **OK**.

Task 4 - Use the View Wizard to create a drafting view layout.

1. Click ![icon] (View Creation Wizard). The View Wizard dialog box opens, enabling you to predefine the configuration of the layout.

2. In the *Minimum distance between each view* field, enter **195**, as shown in Figure 1–106.

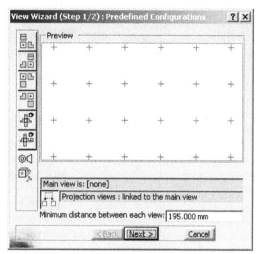

Figure 1–106

3. In the View Wizard dialog box, click 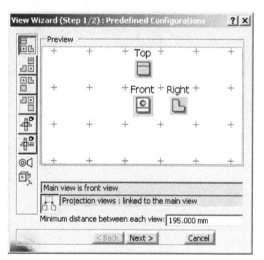. The layout displays in the View Wizard Preview, as shown in Figure 1–107.

Figure 1–107

4. Click **Next**.

5. Click 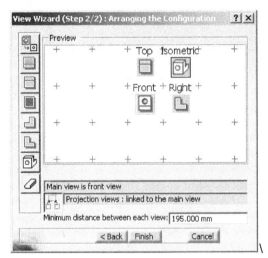 to add an isometric view to the layout. Position the isometric view, as shown in Figure 1–108.

Figure 1–108

6. Click **Finish**.

7. Activate the assembly model window. Rotate the assembly model and select the surface shown in Figure 1–109.

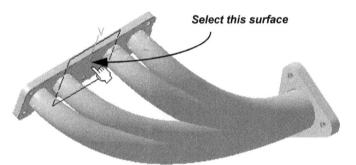

Select this surface

Figure 1–109

8. Accept the views by selecting anywhere in the display. The drawing updates as shown in Figure 1–110.

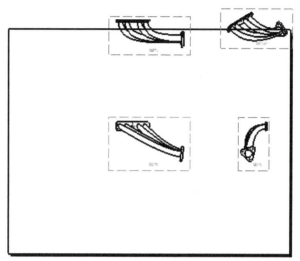

Figure 1–110

9. Move the Front view to the location shown in Figure 1–111. Note that all other views move relative to the Front view.

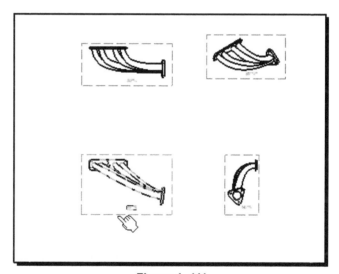

Figure 1–111

10. In the Properties dialog box of **Sheet.1**, change the *Scale* to **1:2**. All of the views update to reflect this change, as shown in Figure 1–112.

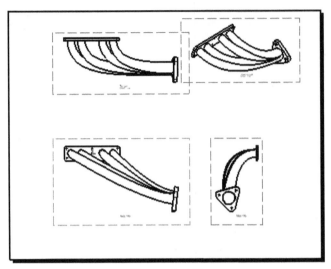

Figure 1–112

11. Modify the *Scale* value of the isometric view to **1:4**, as shown in Figure 1–113.

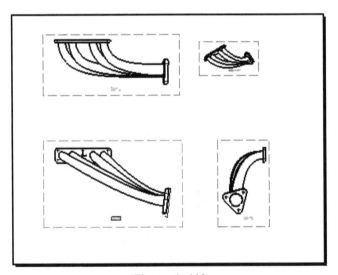

Figure 1–113

12. Move the Right View further to the right, as shown in Figure 1–114.

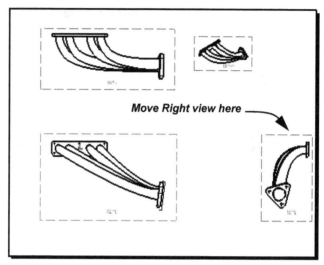

Figure 1–114

Task 5 - Create an Auxiliary view of the exhaust flange.

1. Zoom in on the Front view, as shown in Figure 1–115.

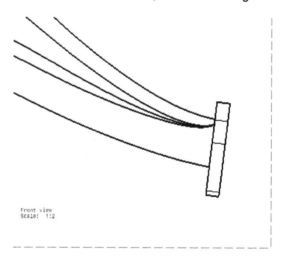

Figure 1–115

2. Ensure that the Front view is the active view.

3. In the Projections toolbar, click 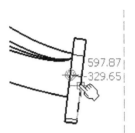 (Auxiliary View).

4. Select the edge of the Front view geometry, as shown in Figure 1–116.

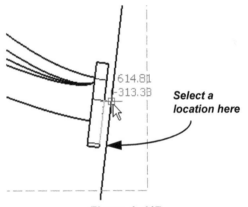

Figure 1–116

5. Select a location to the right of the Front view geometry, as shown in Figure 1–117.

Figure 1–117

6. Move the cursor to the right of the Front view to locate the Auxiliary view, as shown in Figure 1–118. Click the left mouse button to place the view.

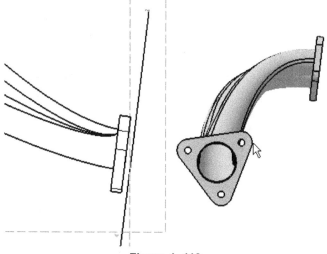

Figure 1–118

Task 6 - Modify the Auxiliary view.

1. Double-click on the directional arrows of the Auxiliary view, as shown in Figure 1–119. The system enters the Edit/ Replace workspace.

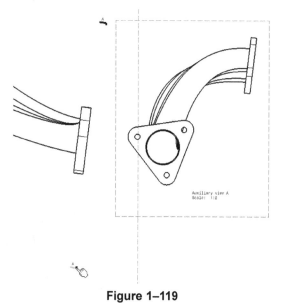

Auxiliary view A
Scale: 1:2

Figure 1–119

2. In the Edit/Replace toolbar, click (Invert Profile Direction) to invert the arrows.

3. Click the left mouse button (click and hold) and drag the lower vertex of the line to the location shown in Figure 1–120.

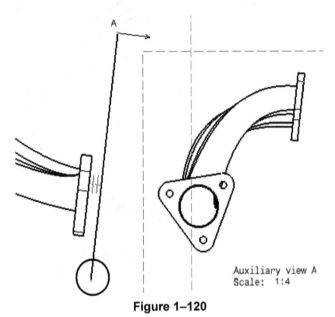

Auxiliary view A
Scale: 1:4

Figure 1–120

4. Move the other end of the line to the location shown in Figure 1–121.

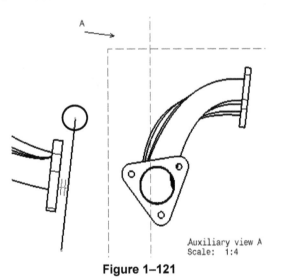

Auxiliary view A
Scale: 1:4

Figure 1–121

5. Click ⬆ (End Profile Edition). The drawing displays as shown in Figure 1–122.

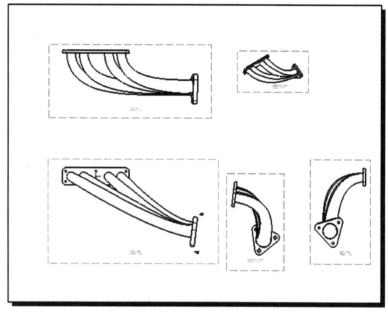

Figure 1–122

6. Move the Auxiliary view to the right and the Projection view to the left, as shown in Figure 1–123.

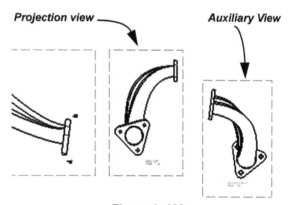

Figure 1–123

7. Save the drawing as **ExhaustManifold**.

8. Close all of the files.

Practice 1e

(Optional) Section & Cut Views

Practice Objectives

- Create a part drawing without instruction.
- Create a Section View with a 3D profile.
- Create a Section Cut with a 3D profile.

In this practice, you will create a part drawing for the handle of a power drill, Handle.CATProduct.

Task 1 - Retrieve a product file.

1. Open **TransitionTube.CATPart**. The part displays as shown in Figure 1–124.

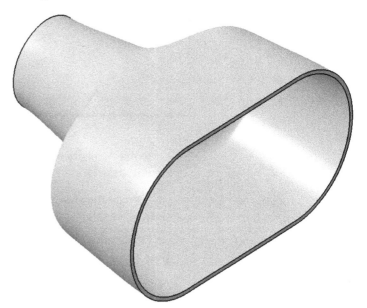

Figure 1–124

2. Create a new Drawing file. For the *Standard*, enter **ANSI** and for the *Sheet Style*, select **D ANSI**.

3. Produce the views shown in Figure 1–125. The section cut views are aligned to the sections used to build the transition tube part. Build these sections in the 3D model to ensure that they are located correctly.

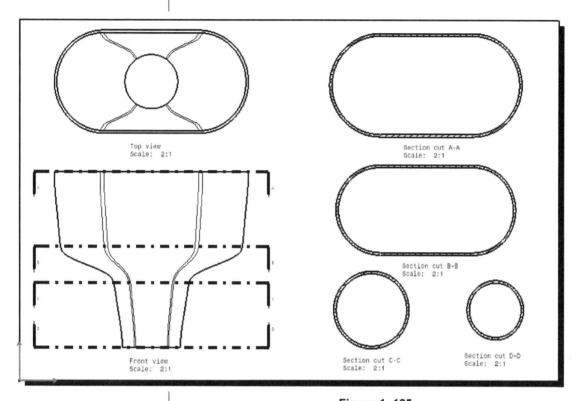

Figure 1–125

4. Save and close all of the files.

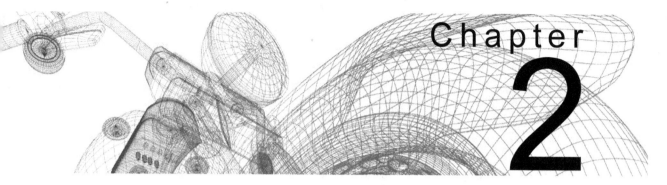

Chapter 2

View Modification

This chapter focuses on the methods available for modifying drawing views.

Learning Objectives in this Chapter

- Understand how to manipulate and position views.
- Recognize and apply the various view properties.
- Recognize and apply the various section and detail view properties.
- Apply various hatching properties.
- Modify profiles.
- Understand the 3D View support.

2.1 View Manipulation

This section describes the following ways of manipulating a view:

- Delete

- Hide/Show

- Show Geometry in All Viewpoints

Delete View

To delete a view, right-click on the view in the display or specification tree and select **Delete**.

Hide/Show

You can hide a view to simplify the sheet. To hide a view, right-click on it in the display or specification tree and select **Hide/Show**.

Hidden views are displayed in the hidden space. Click (Swap visible space) to toggle between visible and hidden space.

Show Geometry in All Viewpoints

If you are not sure how the geometry in a specific view relates to the 3D geometry of the part or product model, you can use the 3D model to assist you. By selecting **Tools>Analyze>Show Geometry in All Viewpoints**, an 3D view of the model displays in a sub-window. Any selected in the drawing geometry highlights in all views as well as in 3D sub-window to help you locate it. If **Animate** option is activated, the model in the sub-window also orients according to the selected view. An example is shown in Figure 2–1.

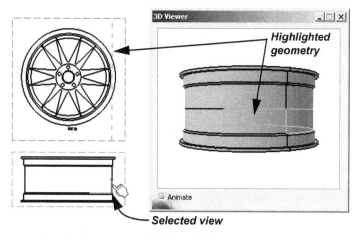

Selected view

Figure 2–1

2.2 View Positioning

This section introduces view positioning commands that can be accessed from the shortcut menu, as shown in Figure 2–2, or by manipulating the view directly on the drawing.

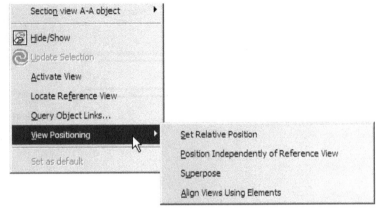

Figure 2–2

The following topics are covered:

*   Moving Views

*   Set Relative Position

*   Superpose

*   Align Views Using Elements

Moving Views

You can move a view in the same sheet or to another sheet. To move a view in the same sheet, select the dashed line frame of the view and drag it to the required location.

If a parent view is moved, any child views are also moved because of the view alignment. To unalign a view, right-click on it in the specification tree and select **View Positioning>Position Independently of Reference View**. You can undo this operation by selecting **View Positioning>Position According to Reference View**.

You can use standard Windows shortcut keys: <Ctrl> + <X> (Cut) and <Ctrl> + <V> (Paste).

To move a view to another sheet, cut and paste it from the display or specification tree. You can press <Ctrl> to select multiple views. When pasting the views, select the required sheet in the specification tree. Once your views have been pasted, you can manipulate their location.

Set Relative Position

When the **View Positioning>Set Relative Position** option is selected, a positioning line and grid display on the model, as shown in Figure 2–3. The positioning line is anchored to the view at the center grid point.

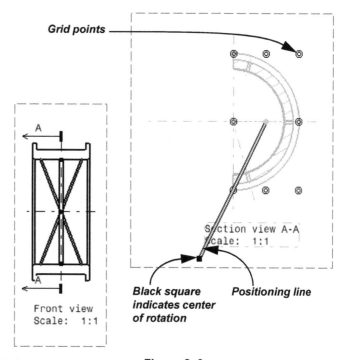

Figure 2–3

How To: Position Relative to Another View

1. Select the black square at the end of the positioning line. The square displays a blinking crosshair.
2. In the specification tree or the frame of another view in the drawing, select a view. The black square snaps to the origin of the selected view, enabling you to position relative to the selected view, as shown in Figure 2–4.

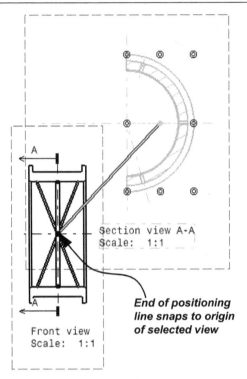

Section view A-A
Scale: 1:1

*End of positioning
line snaps to origin
of selected view*

Front view
Scale: 1:1

Figure 2–4

3. The view can now be repositioned in the following ways:

   • Select and drag the positioning line to translate the view
     along the positioning line.

   • Select and drag on the green dot to rotate the view about
     the black square.

   • Select a grid point to move the positioning line to a new
     anchor location on the view.

Note that when translating or rotating the view, coordinate information is displayed on the drawing, as shown in Figure 2–5.

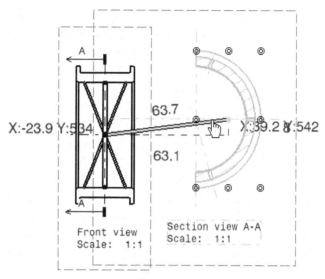

Figure 2–5

4. Once the view has been moved, select anywhere in the drawing background to complete the operation.

If the view is initially aligned to a parent view, the system automatically positions the view independent of the reference view during a **Set Relative Position** operation.

Superpose

Superpose is used to place a view directly on top of another view. The purpose of superposing is to display the various arrangements or the range of motion of an assembly.

To superpose a view, activate the view to be moved, right-click and select **View Positioning>Superpose**. CATIA prompts you to select a view to use as a reference. The view selected first is placed on the center of the view referenced second. The Superposed view is not locked in place. You can still drag and change its location using the available view positioning techniques.

Align Views Using Elements

This operation aligns a view by referencing existing geometry between the two views. Right-click on the view to be moved and select **View Positioning>Align Views Using Elements**. Then select an edge or axis from each view. The system positions the first view so that the two selected elements are co-linear. An example is shown in Figure 2–6.

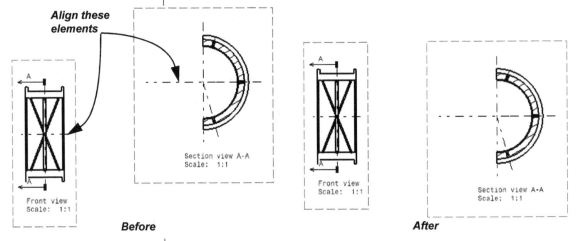

Before

After

Figure 2–6

2.3 View Properties

View properties enable you to customize the display of all views except Quick views. To access view properties, right-click on the view and select **Properties**. The Properties dialog box opens as shown in Figure 2–7.

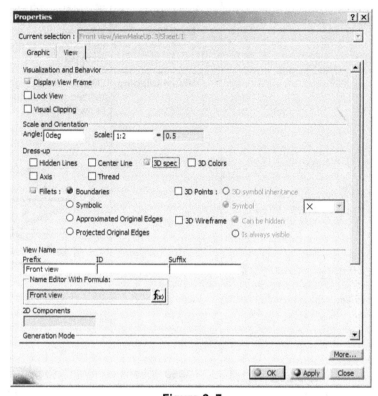

Figure 2–7

The following areas of the View Properties dialog box are covered:

- Visualization and Behavior

- Scale and Orientation

- Dress-Up

- View Name

- Generation Mode

Visualization and Behavior

The options in the *Visualization and Behavior* area are described as follows:

Option	Description
Display View Frame	By disabling this option, the dashed view border is no longer displayed. Once toggled off, the view cannot be moved or manipulated in the main window. It can still be accessed using the specification tree.
Lock View	When enabled, the properties for the view can no longer be modified, nor does the drawing update with 3D model changes.
Visual Clipping	Displays a clipping box on the view, which can be resized and positioned to control the viewable area as shown below.

Scale and Orientation

These options control the scale and angle of the selected view. They can be applied to a child view independent of the parent.

Dress-Up

The *Dress-Up* area controls the display of dress-up elements on the view using the options described below:

Option	Description
Hidden Lines	Displays hidden lines on the view.
Center Line	Displays center lines on the view.
3D Spec	Controls the display of assembly components. When enabled, the settings in the *Drafting* tab in the component's Properties dialog box are applied to the drawing view.

3D Colors	Displays the color(s) assigned to the 3D model in the drawing view.
Axis	Displays axes on the view.
Thread	Displays threads on the view.
Fillets	Controls the display of fillets using the four options shown below. Note that fillets displayed with any option other than **Boundaries** do not inherit 3D colors and do not produce associative dimensions.

Boundaries   *Symbolic*

Approximated Original Edges   *Projected Original Edges*

3D Points	Controls the display of reference point features present in the model. The system can reuse the point symbol assigned in the model by selecting the **3D symbol inheritance** option. To define a custom point display, select an option in the Symbol drop-down list.
3D Wireframe	Controls the display of sketches, wireframe, and surface elements present in the model. With the **Can be hidden** option enabled, the system applies hidden line removal to the elements if the **Hidden Line** option is enabled. If **Is Always visible** is selected, the visibility of the element is controlled by the 3D model.

View Name

The name of the view is controlled using the *Prefix*, *ID*, and *Suffix* fields. The *Name Editor With Formula* field displays the values of *Prefix*, *ID*, and *Suffix* together (by default, as shown in Figure 2–8).

```
1.Plan View_A
Scale:   1:1
```

View Name
Prefix	ID	Suffix
1.	Plan View	_A

Name Editor With Formula:
1.Plan View_A *f(x)*

Figure 2–8

Click *f(x)* to customize the formula.

Generation Mode

Options for the *Generation Mode* area in the View Properties dialog box are described as follows:

Option		Description
Only generate parts larger than		Specify lower limit for size of part displayed in assembly view. This is a good method of eliminating fasteners and other small geometry to improve update times for a view.
Enable occlusion culling		Applies to assemblies that have been opened in Visualization mode. When enabled, the system only loads components that can be seen in the resulting view. Improves update times for the view.
View generation mode		Controls the way CATIA generates view geometry. Selecting an option other than **Exact view** disables access to a variety of options in the View Properties dialog box.
	Exact view	Generates the view from the exact 3D model.
	CGR	Improves view generation time using a Computer Graphics Representation (CGR) to generate the view. This results in a faceted display of the external view geometry so that individual features cannot be selected. With this option, only the **Hidden Lines** and **3D Spec** dress-up options are available.

	Approximate	Improves view generation time using an approximation method to generate the view. Clicking **Options** opens the Approximation mode dialog box, which enables you to control the *Level of Detail* (LOD) as shown below. The higher the LOD value, the more time required to generate the view. 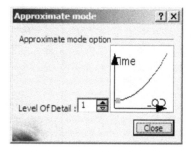 This mode is suited to large, complex assemblies and should not be used on simple part drawing views. With this option, only the **Hidden Lines** and **3D Spec** dress-up options are available.
	Raster	Converts the view to a raster image so that the resulting view is pixelated. Therefore, geometry cannot be selected for dimension creation. Clicking **Options** opens the Generation mode options dialog box, which enables you to display the view using hidden line removal, shading, or shading with edges as shown below. You can also define the visualization and print quality of the view. 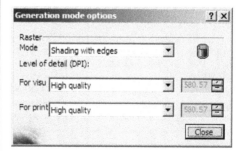 With this option, only the **Hidden Lines**, **3D Spec**, and **3D Colors** dress-up options are available.

2.4 Section and Detail Properties

To modify the callouts for Section and Detail views, right-click on the arrows and select **Properties**. The Properties dialog box opens, as shown in Figure 2–9.

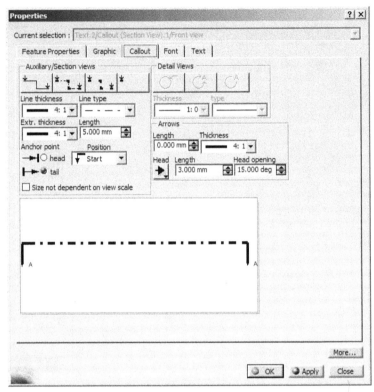

Figure 2–9

Depending on the type of callout selected, either the Auxiliary/ Section views or *Detail Views* field are enabled. This dialog box enables you to customize the style and shape of the callout, and to control how the font and text are displayed.

Recreating the Callout

Callouts for section, detail, and auxiliary views can be recreated if they or the view containing the callout are deleted.

How To: Recreate a Callout

1. Right-click on the section, detail, or auxiliary view, and select **x object>Add Callout**, as shown in Figure 2–10.

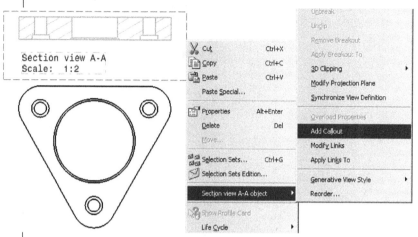

Figure 2–10

2. In the working area or specification tree, select the target view to add the callout, as shown in Figure 2–11.

If the target view that you want to add the callout is in a different sheet, the target view must be selected in the specification tree.

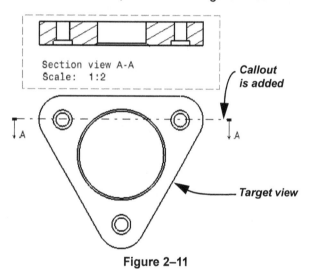

Figure 2–11

2.5 Hatching Properties

To modify section hatching, right-click on a hatch line in the Section view and select **Properties**. The Properties dialog box opens as shown in Figure 2–12.

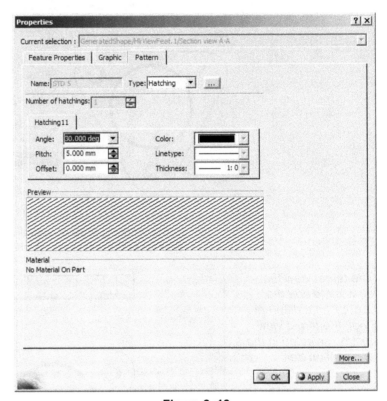

Figure 2–12

The *Pattern* tab enables you to modify the angle, pitch (spacing), offset, color, and line style of the hatching display.

2.6 Profile Modification

Section Profiles

Section profiles can be modified at any time by double-clicking on the section view profile in the parent view. This places you in the Edit/Replace workspace. You can invert and recreate sections using the Edit/Replace toolbar, as shown in Figure 2–13.

Figure 2–13

The icons are described as follows:

Option	Description
⤒	Exits the Edit/Replace workspace.
⫯	Replaces the current profile used to define the section. Once the icon is selected, sketch a new profile in the parent drawing view. The section view does not update until you exit the workspace.
⥮	Inverts the profile direction.

Detail Profiles

Detail profiles can be modified by double-clicking on the detail callout in the parent view. The Edit/Replace toolbar contains two icons, as shown in Figure 2–14.

Figure 2–14

Use ⫯ (Replace Profile) to draw a new detail profile and

⤒ (End Profile Edition) to exit the workspace. At any time in this workspace, you can reposition the existing detail profile by dragging it to a new location on the view.

2.7 3D Support

When creating a model, 3D supports can be added to a CATPart. The support creates a grid on the XY, YZ, and XZ planes of the active axis system. This grid can be used as a reference for the creation of geometry by selecting the vertices or edges of the grid. For example, a wireframe spline can be created by selecting grid locations, as shown in Figure 2–15.

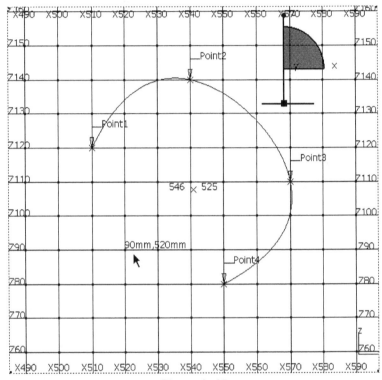

Figure 2–15

This 3D support can be displayed when adding views to a drawing. By displaying the grid, the drawing can automatically convey positional information about the model, specifically for parts that were created using in-place modeling techniques.

For example, a support is displayed in the drawing view shown in Figure 2–16. From this drawing, the manufacturer can determine that the center of this part is located at the 400mm, 0mm location from the assembly axis system.

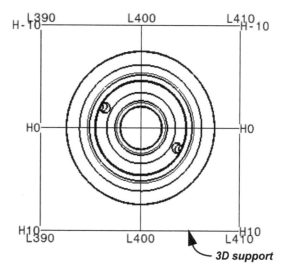

Figure 2–16

To display a 3D support in a drawing view, you must consult your CAD Administrator to have the following configurations set:

- Modify the *Generative Parameters* category in the drawing standards and set the **Tools>Standard>Generative Parameters>Default Generative Style>Generative Shape Design>Work On Support>Extraction** option to **Yes**.

- Clear the **Tools>Options>Mechanical Design>Drafting> Administration tab>Prevent generative view style usage** option.

Practice 2a | View Manipulation

Practice Objectives

- Delete a view.
- Modify a view using Hide/Show.
- Relate a part to a drawing view.

Task 1 - Open the ExhaustFlange.CATDrawing.

1. Select **File>Open** and retrieve **ExhaustFlange_V iew.CATDrawing** and **ExhaustFlange.CATPart** from the *Exhaust Manifold* directory. The drawing displays as shown in Figure 2–17.

    If you completed the previous practice you can continue to use **ExhaustFlange.CATDrawing** instead.

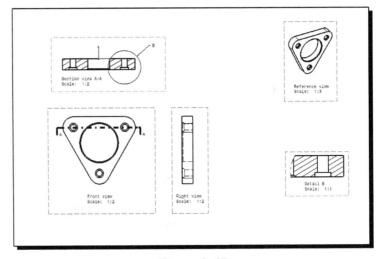

Figure 2–17

Task 2 - Delete a view.

The view frame of an active view displays in red.

1. Before performing modifications, always ensure that the view you intend to modify is set as the active view. In the specification tree, double-click on the Right view to make it active. When active, the view name displays in blue as shown in Figure 2–18.

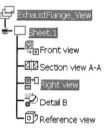

Figure 2–18

2. Right-click on the Right view and select **Delete**. The specification tree displays as shown in Figure 2–19.

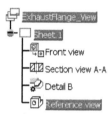

Figure 2–19

Note that the Right view has been removed from the drawing, as shown in Figure 2–20.

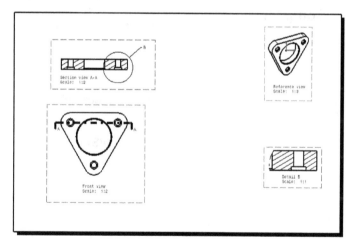

Figure 2–20

3. Select **Edit>Undo** to undo the deletion of the Right view.

*You can also use the Windows **Undo** shortcut (<Ctrl> + <Z>) to undo the operation.*

Task 3 - Hide a view.

1. In the display window or specification tree, right-click on the Right view and select **Hide/Show**. The specification tree displays as shown in Figure 2–21.

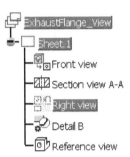

Figure 2–21

2. In the View toolbar, click (Swap visible space). The Right view is located in the invisible display space and has not been permanently removed from the drawing.

Design Considerations

Use the **Hide/Show** and **Swap visible space** tools to simplify the drawing display when reorganizing a drawing. Since the system does not need to update the display of the hidden views, performance improvements can be obtained while working on the drawing in CATIA.

3. Click (Swap visible space) to return to the visible space.

4. In the specification tree, right-click on the Right view and select **Hide/Show**. The Right view displays in the drawing again.

Task 4 - Display a shaded view.

1. In the specification tree, right-click on Reference view and select **Properties**.

2. Change the *Scale* of the view to **1:2**, as shown in Figure 2–22.

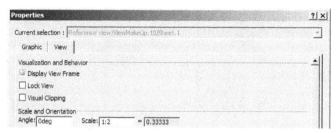

Figure 2–22

3. Scroll to the bottom of the Properties dialog box and locate the *View generation mode* field, as shown in Figure 2–23.

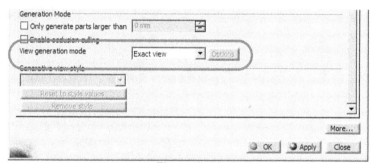

Figure 2–23

4. In the View generation mode drop-down list, select **Raster**.

5. Click **Options**. The Generation mode options dialog box opens as shown in Figure 2–24

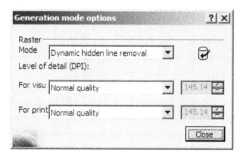

Figure 2–24

6. Make the following selections:

   • *Mode:* **Shading with edges**
   • *For visu:* **High quality**
   • *For print:* **High quality**

7. Click **Close** and click **OK** to apply the view property modifications. The reference view displays as shown in Figure 2–25.

```
Reference view
Scale:  1:2
```

Figure 2–25

8. Save the drawing.

Task 5 - Relate ExhaustFlange.CATPart to the drawing.

---

1. Select **Tools>Analyze>Show Geometry in All Viewpoints**. An isometric view of **ExhaustFlange.CATPart** displays in the 3D Viewer window, as shown in Figure 2–26.

If the part displays as blacked out in the 3D Viewer window, ensure that the part file is loaded in the CATIA session.

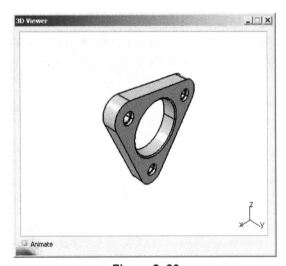

Figure 2–26

Design Considerations

2. Hover the cursor over each drawing view. The model in the 3D Viewer window orients to the drawing view.

When drafting complex parts, geometry and line density can complicate view creation. The **Show Geometry in All Viewpoints** tool helps to ensure that the selected drawing views concisely capture the intent of the drawing.

3. Select the counterbore hole in any view. The selected geometry highlights in all views.

4. Close the 3D Viewer window.

5. Save the drawing and close all of the files.

Practice 2b | View Manipulation II

Practice Objectives

- Move a view between sheets.
- Move a view in a sheet.
- Align views using elements.

Task 1 - Open Tire.CATDrawing.

1. Select **File>Open** and open **Tire.CATDrawing**. The drawing displays as shown in Figure 2–27.

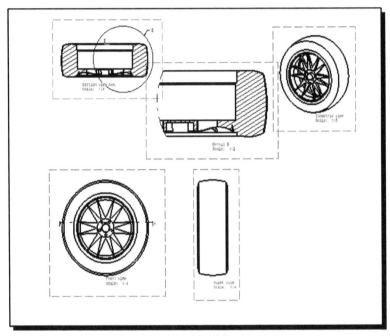

Figure 2–27

Task 2 - Insert a second sheet and insert the Isometric View.

1. Select **Insert>Drawing>Sheets>New Sheet**. A new sheet is added to the drawing.

2. Select the *Sheet.1* tab to toggle back to the first sheet of the drawing.

The Windows shortcut keys, <Ctrl>+<X> (Cut) and <Ctrl>+<V> (Paste), can also be used.

3. In the display or specification tree, double-click on the Isometric view to make it active.

4. Select **Edit>Cut**.

5. In the specification tree, right-click on **Sheet.2** and select **Paste**. The drawing displays as shown in Figure 2–28.

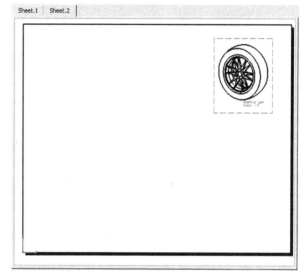

Figure 2–28

Task 3 - Move a view on the same sheet.

1. Activate **Sheet.1** and select the Front view from the specification tree.

2. Use the left mouse button to move the view to a new location on the same sheet. The child views are also moved due to a linked view alignment.

Task 4 - Move the Section View to a new location.

1. Select the dashed-line frame of the Section view and drag it to a different location. The movement is vertically constrained.

2. In the specification tree, right-click on the Section view and select **View Positioning>Position Independently of Reference View**.

3. Drag the Section view again. The movement is no longer constrained to the Front view, as shown in Figure 2–29.

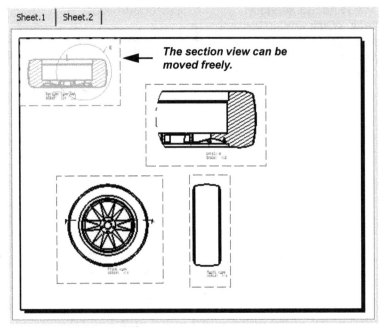

Figure 2–29

4. To realign the Section view with its default reference view, right-click on the view frame of the Section view and select **View Positioning>Position According to Reference View**. The Section view is once again vertically constrained to the Front view.

Task 5 - Align the Detail View with the Front View using elements.

Design Considerations

The **Align Views Using Elements** feature aligns the internal elements of separate views. This enables you to keep a drawing organized without creating referenced alignment constraints.

1. Right-click on the red view frame around the Detail B view and select **View Positioning>Align Views Using Elements**.

2. Select the top edge of the Detail B view and the top edge of the Section view, as shown in Figure 2–30.

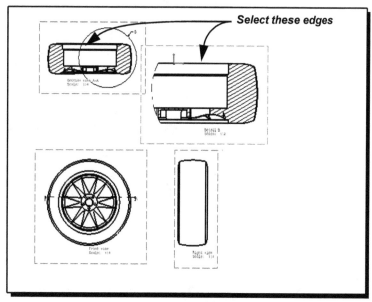

Figure 2–30

3. Select and move the Detail B view. Contrary to a reference alignment, the view is not constrained to the Section view.

Task 6 - Modify the hatching properties of Section view A-A.

---

1. Right-click on the hatching lines of Section view A-A and select **Properties**, as shown in Figure 2–31.

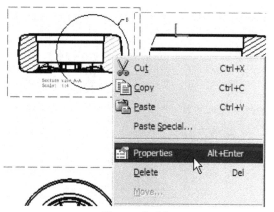

Figure 2–31

---

1. Select the *Pattern* tab, as shown in Figure 2–32.

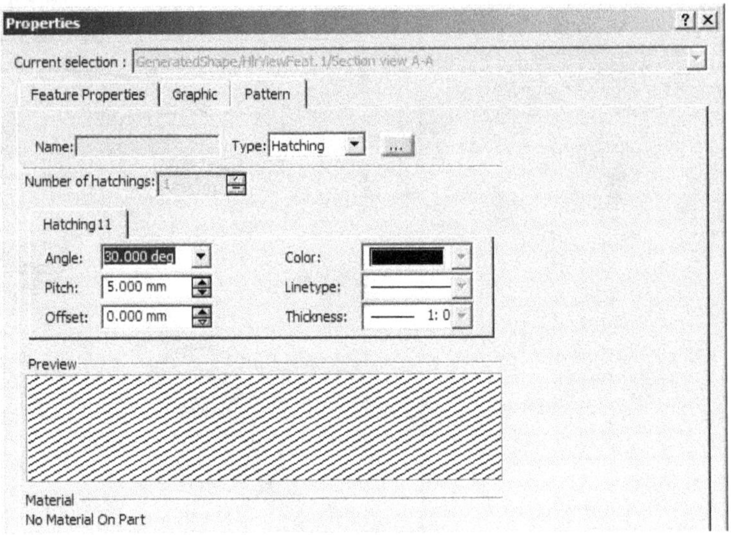

Properties

Current selection : GeneratedShape/HlrViewFeat.1/Section view A-A

Feature Properties | Graphic | Pattern

Name: Type: Hatching ...

Number of hatchings: 1

Hatching 11

Angle: 30.000 deg   Color: ████

Pitch: 5.000 mm   Linetype: ──────

Offset: 0.000 mm   Thickness: ──── 1: 0

Preview

Material
No Material On Part

Figure 2–32

2. Make the following changes:

   • *Angle:* **60 deg**
   • *Pitch:* **2mm**

3. Click **Apply**. The view displays as shown in Figure 2–33. Keep the Properties dialog box open.

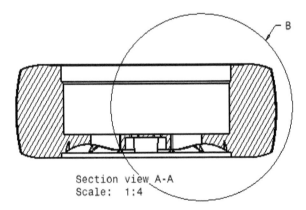

Section view A-A
Scale: 1:4

Figure 2–33

4. In the Type drop-down list, select **Coloring** as shown in Figure 2–34. This creates a filled section.

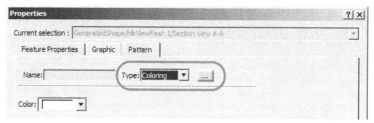

Figure 2–34

5. In the Color drop-down list, select **Black**.

6. Click **OK**. The drawing displays as shown in Figure 2–35.

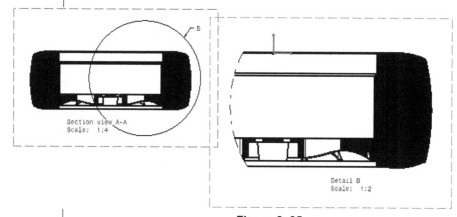

Figure 2–35

Design Considerations

Since the Detail B view was created from Section view A-A, both views display the modifications to the hatching properties.

Task 7 - Modify section profile properties.

1. Double-click on the section view profile in the Front view. The system places you in the Edit/Replace workspace.

2. Click ![icon] (Replace profile). This tool enables you to draw a new profile to be used to define the section.

3. Sketch a horizontal section line that is coincident with the center of the tire, as shown in Figure 2–36. Do not forget to double-click when placing the end point of the line to complete the profile.

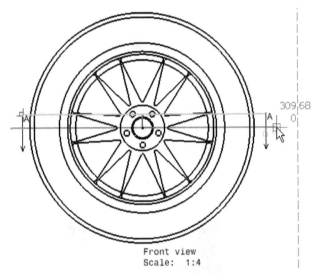

Front view
Scale: 1:4

Figure 2–36

Once complete, the system replaces the old profile with the newly sketched one, as shown in Figure 2–37. The section view does not update until you have exited the Edit/Replace workspace.

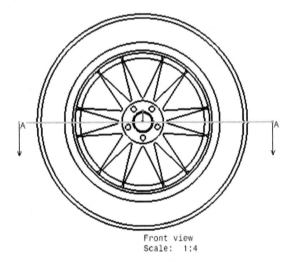

Front view
Scale: 1:4

Figure 2–37

4. Click 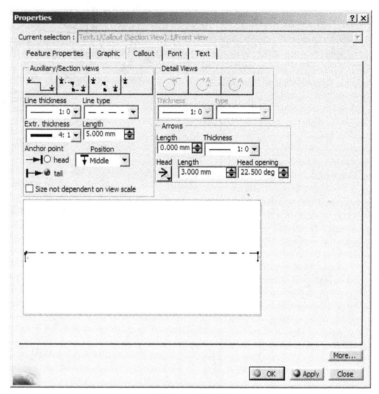 (End Profile Edition) to exit the Edit/Replace workspace. Section view A-A updates with the new profile.

Task 8 - Modify the section callout properties.

1. In the Front view, right-click on the section profile and select **Properties**. Select the *Callout* tab, and the Properties dialog box displays as shown in Figure 2–38.

Figure 2–38

2. Click ⌐ to define a solid callout line with a *thickness* of **1**.

3. Change the *Extr. thickness value* to **3**.

4. Click **OK** to complete the operation. The Front view displays as shown in Figure 2–39.

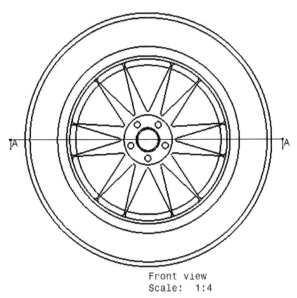

Front view
Scale: 1:4

Figure 2–39

5. Save the drawing and close all of the files.

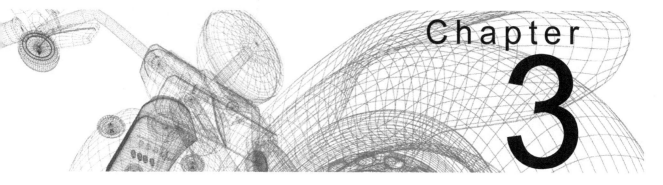

Chapter

3

Dimensioning

Detailing a drawing involves adding information from the model to the drawing so that all design information is effectively communicated. Detail items can include dimensions and notes.

Learning Objectives in this Chapter

- Add dimensions manually.
- Add dimensions automatically.
- Use One step dimensioning.
- Apply step by step dimensioning.
- Recognize and apply dimension generation settings.
- Modify dimension properties.

3.1 Manual Dimensioning

The Generative Drafting workbench provides the following two options to dimension a drawing:

*   Manual dimensioning

*   Automatic dimension generation

Use the Dimensions toolbar shown in Figure 3–1, to manually create dimensions.

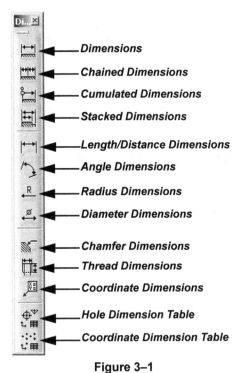

Figure 3–1

The dimension types are described as follows:

Dimension Type	Description
Dimensions	Creates a length/distance, angle, radius, or diameter dimension from the selected reference(s). The dimension type (length, distance, angle, etc.) is determined by the type and number of selected references. For example, selecting two parallel lines will result in a distance dimension, or selecting a circle will result in a diameter dimension. This default behavior can be over-ridden by the user through the contextual menu. Each dimension acts independently when moved, modified, or deleted.
Chained Dimensions	Creates a chain of distance or angle dimensions by using the last selected reference to create the next dimension as shown below. The chain of dimensions is moved, modified, or deleted as a single element. To delete dimensions separately, toggle off (Dimension system selection mode) in the Tools toolbar.
Cumulated Dimensions	Creates a cumulated dimension. The first reference selected becomes the base dimension. All additional references are located with respect to the base as shown below. The cumulated dimensions are moved, modified, or deleted as a single element. To delete dimensions separately, toggle off (Dimension system selection mode) in the Tools toolbar.

Stacked Dimensions	Creates a stack of length dimensions using the first reference to create the next dimension as shown below. The stack of dimensions are moved, modified, or deleted as a single element. To delete dimensions separately, toggle off 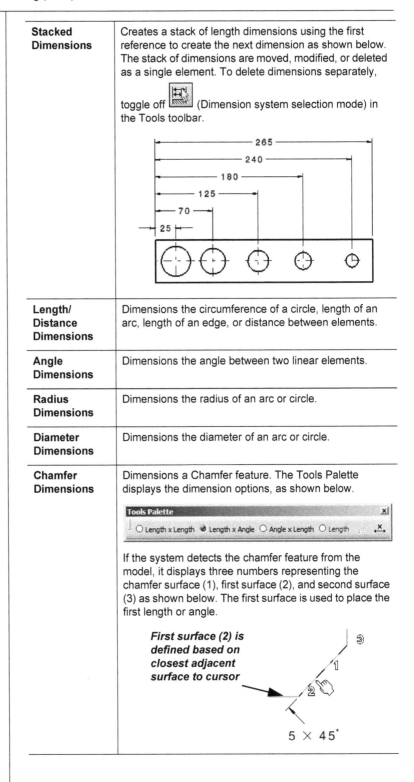 (Dimension system selection mode) in the Tools toolbar.
Length/ Distance Dimensions	Dimensions the circumference of a circle, length of an arc, length of an edge, or distance between elements.
Angle Dimensions	Dimensions the angle between two linear elements.
Radius Dimensions	Dimensions the radius of an arc or circle.
Diameter Dimensions	Dimensions the diameter of an arc or circle.
Chamfer Dimensions	Dimensions a Chamfer feature. The Tools Palette displays the dimension options, as shown below.

If the system detects the chamfer feature from the model, it displays three numbers representing the chamfer surface (1), first surface (2), and second surface (3) as shown below. The first surface is used to place the first length or angle.

First surface (2) is defined based on closest adjacent surface to cursor

5 × 45°

Thread Dimensions	Displays thread parameters on the model of a selected thread surface as shown below. Thread surfaces are displayed by enabling the **Thread** option in the View Properties dialog box. 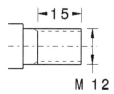
Coordinate Dimensions	Dimensions the horizontal and vertical coordinates of a selected vertex or point relative to the view origin as shown below. 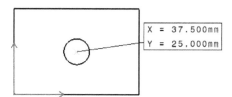
Hole Dimension Table	Creates a hole dimension table that displays the X- and Y-coordinates and diameters of all selected holes, relative to a user-defined origin as shown below. Select all holes using <Ctrl> before creating the hole dimension table. The dimensions are created with the same unit, which is set in the CATIA options. 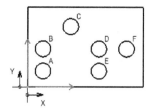
Coordinate Dimension Table	Creates a coordinate dimension table that displays the X-, Y-, and Z- (if applicable) coordinates for all selected points relative to a user-defined origin as shown below. Select all points using <Ctrl> before creating the coordinate dimension table. 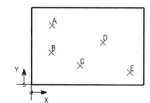

3.2 Manually Create Dimensions

General Steps

Use the following general steps to manually create dimensions:

1. Set dimension creation options.
2. Select the appropriate dimensioning tool.
3. Select the appropriate elements of the view.
4. Manipulate dimensions, as required.

Step 1 - Set dimension creation options.

Select **Tools>Options>Mechanical Design>Drafting>**
Dimension tab. The dimension creation options display as shown
in Figure 3–2.

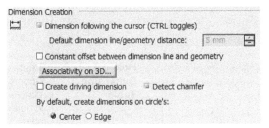

Figure 3–2

To take advantage of the full associativity of CATIA V5, click
Associativity in 3D and select the **Never create
non-associative dimensions** option in the Dimensions
associativity on 3D dialog box, as shown in Figure 3–3.

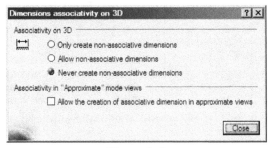

Figure 3–3

This option ensures that drawing dimensions update with
changes to the referenced 3D geometry.

Step 2 - Select the appropriate dimensioning tool.

Select the appropriate dimensioning tool in the Dimensions toolbar, as shown in Figure 3–4.

Figure 3–4

Step 3 - Select the appropriate elements of the view.

Select the appropriate element(s) that correspond to the type of dimensioning tool.

For example, to obtain a diameter dimension, select the **Diameter** tool in the Dimensions toolbar and select the hole to dimension. Click the left mouse button to place the dimension, as shown in Figure 3–5.

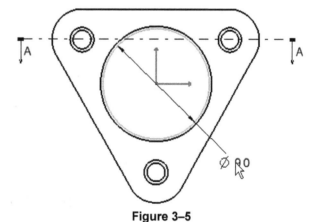

Figure 3–5

Tools Palette

The Tools Palette toolbar displays when you are placing a dimension, as shown in Figure 3–6. It enables you to select a forced dimension placement mode. These options ensure that the dimension is created correctly.

Figure 3–6

The options are described as follows:

Force Mode		Description
		Projected dimension according to cursor position.
		Force dimension on element.
		Force horizontal dimension.
		Force vertical dimension.
		Force dimension along a direction.
		True length dimension.
		Detect an intersection point.

Step 4 - Manipulate dimensions, as required.

Moving Dimensions

You can move dimensions once they have been created using the following methods (shown in Figure 3–7):

• Click and drag on a handle to move both witness lines.

• Click and drag on a dimension to move it left, right, up, or down.

• Click on an arrow head to flip it.

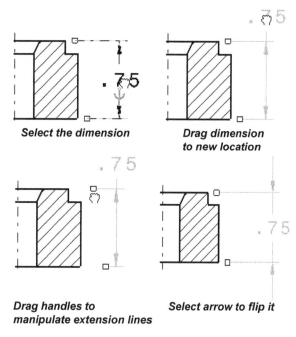

Select the dimension   **Drag dimension
to new location**

**Drag handles to
manipulate extension lines**   **Select arrow to flip it**

Figure 3–7

Dimension Properties

Dimension Properties & Numerical Properties toolbars

You can modify the tolerance format and value of a dimension using the Dimension Properties toolbar options. The Numerical Properties toolbar options enable you to modify the units and the number of decimal places of a dimension. The toolbars are shown in Figure 3–8.

Figure 3–8

Properties dialog box

You can modify dimension properties using the Properties dialog box. To change dimension properties using the dialog box, right-click on the dimension and select **Properties**. The Properties dialog box contains various options (categorized under tabs) that you can use to change the properties of the selected dimension, as shown in Figure 3–9.

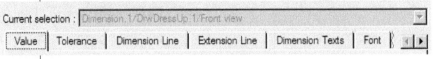

Figure 3–9

The following tabs are described:

- Value

- Tolerance

- Dimension Line

- Extension Line

- Dimension Texts

Value tab

The *Value* tab enables you to orient a dimension, enter an offset value, enable dual dimensioning, and change the format of the value, as shown in Figure 3–10 and Figure 3–11.

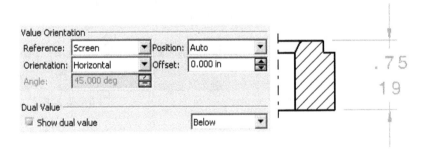

Figure 3–10

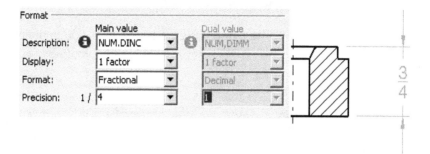

Figure 3–11

Tolerance tab

The *Tolerance* tab enables you to enter tolerance values and apply the values to a dimension, as shown in Figure 3–12.

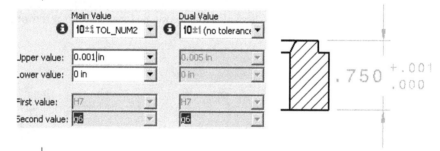

Figure 3–12

Dimension Line tab

The *Dimension Line* tab enables you to modify the color, line thickness, and arrow shape of a dimension, as shown in Figure 3–13.

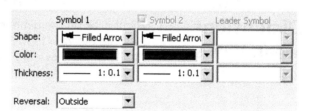

Figure 3–13

Extension Line tab

The *Extension Line* tab enables you to define a funnel for a dimension, as shown in Figure 3–14.

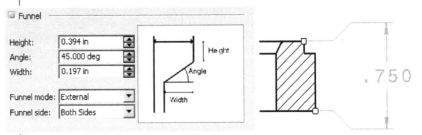

Figure 3–14

Dimension Texts tab

The *Text* tab enables you to add text to dimensions. You can add text above, below, before, or after a dimension value, as shown in Figure 3–15.

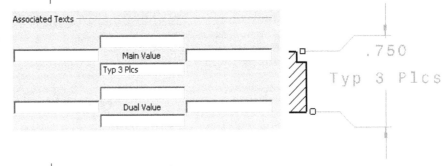

Figure 3–15

Transfer Dimensions Between Views

How To: Transfer Dimensions Between Views

1. Right-click on the dimension and select **Cut**.
2. Activate the view to which you want to transfer the dimension, right-click, and select **Paste**.

3.3 Automatic Dimensions

You can use one of the following methods to automatically create dimensions on your drawing:

- One Step Dimensioning

- Step by Step Dimension Generation

The One Step dimension generation method enables you to place all dimensions onto the drawing at the same time. You can reposition these dimensions after placement.

The Step by Step dimension generation method enables you to step through the creation of each dimension, as shown in Figure 3–16.

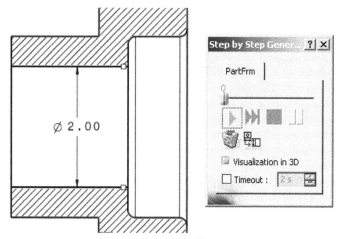

Figure 3–16

3.4 One Step Dimensioning

General Steps

Use the following general steps to create dimensions in one step:

1. Select the view to be dimensioned.
2. Start the creation of dimensions.
3. Reposition the dimensions.

Step 1 - Select the view to be dimensioned.

Select the view to be dimensioned from the sheet or specification tree (the view does not need to be active).

CATIA dimensions all views on the current sheet if you do not select a view to be dimensioned.

Step 2 - Start the creation of dimensions.

Click (Generate Dimensions) in the Dimension Generation toolbar. All possible dimensions display for the view, as shown in Figure 3–17. All views are dimensioned appropriately if you did not select a view.

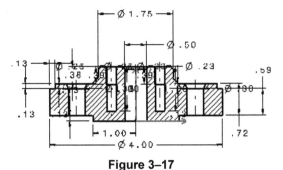

Figure 3–17

Step 3 - Reposition the dimensions.

Activate the view containing the dimensions and select
Tools>Positioning>Dimension Positioning to automatically
reposition all linear dimensions, as shown in Figure 3–18. Radial
dimension positions are not affected and must be manually
repositioned.

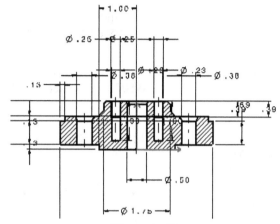

Figure 3–18

3.5 Step by Step Dimensioning

General Steps

Use the following general steps to create dimensions step by step:

1. Start the creation of dimensions.
2. Enter a timeout value.
3. Generate dimensions.
4. Remove or transfer dimensions.
5. Reposition dimensions.

Step 1 - Start the creation of dimensions.

Select the view before beginning the options if you only want to dimension one view.

Click  (Generate Dimensions Step by Step) in the Dimension Generation toolbar to start the creation of dimensions.

Step 2 - Enter a timeout value.

Enter a timeout value in seconds or clear the **Timeout** option to proceed manually, as shown in Figure 3–19.

Figure 3–19

Step 3 - Generate dimensions.

Click ▶ (Next Dimension Generation) to begin generating dimensions. The first dimension displays on an appropriate view. The system pauses the length of time entered in the *Timeout* field and creates the next dimension.

Step 4 - Remove or transfer dimensions.

Click ▐▐ (Pause in Dimension Generation) to pause the dimension generation. When dimension generation has been paused, 🗑 (Not Generated) and ⧉ (Transferred) become available:

- Click 🗑 (Not Generated) to remove a dimension that is not required.

- Click ⧉ (Transferred) to switch from the current view to a different view by selecting the different view.

Step 5 - Reposition dimensions.

Manually reposition the dimensions or activate the view, and then select **Tools>Positioning>Dimension Positioning** to automatically reposition all of the linear dimensions. Radial dimension positions are not affected and must be repositioned manually.

3.6 Dimension Generation Settings

You can modify dimension settings to generate dimensions on your drawing more effectively. Select **Tools>Options> Mechanical Design>Drafting** to change the default dimension generation settings. When the Options dialog box opens, select the *Generation* tab.

The *Dimension Generation* area is shown in Figure 3–20 and the options are described in the table below.

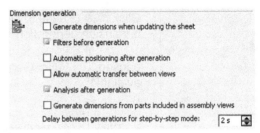

Figure 3–20

Option	Description
Generate dimensions when updating the sheet	Automatically adds dimensions for new features when drawing is updated.
Filters before generation	Opens the Dimension Generation Filters dialog box, as shown below.

Automatic positioning after generation	Automatically cleans the display of dimensions after One Step dimension generation.
Allow automatic transfer between views	Enables transfer of dimensions between views using (Transferred).
Analysis after generation	Automatically opens the Generated Dimension Analysis dialog box after the dimension generation, which displays the number of constraints in the 3D model and the number of dimensions generated on the drawing. The dialog box also enables visual review of the 3D constraints and corresponding dimensions.
Generate dimensions from parts included in assembly views	Extracts 3D part constraints, in addition to assembly constraints, when generating assembly dimensions.

3.7 Modifying Dimension Properties

Automatically generated dimensions might contain lines and text that are difficult to read and interpret. Furthermore, they might not fulfill corporate standards in tolerancing and graphical representations. Dimension properties can be manually modified to improve drawing readability and to customize dimension tolerances and graphics.

The standard Windows shortcut keys <Alt> + <Enter> can also be used to access Properties.

To display dimension properties, select the dimension and select **Edit>Properties**. Select multiple dimensions by pressing <Ctrl>. The Properties dialog box opens as shown in Figure 3–21. It covers the following tabs: *Value, Tolerance, Dimension Line, Extension Line, Dimension Texts, Font, Text.*

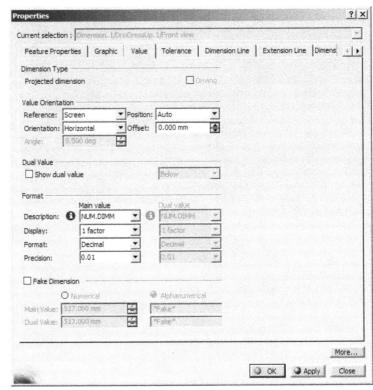

Figure 3–21

Value Tab

Projected Dimension

The **Driving** option controls the associativity of dimensions that have been added to geometry that is not imported from the 3D model, but rather sketched in the Drafting workbench using tools such as Line, Circle, Profile, etc. When activated, this option enables you to modify the dimension values that drive the sketched geometry. Dimensions with the **Driving** option enabled display in blue in the drawing display. Double-click on the value to modify it in the Dimension Value dialog box, as shown in Figure 3–22.

*The **Drive geometry** option can also be selected in the Dimension Value dialog box.*

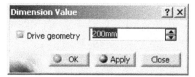

Figure 3–22

Value Orientation

The dimension value can be oriented horizontally, vertically, or at a fixed angle by changing the **Orientation** type. It can also be offset from the dimension line by an **Offset** distance. The value can be placed in or outside the extension lines by modifying **Position**. The dimension shown in Figure 3–23 is oriented at a fixed angle of 45 degrees and is offset from the dimension line (center) by 4.5mm.

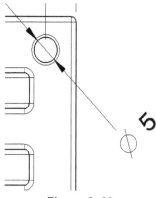

Figure 3–23

Dual Value

Selecting the **Show dual value** option inserts a second dimensional value below, beside, or as a fraction of the first dimensional value. The format options enable you to specify the units, precision, and display format for both the first and dual value dimensions.

A dual value in inches, with a decimal format with one-thousandth precision, and located below the first dimension value is shown in Figure 3–24.

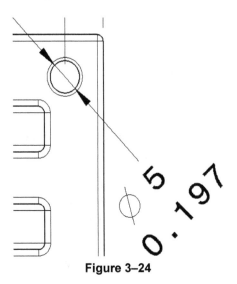

Figure 3–24

Fake Dimension

True dimension values can be replaced with user-defined numerical or alphanumeric values. Fake dimensions are limited to six characters; for longer strings, dimension text annotation should be used. Dimensions containing fake values display in brown on the drawing display.

Fake dimensions are useful when dimensioning a part that includes a design table. A symbolic dimension can be applied using a fake dimension. This symbol can then be related to a table on the drawing that defines the possible sizes in the design table, as shown in Figure 3–25.

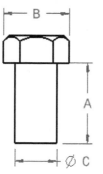

PartNumber	A	B	C
Bolt01	30	12.5	7.5
Bolt02	30	12.5	8
Bolt03	30	12.5	8.5
Bolt04	40	15	9
Bolt05	40	15	9.5
Bolt06	40	15	10

Figure 3–25

Tolerance Tab

Tolerance values can be created for the main and dual value dimensions separately. To create a tolerance, select the type in the drop-down list, and enter the upper and lower limits in the *Upper Value* and *Lower Value* fields. The tolerance value displays as shown in Figure 3–26.

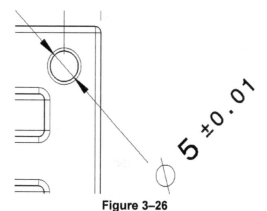

Figure 3–26

Dimension Line Tab

Change the dimension line graphics and symbol types. Select either the regular, two part, or leader-type line type in the Representations drop-down list, and customize the line and symbol thickness and color. The Reversal drop-down list switches the orientation of the dimension lines from inside to outside the extension lines.

The dimension line representation has been changed to **Two Parts** and *thickened* to **1** in Figure 3–27.

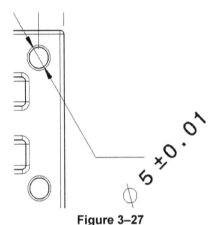

Figure 3–27

Extension Line Tab

Change the color and thickness of the extension lines, or disable them altogether by clearing the **Display extension line** option. By default, extension lines are perpendicular to the dimensioned edge. Skew the lines by entering a **Slant** angle.

Extremities

Overrun specifies the distance that an extension line extends past the dimension line. The **Blanking** option enables the extension line to be offset from the dimensioned face.

Funnel

Specify the height, width, and angle of an extension line funnel. **Funnel side** specifies which extension line to funnel, and **Funnel mode** switches between an external and internal funnel.

A slant angle of 5 degrees and a top funnel have been applied to the dimension shown in Figure 3–28.

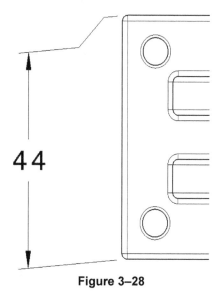

Figure 3–28

Dimension Texts Tab

Dimension texts are used to annotate dimensions. **Main value** represents the main dimension value text. The orientation of the text fields in this tab indicate the orientation of the text in the drawing view. You can also enter **Prefix-suffix** and **Associated Texts**, which can contain symbols.

The Typ annotation has been added as a suffix on the dimension shown in Figure 3–29.

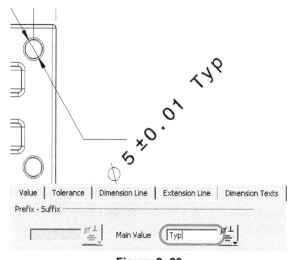

Figure 3–29

Font Tab Customize dimension font style, size, and character ratio/ spacing.

Text Tab Create text frames and set text positioning, as shown in Figure 3–30.

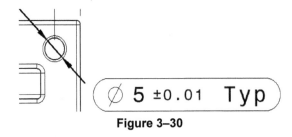

Figure 3–30

Practice 3a

Annotate a Drawing

Practice Objectives

- Create and manipulate dimensions.
- Create tolerances.

In this practice, you will continue developing the **ExhaustFlange** drawing by adding dimensions and other annotations. The annotated Front view is shown in Figure 3–31.

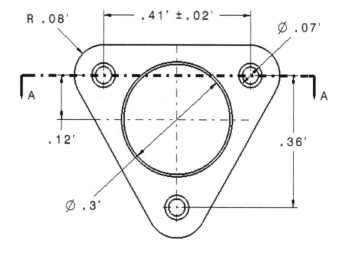

Front view
Scale: 1:2

Figure 3–31

Task 1 - Open the ExhaustFlange.CATDrawing.

1. Open **ExhaustFlange_Dims.CATDrawing** and **ExhaustFlange.CATPart** from the *ExhaustManifold* directory.

   If you completed the previous practice you can continue to use **ExhaustFlange.CATDrawing** instead.

The drawing displays as shown in Figure 3–32.

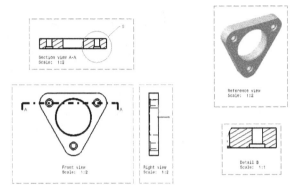

Figure 3–32

Task 2 - Show the Axis and Center Lines of a view.

1. Activate the Front view.

2. In the specification tree, select the Front view.

3. In the specification tree, hold <Shift> and select the **Detail B** view. All of the views in between should be highlighted, as shown in Figure 3–33.

Figure 3–33

4. In the specification tree, right-click on any view and select **Properties**. The Properties dialog box opens.

5. In the Properties dialog box, in the *Dress-up* area, select the **Axis**, **Center Line**, and **3D spec** options as shown in Figure 3–34. Apply the changes and note the result.

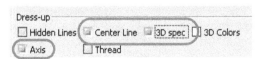

Figure 3–34

6. Click **OK**.

Task 3 - Add dimensions to the drawing.

1. Ensure that the Front view is active.

2. Zoom in on the Front view. In the Dimensions toolbar, click

   (Dimensions).

3. Select the hole on the left side for the first dimension reference, as shown in Figure 3–35. The system creates a diameter dimension.

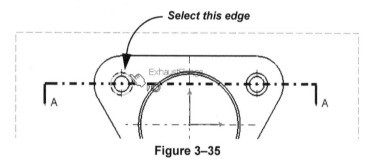

Figure 3–35

4. Select the hole on the right side for the second dimension reference, as shown in Figure 3–36. A length dimension displays between the two references.

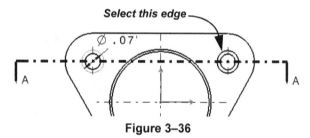

Figure 3–36

5. Drag the dimension line to the position shown in Figure 3–37 and place the dimension by clicking the left mouse button.

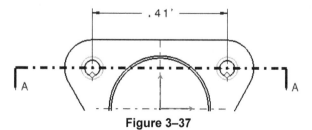

Figure 3–37

Task 4 - Create a dimension.

1. Double-click (Dimensions) to create the dimensions shown in Figure 3–38.

Use the Force dimension placement mode options in the Tools Palette toolbar to force the dimension to be vertical, as required.

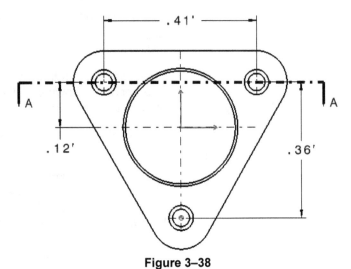

Figure 3–38

2. Double-click (Diameter Dimensions) to create the two diameter dimensions shown in Figure 3–39.

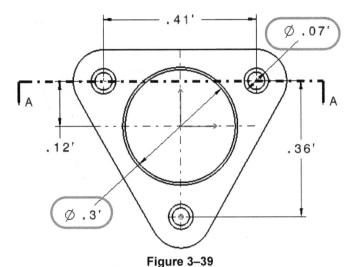

Figure 3–39

3. Click [R←] (Radius Dimensions) to create the R.08'
   dimension shown in Figure 3–40.

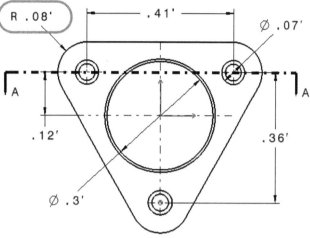

Figure 3–40

4. Use [↔] (Dimensions) and [ø↔] (Diameter Dimensions) to
   create the dimensions shown in Figure 3–41.

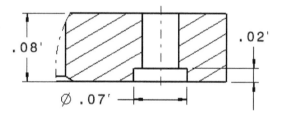

Detail B
Scale: 1:1
Figure 3–41

Task 5 - Manipulate dimensions.

1. Select the **.08' dimension** from Detail B. Right-click and select **Cut**, as shown in Figure 3–42.

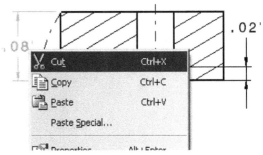

Figure 3–42

2. Click  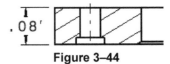 (Fit All In) to display the complete drawing.

3. In the specification tree, right-click on Section view A-A and select **Paste**, as shown in Figure 3–43.

Figure 3–43

4. Move the .08' dimension to the position shown in Figure 3–44.

Figure 3–44

Task 6 - Add tolerance to a dimension.

1. Select the **.41' dimension**. The Dimension Properties and Numerical Properties toolbars become active, as shown in Figure 3–45.

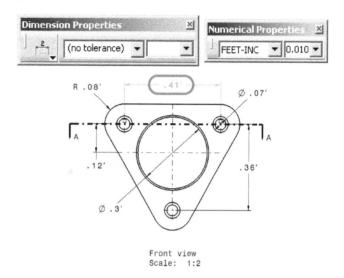

Front view
Scale: 1:2

Figure 3–45

2. In the Tolerance type drop-down list, select **ANS_NUM2** as shown in Figure 3–46.

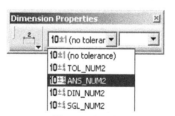

Figure 3–46

The .41' dimension updates, as shown in Figure 3–47.

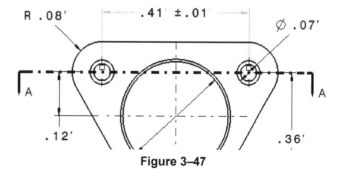

Figure 3–47

3. Select **+-0.20** as the value of the tolerance, as shown in Figure 3–48.

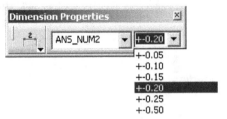

Figure 3–48

The .41' dimension updates, as shown in Figure 3–49.

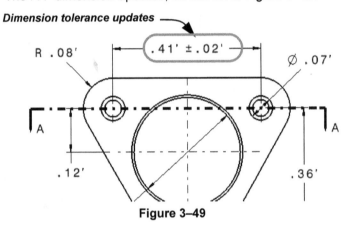

Figure 3–49

4. Zoom in on the Detail view and select the **.02' dimension**, as shown in Figure 3–50.

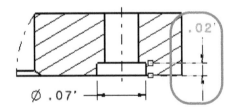

Detail B
Scale: 1:1

Figure 3–50

5. Right-click and select **Properties**.

6. Select the *Tolerance* tab and set the following values as shown in Figure 3–51:

    - *Main Value:* **ANS_NUM2**
    - *Upper value:* **0.008**
    - *Lower value:* **-0.004**

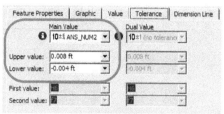

Figure 3–51

7. Click **OK**. The drawing displays as shown in Figure 3–52.

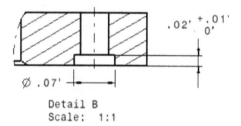

Figure 3–52

Note that the tolerance reads 0'. This is because the dimension precision is currently set to 0.01. In the next steps, you will increase the precision so that the tolerance can be seen.

8. Open the Properties dialog box for the .02' dimension and select the *Value* tab. Set the following values as shown in Figure 3–53:

    - *Display:* **2 factors**
    - *Precision:* **0.001**

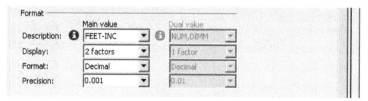

Figure 3–53

9. Click **OK**. The drawing updates as shown in Figure 3–54. Note that the dimensions have changed to inches.

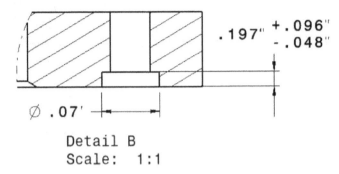

Detail B
Scale: 1:1

Figure 3–54

Task 7 - Create a chamfer dimension.

1. Zoom in on the Right view, as shown in Figure 3–55.

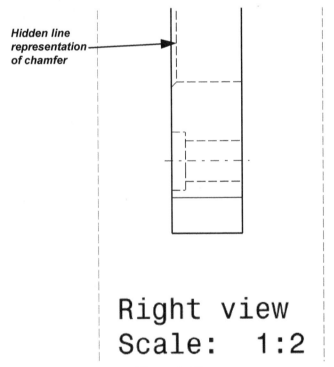

Figure 3–55

2. Click  (Chamfer Dimensions). The Tools Palette displays with the options for controlling the chamfer dimension, as shown in Figure 3–56.

Figure 3–56

3. Select the **Length x Angle** option and select the three references shown in Figure 3–57.

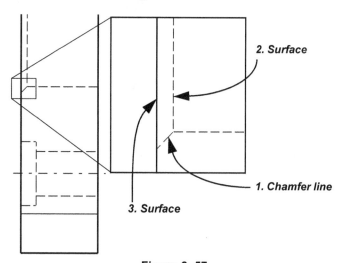

Figure 3–57

4. Place the chamfer dimension. The drawing displays as shown in Figure 3–58.

*If the dimension does not look like the one in Figure 3–58, right-click and select **Length x Angle** before placing the dimension.*

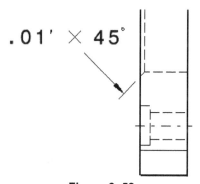

Figure 3–58

Task 8 - Create a thread dimension.

In this task, you will add a thread dimension to the drawing. The thread dimension can only be shown by selecting the representation of a thread surface. You must enable thread display in the drawing view.

1. In the specification tree, press and hold <Ctrl>, select Section View A-A and Detail B, then right-click and select **Properties**.

2. Enable the **Thread** option, as shown in Figure 3–59.

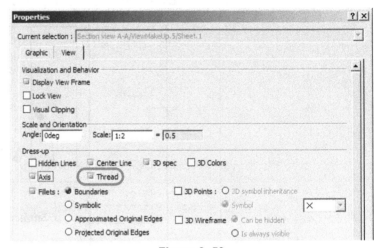

Figure 3–59

The updated drawing view displays as shown in Figure 3–60.

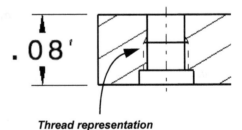

Thread representation

Figure 3–60

3. Zoom in on Section A-A View and click (Thread Dimension) and select the thread representation.

4. Arrange the dimensions so that the drawing displays as shown in Figure 3–61.

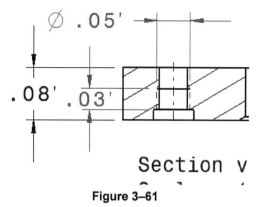

Figure 3–61

Task 9 - Create a true length dimension.

---

1. Zoom in on the Reference view.

2. Click 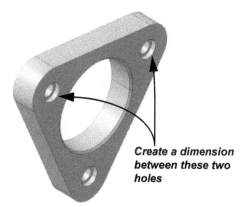 (Length/Distance Dimensions) to create a Length/Distance dimension between the two holes shown in Figure 3–62.

Create a dimension between these two holes

Figure 3–62

Note that you cannot create the dimension because the view generation mode is currently set to **Raster**. To create the dimension, the view generation mode must first be changed to **Exact view**.

3. Click (Length/Distance Dimensions) again to deactivate it.

4. In the specification tree, right-click on **Reference** view and select **Properties**.

5. In the *View* tab, in the View generation mode drop-down list, select **Exact view**.

6. Click **OK**.

7. Create a Length/Distance dimension between the two holes shown in Figure 3–63.

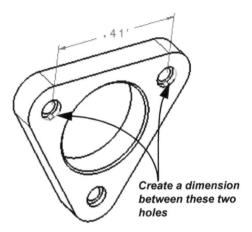

Create a dimension between these two holes

Figure 3–63

Design Considerations

When dimensioning an isometric view, the system automatically switches the dimension representation to **True Length Dimension**, as indicated by the highlighted icon in the Tools Palette, as shown in Figure 3–64.

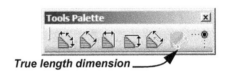

True length dimension

Figure 3–64

8. Place the dimension on the drawing. The extension lines of the dimension are not exactly vertical. To change this orientation, you will use the Dimension Properties dialog box.

9. Right-click on the .41' dimension and select **Properties**. Select the *Extension Line* tab, as shown in Figure 3–65.

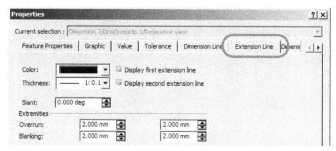

Figure 3–65

10. Enter a *Slant value* of **7deg** and click **OK**. The drawing displays as shown in Figure 3–66.

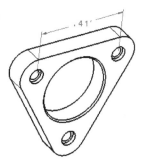

Figure 3–66

Task 10 - Create a drawing sheet and add a view.

1. In the Drawing toolbar, click [ ] (New Sheet) to create a new sheet. **Sheet.2** is added to the specification tree.

2. Create a Front view on **Sheet.2**. Select the surface from the 3D model shown in Figure 3–67.

Select surface opposite side with counter-bores

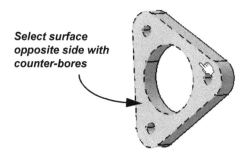

Figure 3–67

3. Place the view on the sheet.

4. Change the *scale* of the view to **1:2**. The Front view displays as shown in Figure 3–68.

Figure 3–68

Task 11 - Create a hole table.

Design Considerations

The units defined in the Options dialog box affect the creation of the hole dimension table. To create a hole dimension table in inches, the default unit system must be also be in inches.

1. Select **Tools>Options>General>Parameters and Measure**, and select the *Units* tab.

2. In the list, select **Length**. Change the *Units* to **Inch**, as shown in Figure 3–69.

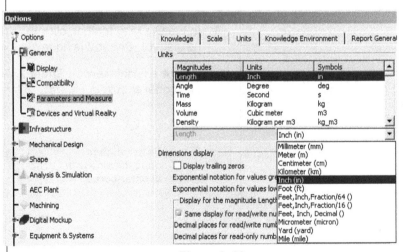

Figure 3–69

3. Click **OK**.

4. Hold <Ctrl> and select the three holes shown in Figure 3–70.

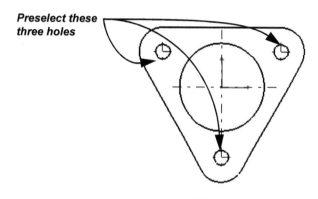

Front view
Scale: 1:2

Figure 3–70

5. In the Dimensions toolbar, click 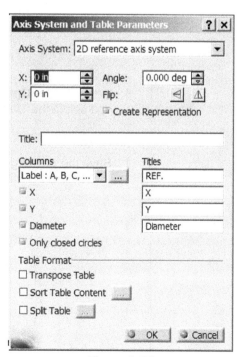 (Hole Dimension Table). The Axis System and Table Parameters dialog box opens as shown in Figure 3–71.

Figure 3–71

6. Click **OK** to accept all of the default values.

7. Drag the hole table to a location, as shown in Figure 3–72. Click the left mouse button to finalize the creation of the hole table.

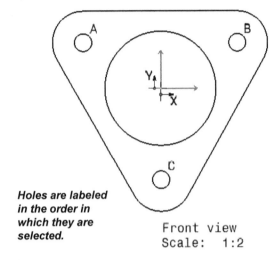

Holes are labeled in the order in which they are selected.

Front view
Scale: 1:2

REF.	X	Y	Diameter
A	-2.46	1.42	0.54
B	2.46	1.42	0.54
C	0	-2.84	0.54

Figure 3–72

8. Select **Tools>Options>General>Parameters and Measure**, and select the *Units* tab.

9. Reset the *default unit* to **Millimeter**.

10. Save the drawing and close all of the files.

Practice 3b | Linear Dimensioning

Practice Objectives

- Create Length/Distance Dimensions.
- Create Chained Dimensions.
- Create Stacked Dimensions.
- Create Cumulated Dimensions.

This practice is intended to demonstrate the differences between the four linear dimensions tools in the Drafting workbench. The drawing created in this practice is not intended to be fully detailed. It is only used to demonstrate the chained, cumulated, and stacked dimension tools.

The completed drawing displays as shown in Figure 3–73.

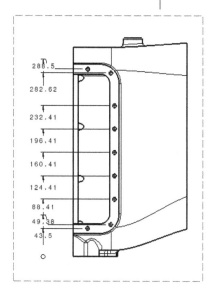

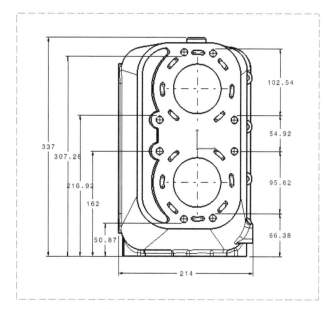

Figure 3–73

Task 1 - Open LinearDimensioning.CATDrawing.

1. Open **LinearDimensioning.CATDrawing** and **LinearDimensioning.CATPart**. The drawing displays as shown in Figure 3–74.

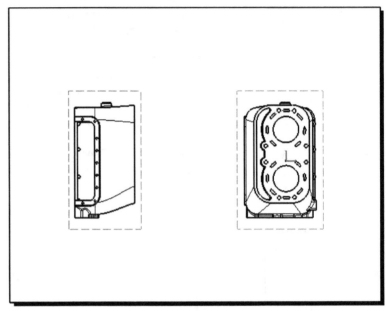

Figure 3–74

Task 2 - Create a length dimension.

In this task, you will create an overall height and width dimension for the view on the right side of the drawing.

1. Expand the Dimensions flyout and drag the toolbar to a floating position on the interface, as shown in Figure 3–75.

Figure 3–75

2. Zoom in on the Front view, activate it, and click

   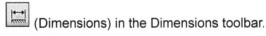 (Dimensions) in the Dimensions toolbar.

3. Create the two dimensions shown in Figure 3–76.

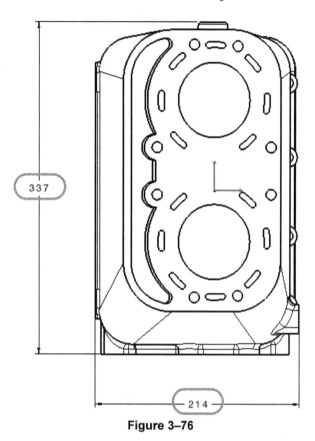

Figure 3–76

Design Considerations

The **Dimensions** icon is used to create a variety of independent dimensions. Each dimension can be modified, moved, and deleted independent of the rest.

___

Task 3 - Create a chained dimension.

___

1. Click ▦ (Chained Dimensions).

2. In the Tool Palette toolbar, click ▧ (Force Vertical Dimension).

3. Begin the chain by selecting the bottom edge of the front view, as shown in Figure 3–77.

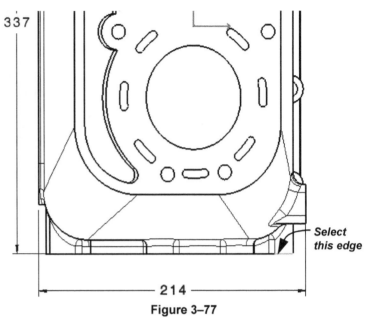

Figure 3–77

4. Select the hole shown in Figure 3–78.

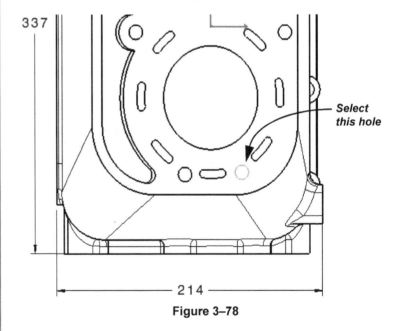

Figure 3–78

A length dimension displays between the two selected entities, as shown in Figure 3–79. Do not place the dimension.

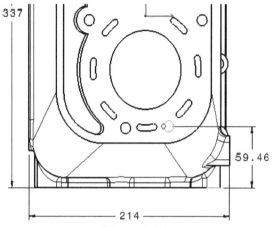

Figure 3–79

5. Continue to select the three holes as shown in Figure 3–80. A chain of dimensions is created.

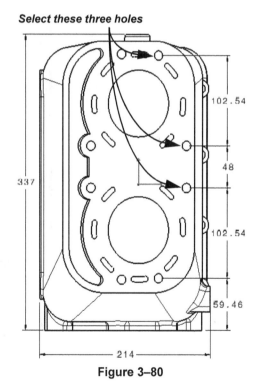

Figure 3–80

6. To complete the creation of the dimension chain, select a placement location on the drawing.

7. Select and drag any of the dimensions. Since the dimensions were created as a chain, all four dimensions move together.

Design Considerations

A dimension chain is a quick method of developing a series of connected dimensions. It minimizes the number of references selected.

Task 4 - Create a stacked dimension.

To compare the results of chained and stacked dimensions, you will create a similar set of dimensions on the left side of the Front view.

1. Click [icon] (Stacked Dimensions).

2. Select the edge and the holes as shown in Figure 3–81.

To lock the orientation of the dimensions, hold <Ctrl>.

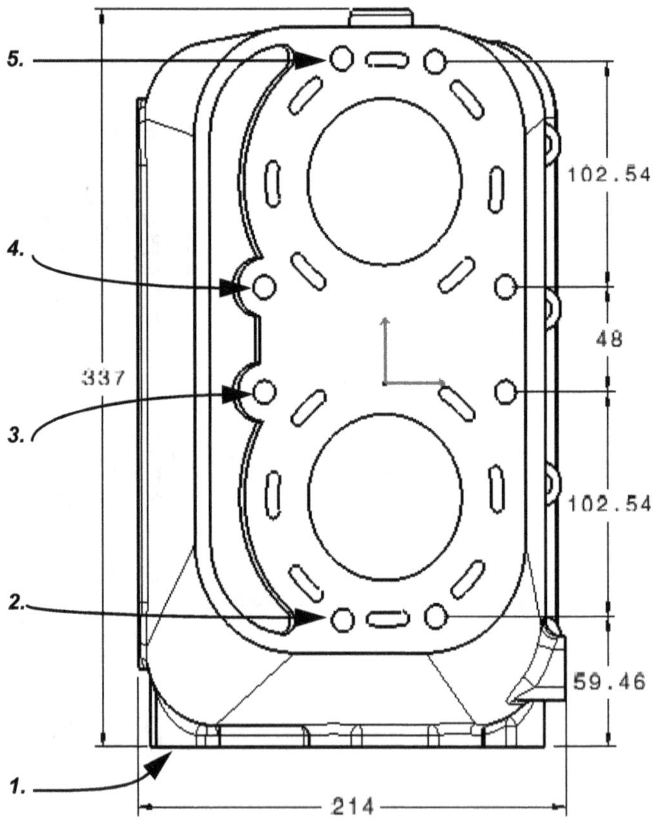

Figure 3–81

3. As you place the dimension, note that the order of dimensions automatically adjusts, depending on the side of the selected features on which the dimension is placed.

4. Place the dimension. You will need to adjust the position of the 337 dimension, as shown in Figure 3–82.

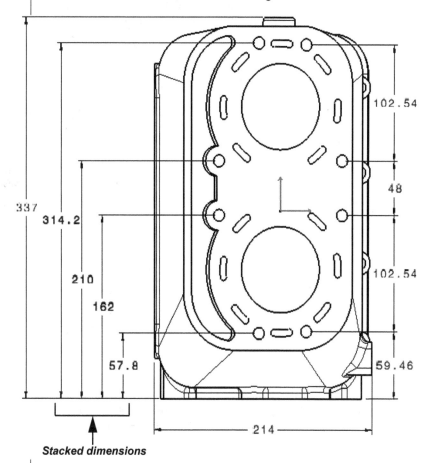

Stacked dimensions

Figure 3–82

Design Considerations

Stacked dimensions behave in the same way as chained dimensions. To delete the dimensions independently, toggle off

(Dimension system selection mode) in the Tools toolbar.

Unlike chained dimensions, stacked dimensions share a common baseline, defined by the first selection.

Task 5 - Create a cumulated dimension.

In this task, you will create a cumulated dimension to dimension the hole positions in the left view. A cumulated dimension is similar to a stacked dimension, because it uses the baseline defined by the first selection. The difference lies in the way the dimensions are represented.

1. Activate the Left view.

2. Click (Cumulated Dimensions).

3. Select the bottom edge of the left view and select the hole to create the dimension shown in Figure 3–83. Do not place the dimension.

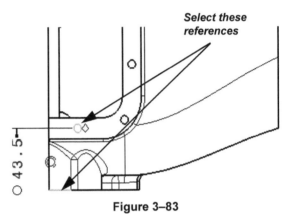

Select these references

Figure 3–83

Design Considerations

Note the default orientation of the dimension. To dimension all of the holes on the bottom mounting surface, the orientation should be rotated 90 degrees. This is done using the **Value Orientation** option.

4. Before placing the dimension, right-click on it and select **Value Orientation**.

5. In the Orientation drop-down list, select **Perpendicular** and click **OK**. The system displays the dimension horizontally.

6. Continue to select the remaining eight holes to create the dimensions shown in Figure 3–84.

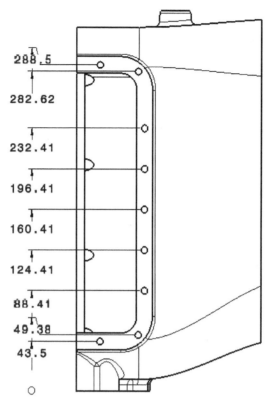

288.5
282.62
232.41
196.41
160.41
124.41
88.41
49.38
43.5

Figure 3–84

7. Save all of the files and close all of the windows.

Design Considerations

The units of a dimension can be changed after it has been created using the options in the Numerical Properties toolbar. Note that changing the default units of dimensions must be done by a CAD Administrator from the Drawing Standards file.

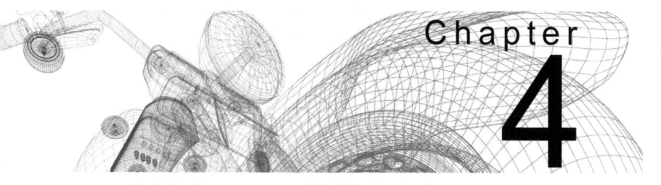

Geometric Tolerancing

Geometric tolerancing is used to display manufacturing and assembly tolerances in the drawing.

Learning Objectives in this Chapter

- Review Geometric Tolerancing terminology.
- Create Geometric Tolerances.

4.1 Geometric Tolerancing Terminology

In many cases, the manufacturing process inherently controls the accuracy of machined parts. If there is doubt about the adequacy of the manufacturing control or if a particular form must be held within closer limits to meet functional or interchangeability requirements, a geometrical tolerance must be specified.

Geometrical tolerances control the position of features or the form, orientation, or location of surfaces. Geometrical tolerances are created using the Tolerancing toolbar, as shown in Figure 4–1.

Figure 4–1

Figure 4–2 shows an example of a geometrical tolerance control frame.

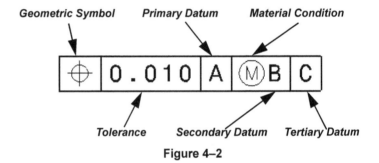

Figure 4–2

Definition of Terms

The datum, material condition, and supplementary symbols are described as follows:

Symbol	Description
A	Datum Feature
Ø	Diameter

Symbol	Description
Ⓔ	Envelope
Ⓕ	Free State
Ⓛ	Least Material Condition
Ⓜ	Maximum Material Condition
Ⓟ	Projected Tolerance Zone
Ⓢ	Regardless of Feature Size
Ⓣ	Tangent Plane
⟨ST⟩	Statical Tolerance
Ⓤ	Unequally
⟨↔⟩	Between

The geometric characteristic symbols used to define geometric tolerances are described as follows:

Symbol	Description	Symbol	Description
⌀⟂≣	None	⟂	Perpendicularity
—	Straightness	//	Parallelism
▱	Flatness	⊕	Position
○	Circularity	◎	Concentricity
⌀⁄	Cylindricity	≡	Symmetry

	Line Profile		Circular Runout
	Surface Profile		Total Runout
	Angularity		

4.2 Create Geometric Tolerances

General Steps

Use the following general steps to create geometric tolerances:

1. Create datum features.
2. Create geometric tolerances.

Step 1 - Create datum features.

How To: Create a Datum Feature

1. In the Geometric Tolerance toolbar, click [A] (Datum Feature).
2. Select elements from the view to locate the datum features, as shown in Figure 4–3.

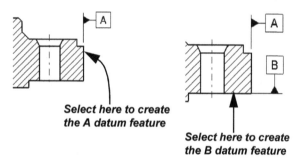

Select here to create the A datum feature

Select here to create the B datum feature

Figure 4–3

3. Enter the datum identifier in the Datum Feature Creation dialog box, as shown in Figure 4–4. The system automatically enters the next sequential letter. Click **OK**.

Figure 4–4

4. Drag the datum tag to the required location.

Step 2 - Create geometric tolerances.

How To: Create a Geometric Tolerance

1. In the Tolerancing toolbar, click  (Geometrical Tolerance).
2. Select a dimension or feature to place the control frame.
3. In the Geometrical Tolerance dialog box, enter the required information as shown in Figure 4–5. Additional frames can be added using the icons in the *Add Tolerances* area.

Figure 4–5

4. Drag the control frame to the required location. The geometrical tolerance control frame displays as shown in Figure 4–6.

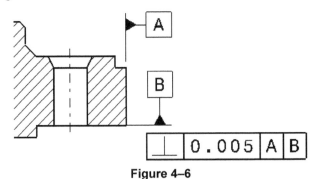

Figure 4–6

Practice 4a

Geometric Tolerances I

Practice Objectives

- Create geometric tolerances.
- Modify geometric tolerances.

In this practice, you will create and modify geometry tolerances for the drawing of **Arm.CATPart**. Once complete, the drawing displays as shown in Figure 4–7.

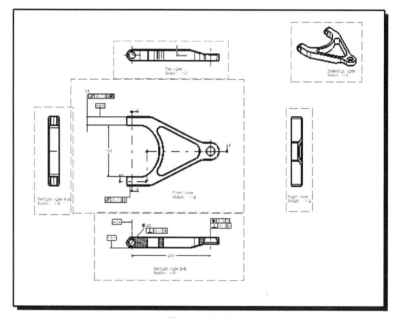

Figure 4–7

Task 1 - Open a CATDrawing.

1. Open **Arm.CATDrawing**. The drawing displays as shown in
    Figure 4–8.

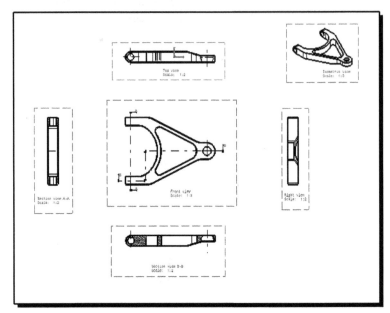

Figure 4–8

Task 2 - Use Links to open the associated part file.

1. Select **Edit>Links**.The Links of document dialog box opens
    as shown in Figure 4–9.

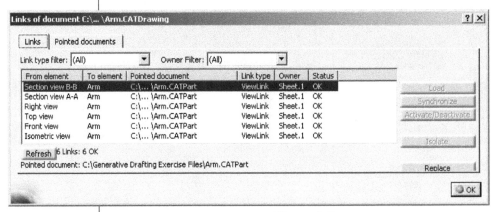

Figure 4–9

2. Select the *Pointed documents* tab. The Links of document dialog box reports the file path to the referenced 3D model, as shown in Figure 4–10.

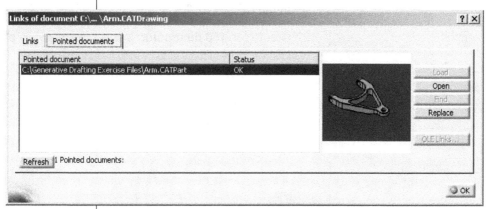

Figure 4–10

3. Click **Open**. The **Arm.CATPart** file opens, as shown in Figure 4–11.

Figure 4–11

4. Activate the **Arm.CATDrawing** window.

Task 3 - Create dimensions.

1. In the Update toolbar, click 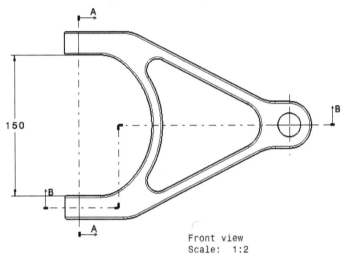 (Update) if required.

2. Create the **150 dimension** in the Front view, as shown in Figure 4–12.

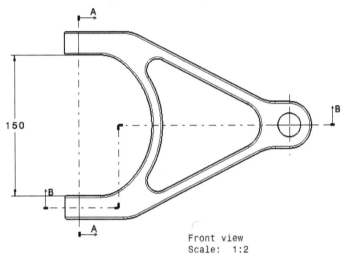

Front view
Scale: 1:2

Figure 4–12

3. Create the **two dimensions** in the Section view B-B, as shown in Figure 4–13.

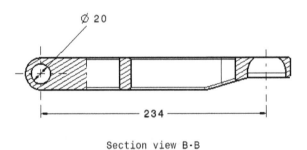

Section view B-B
Scale: 1:2

Figure 4–13

Task 4 - Create a datum.

1. In the Tolerancing toolbar, click 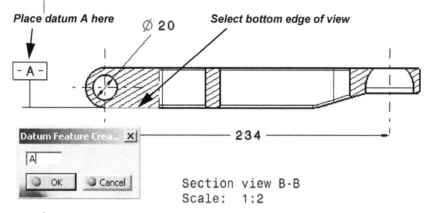 (Datum Feature).

2. Select the bottom edge of the geometry in Section view B-B and place the datum feature, as shown in Figure 4–14.

Place datum A here   Ø 20   *Select bottom edge of view*

Section view B-B
Scale: 1:2

Figure 4–14

3. Ensure that the datum label is **A** and click **OK** to complete the datum feature.

4. Create datum feature **B**, as shown in Figure 4–15.

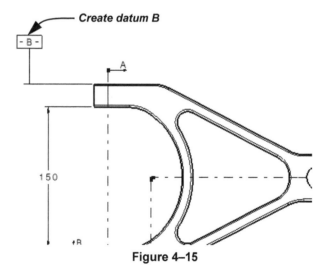

Create datum B

Figure 4–15

Task 5 - Create a geometrical tolerance.

1. In the Tolerances toolbar, click (Geometrical Tolerance).

2. Select the diameter dimension, as shown in Figure 4–16.

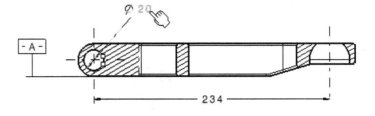

Section view B-B
Scale: 1:2

Figure 4–16

3. In the *Edit Tolerance* area, select the **perpendicularity symbol**, and entering **0.10** to define the geometrical tolerance.

4. Clear the *Reference* area by clicking (Erase).

5. In the *Datum features* area, select **datum B,** as shown in Figure 4–17.

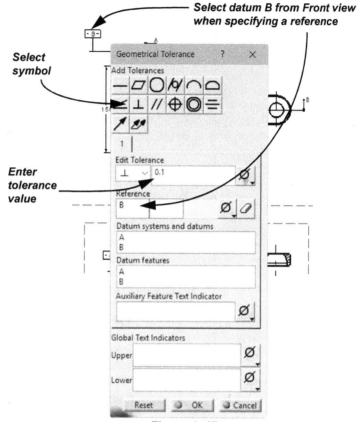

Figure 4–17

6. Click **OK** to complete the feature. The Section view displays as shown in Figure 4–18.

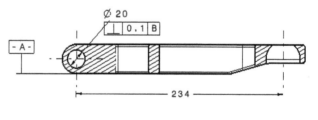

Section view B-B
Scale: 1:2

Figure 4–18

7. Create the 25 dimension in the Front view, as shown in Figure 4–19.

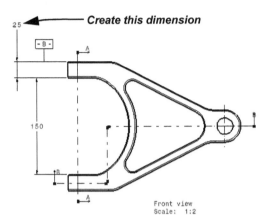

Front view
Scale: 1:2

Figure 4–19

8. Create the geometrical tolerance, as shown in Figure 4–20.

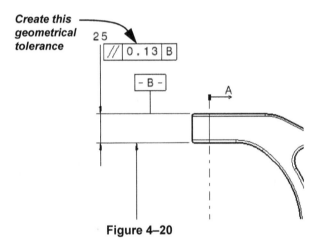

Figure 4–20

9. Create a geometrical tolerance to control the surface shown in Figure 4–21.

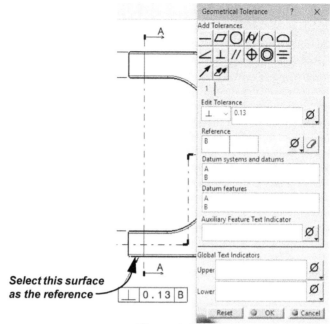

Select this surface as the reference ⟶

Figure 4–21

10. Click **OK**. The feature displays with handles.

11. Select the circle handle (not the middle of the circle) and drag it to the position shown in Figure 4–22.

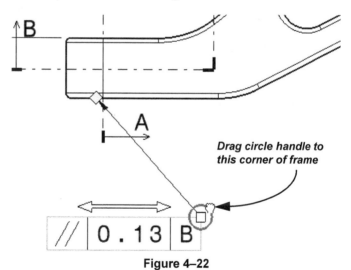

Drag circle handle to this corner of frame

Figure 4–22

12. Use the double-headed arrow to move the geometrical tolerance frame to the location shown in Figure 4–23.

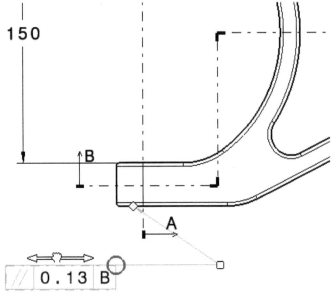

Figure 4–23

13. Select the handle to move the line, as shown in Figure 4–24.

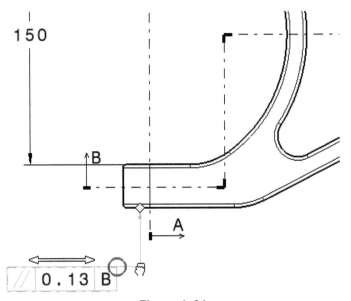

Figure 4–24

14. Select anywhere on the sheet to complete the placement, as shown in Figure 4–25.

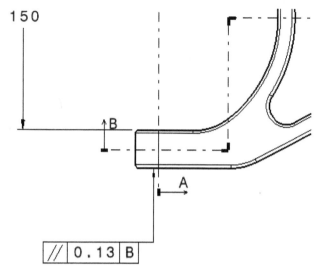

Figure 4–25

15. Save the drawing.

Task 6 - Modify a geometrical tolerance.

1. Double-click on the geometrical tolerance created for the 25 value of the Front view. The Geometrical Tolerance dialog box opens.

2. In the *Reference* field, click to the right of letter B. In the Symbol selection pull-down list, select the **Maximum Material condition** symbol, as shown in Figure 4–26.

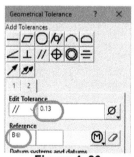

Figure 4–26

3. Click **OK** to complete the modification. The geometrical tolerance displays as shown in Figure 4–27.

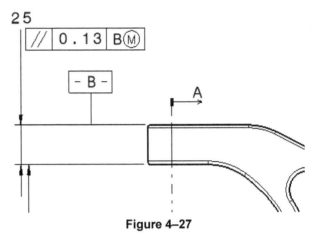

Figure 4–27

Task 7 - Create a datum feature.

1. Create the **C** datum on the axis of the hole in Section view B-B, as shown in Figure 4–28.

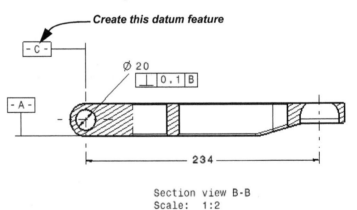

Section view B-B
Scale: 1:2

Figure 4–28

2. Create the geometrical tolerance frame defining the position of the feature, as shown in Figure 4–29. In the Geometrical Tolerance dialog box, in the *Add Tolerances* area, click

⊥ (Perpendicularity) to enter information in the second line.

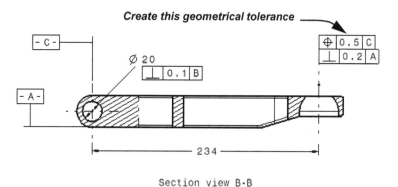

Create this geometrical tolerance

Section view B-B
Scale: 1:2

Figure 4–29

The drawing displays as shown in Figure 4–30.

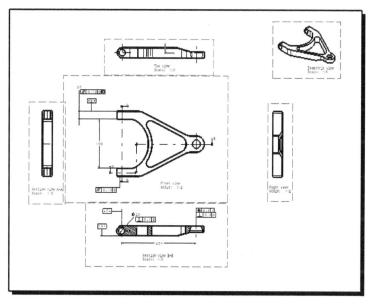

Figure 4–30

3. Save the drawing and close all of the files.

Practice 4b | Geometric Tolerances II

Practice Objectives

- Create dimensions with tolerances.
- Create geometric tolerances.

This practice can be completed at any time during the course, as time permits.

Task 1 - Open files.

1. Open **Cover.CATPart** and **Cover.CATDrawing**.

2. Create a Front view and a Section view, as shown in Figure 4–31. Refer to Figure 4–32 and Figure 4–33 for details.

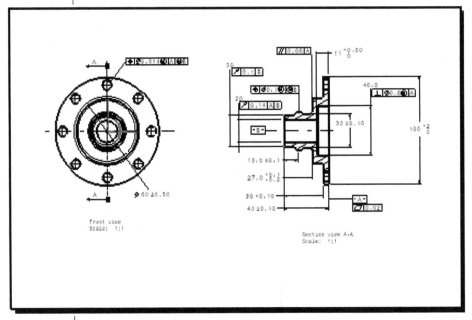

Figure 4–31

3. Create dimensions and geometrical tolerances, as shown in Figure 4–32 and Figure 4–33. The Tolerance format used is **ANS_NUM2**.

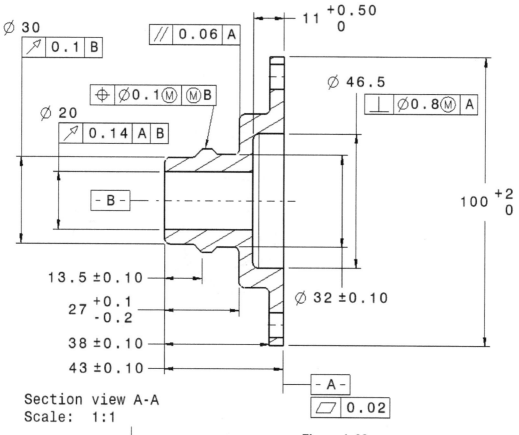

Section view A-A
Scale: 1:1

Figure 4–32

Design Considerations

To change the orientation of a Geometric Tolerance, access its Properties dialog box and change the **Orientation** in the *Text* tab.

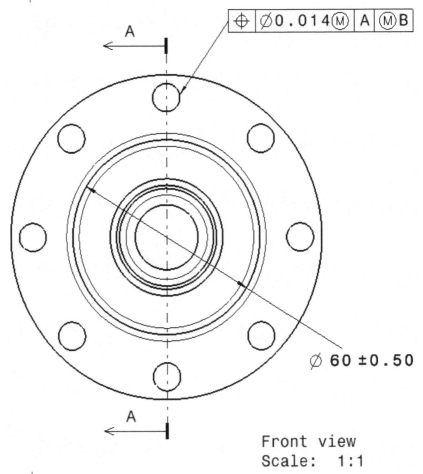

Front view
Scale: 1:1

Figure 4–33

4. Save the files and close all windows.

Design Considerations

The units of a dimension can be changed after it has been created using the options in the Numerical Properties toolbar. Note that changing the default units of dimensions must be done by a CAD Administrator from the Drawing Standards file.

In CATIA R20, view callout styles for projection and section views were modified. Callouts generated in drawings created before R20 will still display using the older style.

Practice 4c

Geometric Tolerances III

Practice Objectives

- Create dimensions with tolerances.
- Create geometric tolerances.

This practice can be completed at any time during the course, as time permits.

Task 1 - Open a part file.

1. Open **Spindle.CATPart**.

2. Create a drawing file in the **C ANSI** format.

3. Create the Front view, Section view, and Isometric view, as shown in Figure 4–34.

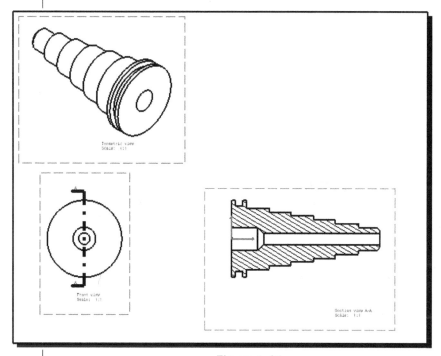

Figure 4–34

4. Create datum features and geometrical tolerances on the section view, as shown in Figure 4–35.

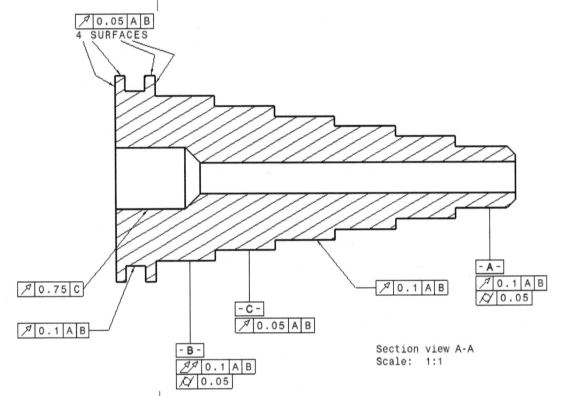

Section view A-A
Scale: 1:1

Figure 4–35

Design Considerations

To add a break to a leader (such as the four surface circular runout tolerance), right-click on the yellow square of the leader and select **Add a Breakpoint**.

5. Save the drawing as **Spindle.CATDrawing** and close all of the files.

Detailing

Detailing a drawing involves adding information to the drawing so that all of the design information is effectively communicated. A fully detailed drawing should communicate enough information to manufacture the part. Detail items include, but are not limited to, notes, tables, and symbols.

Learning Objectives in this Chapter

- Understand annotation creation.
- Create text annotations with and without leaders.
- Edit text with leaders.
- Understand how to organize annotations by alignment.
- Create symbols such as roughness and weld.
- Annotate dress-up elements.
- Learn how to create tables.
- Understand and apply attribute links and dimension and annotation settings.

5.1 Annotation Creation

Text is used to communicate information that cannot be communicated through views or dimensions. You can create two types of text in CATIA V5 generative drafting:

- Free Text

- Associative Text

Free text is added to the Background or to the active view when working in Working Views mode. By default, text displays in a horizontal orientation as shown in Figure 5–1.

Break All Sharp Edges

Figure 5–1

Hold <Ctrl> when selecting a location in which to place vertically oriented text, as shown in Figure 5–2.

Break All Sharp Edges

Figure 5–2

Text associated with a dimension follows any changes to the position of the dimension. Text can be associated with existing dimensions by pressing <Shift> or using the shortcut menu.

To associate text with a dimension, hold <Shift> and select the dimension to which associativity is required when placing the text.

5.2 Create Text Annotations

General Steps

Use the following general steps to create text:

1. Select the view to which to add text.
2. Activate the **Text** tool.
3. Select a location for the text.
4. Enter text.
5. Complete the creation of text.

Step 1 - Select the view to which to add text.

Activate the view in which you want to add text or select **Edit>Sheet Background** to add text to the background. Text added to the background is not associated to any view. Generally, you use this mode to fill in information in the titleblock and revision columns.

Step 2 - Activate the Text tool.

Click ⊞ **T** (Text) in the Text toolbar.

Step 3 - Select a location for the text.

Select a location for the text. The view frame expands to include the text if it is being placed in a view.

Step 4 - Enter text.

The Text Editor dialog box opens once a location for the text has been selected. Enter the text in the Text Editor, as shown in Figure 5–3. To add another line of text to a note, press <Shift> + <Enter>.

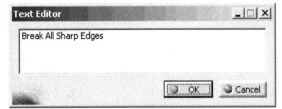

Figure 5–3

Step 5 - Complete the creation of text.

When the required text has been entered, click **OK** and select anywhere in the display to complete the creation of text.

Linking Existing Text

If the text already exists and you require associativity to a dimension, do the following:

1. Move the text to an appropriate location with respect to the dimension to which it is going to be associated.
2. Right-click on the text and select **Positional Link>Create**.
3. Select the dimension to which you want to link the text.

5.3 Create Text with Leader

Text that is added to a drawing can also be attached to a drawing view or other geometry using a leader. An example of text with a leader is shown in Figure 5–4.

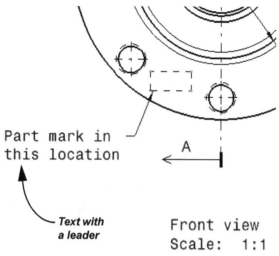

Figure 5–4

General Steps

Use the following general steps to create text with a leader:

1. Activate the **Text with Leader** tool.
2. Select an attachment reference for the leader.
3. Select a location for the text.
4. Enter the text.
5. Complete the creation of text.

Step 1 - Activate the Text with Leader tool.

Click  (Text with Leader) in the Text toolbar.

Step 2 - Select an attachment reference for the leader.

Select an element in the active view to which to attach the leader, as shown in Figure 5–5.

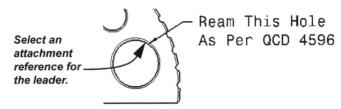

Figure 5–5

Step 3 - Select a location for the text.

Select a location for the text. The view frame expands to include the text.

Step 4 - Enter text.

The Text Editor dialog box opens once a location for the text has been selected. Enter text in the Text Editor, as shown in Figure 5–6.

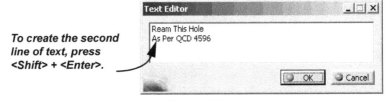

Figure 5–6

Step 5 - Complete the creation of text.

When the required text has been entered, click **OK** and select anywhere in the display to complete the creation of text.

5.4 Edit Text with Leader

Use the following methods to edit the properties of text with a leader.

Handling Annotation Leaders

Select the yellow box on the leader and right-click to display the handling options, as shown in Figure 5–7 and Figure 5–8.

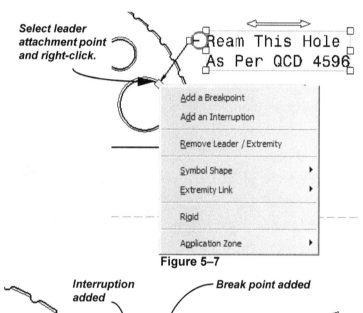

Figure 5–7

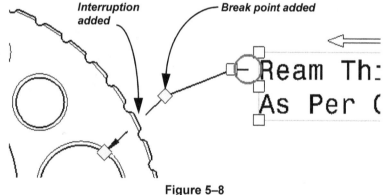

Figure 5–8

You can change the Attachment Symbol Shape, as shown in Figure 5–9.

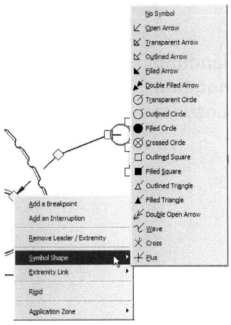

Figure 5–9

Adding Frames

How To: Add a Frame to a Dimension or Text

1. Select the dimension or text.

2. In the Text Properties toolbar, click $\boxed{\text{A None} \quad \vee}$.

3. In the flyout menu, select the required frame as shown in Figure 5–10.

Figure 5–10

A basic dimension is shown in Figure 5–11, indicated by a rectangular frame.

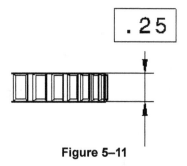

Figure 5–11

Copy Object Graphical Format

The graphical format can be copied from a dimension or text to one or multiple dimensions or text.

How To: Copy the Graphical Format of an Annotation

1. Select one or more annotations to change.

2. In the Graphic Properties toolbar, click ![icon](Copy object format).

3. Select the annotation from which to copy the format, as shown in Figure 5–12.

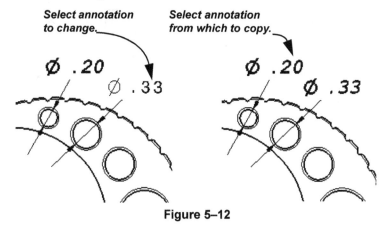

Figure 5–12

5.5 Organizing Annotations - Align Text

You can align and space dimensions and annotation elements (e.g., text) to organize the appearance of drawings.

General Steps

Use the following general steps to align text in your drawing:

1. Select annotation elements.
2. Activate element positioning.
3. Specify alignment conditions.
4. Complete the positioning.

Step 1 - Select annotation elements.

Select the annotation elements by holding <Ctrl>. Selected elements are shown in Figure 5–13.

All selected elements must be from the same view.

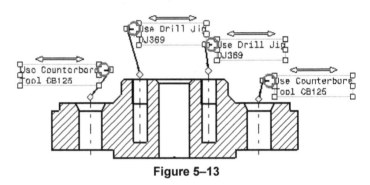

Figure 5–13

Step 2 - Activate element positioning.

Select **Tools>Positioning>Element Positioning**. The Positioning dialog box opens as shown in Figure 5–14.

Figure 5–14

Step 3 - Specify alignment conditions.

Specify the alignment and spacing as required. The text elements shown in Figure 5–15 have been aligned by clicking

 (Align to Top) in the *Align* area in the Position dialog box.

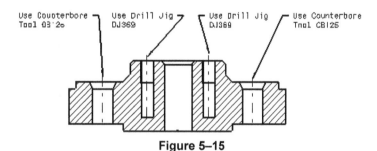

Figure 5–15

Step 4 - Complete the positioning.

Complete the element positioning by selecting **OK** in the Position dialog box and selecting the display.

5.6 Organizing Annotations - Align Dimensions

You can align and space dimensions and annotation elements (e.g., text) to organize the appearance of drawings.

General Steps

Use the following general steps to align dimensions in your drawing:

1. Select the dimensions to be aligned
2. Activate the **Line-Up** tool.
3. Select a reference element.
4. Specify alignment conditions.
5. Complete the positioning.

Step 1 - Select the dimensions to be aligned

Select the dimensions to be aligned. Press <Ctrl> while selecting the dimensions to highlight multiple entities at the same time. Selected dimensions are shown in Figure 5–16.

All selected elements must be from the same view.

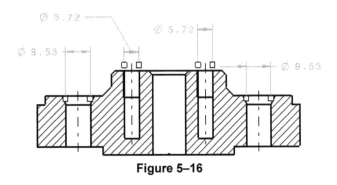

Figure 5–16

Step 2 - Activate the Line-Up tool.

Select **Tools>Positioning>Line-Up** to align the dimensions.

Step 3 - Select a reference element.

Select a reference element relative to which all other dimensions are going to be aligned. The reference element can be a dimension or an element in the view. In the example shown in Figure 5–17, a dimension has been selected as the reference element.

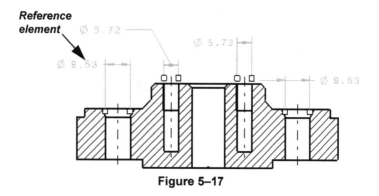

Figure 5–17

Step 4 - Specify alignment conditions.

The Line-Up dialog box opens once a reference element has been selected. Enter the required line-up conditions, as shown in Figure 5–18.

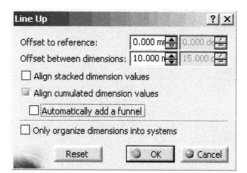

Figure 5–18

Step 5 - Complete the positioning.

Complete the dimension positioning by clicking **OK** in the Line-Up dialog box and selecting in the display area. Dimensions that have been aligned relative to the selected reference display as shown in Figure 5–19.

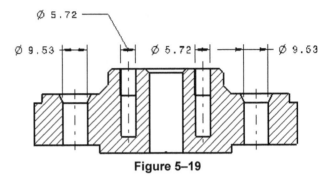

Figure 5–19

5.7 Create Roughness Symbols

Roughness symbols are used to communicate the surface finish texture of a drawing view. The **Roughness** tool can be found in the Symbols toolbar, as shown in Figure 5–20.

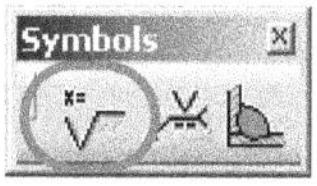

Figure 5–20

General Steps

Use the following general steps to create a roughness symbol:

1. Activate the **Roughness** tool.
2. Select the geometry representing a surface.
3. Specify symbol properties.
4. Complete the symbol creation.

Step 1 - Activate the Roughness tool.

Click ⌐ (Roughness Symbol) in the Symbols toolbar.

Step 2 - Select the geometry representing a surface.

Select the geometry representing the machined surface for which you want to specify a roughness value, as shown in Figure 5–21.

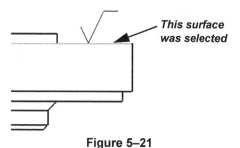

This surface was selected

Figure 5–21

Step 3 - Specify symbol properties.

The Roughness Symbol Editor opens once a reference has been selected. Specify roughness symbol properties by entering text and using the flyout arrows to specify roughness symbology, as shown in Figure 5–22.

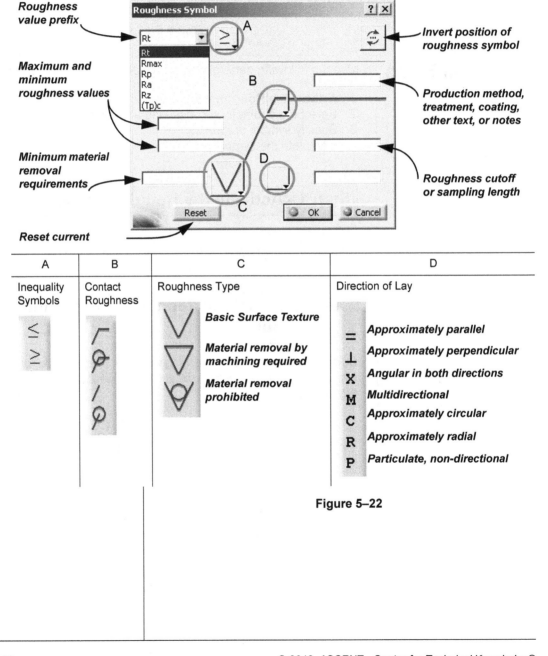

Figure 5–22

A	B	C	D
Inequality Symbols	Contact Roughness	Roughness Type	Direction of Lay

Step 4 - Complete the symbol creation.

Click **OK** in the Roughness Symbol Editor dialog box to complete the creation of the symbol. A completed roughness symbol is shown in Figure 5–23.

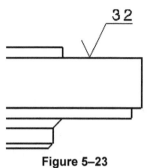

Figure 5–23

5.8 Create Weld Symbols

Two types of weld symbols can be created in a drawing view. The weld symbols can be created from the weld icons found in the Symbols toolbar, as shown in Figure 5–24.

Figure 5–24

General Steps

Use the following general steps to create a welding symbol:

1. Activate the **Welding Symbol** tool.
2. Select a reference.
3. Select a location.
4. Specify weld symbol properties.
5. Complete the weld symbol.

Step 1 - Activate the Welding Symbol tool.

Click ⚒ (Welding Symbol) in the Symbols toolbar.

Step 2 - Select a reference.

Select geometry to define the location of the arrow of the welding symbol, as shown in Figure 5–25.

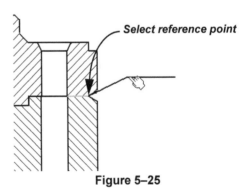

Figure 5–25

Step 3 - Select a location.

Select a location for the welding symbol, as shown in Figure 5–26.

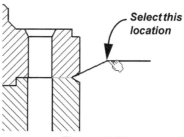

Figure 5–26

Step 4 - Specify weld symbol properties.

The Welding creation dialog box opens once a location for the welding symbol has been selected. Specify welding symbol properties as required by entering values and text, and using the flyout menus to define symbol geometry. The dialog box is shown in Figure 5–27.

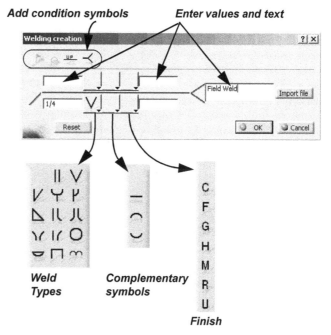

Figure 5–27

Step 5 - Complete the weld symbol.

Click **OK** in the Welding creation dialog box to complete the creation of the welding symbol. The completed welding symbol displays as shown in Figure 5–28.

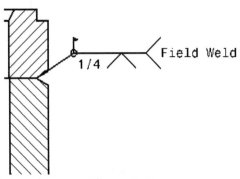

Figure 5–28

Weld Creation

Click 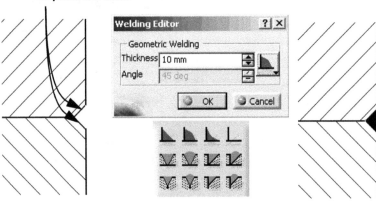 (Weld) to create a graphical representation of a weld. Select the appropriate references and specify the thickness and bead type, as shown in Figure 5–29.

Select references
to place the weld.

Figure 5–29

5.9 Dress-Up Elements

You can create threads, axis, and center lines while generating the view, provided those options have been set in the Properties dialog box, as shown in Figure 5–30.

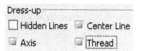

Figure 5–30

If the features have not been generated with the view, have been deleted, or if you only want to display one or two features of a single type, you can create dress-up features in the Dress-up toolbar, as shown in Figure 5–31.

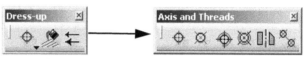

Figure 5–31

Center Line

Click ⊕ (Center Line) to create a center line without a

reference or ⊗ (Center Line with Reference) to create a center line with a reference. The no-reference center line creates a center line that is oriented horizontally and vertically. The reference center line enables you to select a reference to define the orientation of the center line. Note that a center line with a reference cannot be created on an ellipse. The two types of center lines are shown in Figure 5–32.

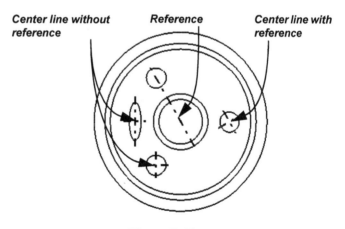

Figure 5–32

Thread

Click ⊕ (Thread) to create a thread without a reference or

⊗ (Thread with Reference) to create a thread with a reference. The no-reference thread is created with a center line that is oriented horizontally and vertically. The reference thread enables you to select an object to determine the orientation of the thread center line. The two types of threads are shown in Figure 5–33.

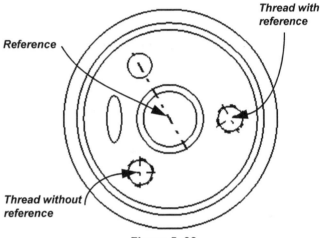

Reference

Thread with reference

Thread without reference

Figure 5–33

Axis Line

Click ⊞ (Axis Line) to create an axis line. If you are working with a section that has been cut through a hole in the part, you only need to select this icon and a reference line to create an axis, as shown in Figure 5–34.

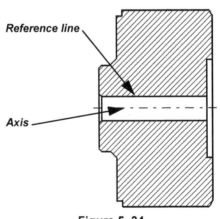

Reference line

Axis

Figure 5–34

If you want to add an axis line between two lines anywhere in a view, click 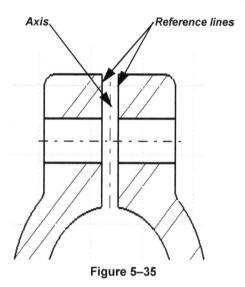 (Axis Line) and select the two lines between which you want to locate the axis line, as shown in Figure 5–35.

Axis ➘   ➚ Reference lines

Figure 5–35

Axis Line and Center Line

Click (Axis line and Center line) and select two holes. The resulting axis and center line are shown in Figure 5–36.

Axis   Centerline

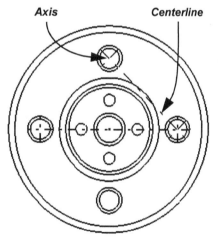

Figure 5–36

Area Fill

Click 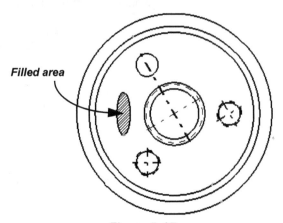 (Area Fill) to fill a selected area or profile with hatching or a solid color. A filled area is shown in Figure 5–37.

Filled area

Figure 5–37

5.10 Create Tables

Using tables in a drawing is an effective method of conveying information. The Generative Drafting workbench provides two types of tables: *Table* and *Table from CSV*.

General Steps

Use the following general steps to create a table:

1. Select the view or background.
2. Activate the **Table** tool.
3. Specify the number of rows and columns.
4. Select a location.
5. Enter the required data.
6. Complete the table.
7. Modify the table, as required.

Step 1 - Select the view or background.

You can add a table to the active view or background. Double-click on the appropriate view to select a view or select **Edit>Background** to activate the background.

Step 2 - Activate the Table tool.

Click ⊞ (Table) in the Table toolbar.

Step 3 - Specify the number of rows and columns.

The Table Editor dialog box opens as shown in Figure 5–38. Enter the required number of columns and rows and click **OK**.

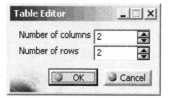

Figure 5–38

Step 4 - Select a location.

Select a location on the drawing sheet to place the table. The table displays as shown in Figure 5–39.

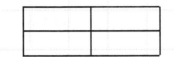

Figure 5–39

Step 5 - Enter the required data.

Double-click on the table. Rows and columns display in orange on the screen and the outside border displays, as shown in Figure 5–40.

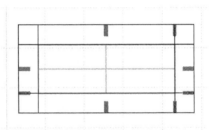

Figure 5–40

Double-click on a cell to add text, as shown in Figure 5–41.

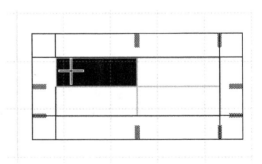

Figure 5–41

Enter the required text in the Text Editor, as shown in
Figure 5–42.

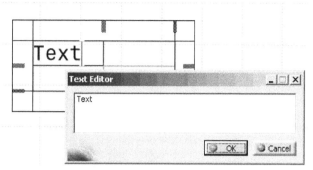

Figure 5–42

Click **OK**.

Step 6 - Complete the table.

Select anywhere on the drawing sheet to deactivate the table.
The table with text displays as shown in Figure 5–43.

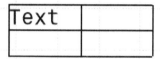

Figure 5–43

Step 7 - Modify the table, as required

You might need to make changes to the table once it has been completed. Double-click on the table to make it active. Drag the handles in the border, as shown in Figure 5–44, to modify the column and/or row size.

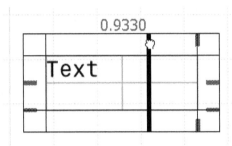

Figure 5–44

Right-click on the border to display the options for changing the table attributes. For example, the shortcut menu displays (shown on the right in Figure 5–45) when the cursor displays (shown on the left in Figure 5–45). This menu enables you to manipulate the selected row. Depending on where the cursor is located on the border, the shortcut menu displays different options that enable you to insert, delete, clear, or resize the rows and columns.

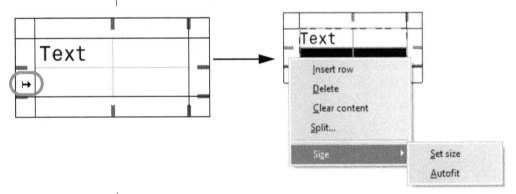

Figure 5–45

Table from CSV

If you want to insert existing data from an Excel spreadsheet, the (.XLS) file must be saved as a (.CSV) (comma-delimited) file format.

How To: Insert a Table from CSV

1. In the Table toolbar, click ⊞ (Table From CSV).
2. Browse to the required (.CSV) file.
3. Select a location on the drawing sheet in which to place the table.

   Figure 5–46 shows an example of an inserted table from CSV. This functionality can be used to display design table information on a drawing.

PartNumber	Width (mm)	Radius (mm)
B121463	20	22.5
B121464	20	23
B121465	20	23.5
B121466	20	24
B121467	20	24.5
B121468	20	25
B121469	25	25.5
B121470	25	26

Figure 5–46

5.11 Attribute Links

Attribute links enable table and annotation text to be linked to model parameter values. Inserting an attribute link in place of static text increases drawing effectiveness and flexibility. When a pointed parameter value changes, linked text automatically updates with the drawing as shown in Figure 5–47.

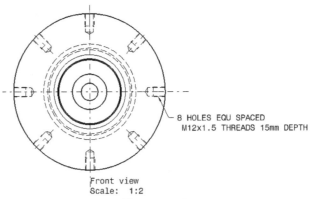

Figure 5–47

Creating an Attribute Link

To create an attribute link, open the Text Editor dialog box by double-clicking on the text box in the drawing display. In the Text Editor, highlight the text to be replaced. Right-click on the highlighted text (or specify a new insertion point by left-clicking with the cursor) in the display area and select **Attribute link**, as shown in Figure 5–48.

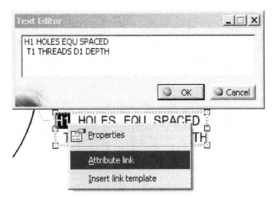

Figure 5–48

Activate the CATPart or CATProduct window and select the parameter or feature to which to link (in the specification tree). Selecting a parameter automatically completes the attribute link.

If a feature has been selected, the Attribute Link Panel dialog box opens as shown in Figure 5–49. The names and values of the parameters associated with the feature are listed in the *Attribute List* area.

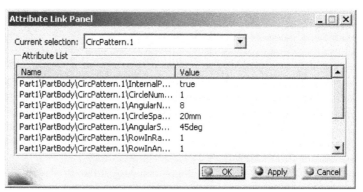

Figure 5–49

Select the parameter in the *Attribute List* and click **OK**. The Text Editor dialog box updates as shown in Figure 5–50.

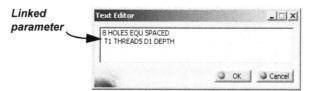

Figure 5–50

Managing Attribute Links

To view properties and synchronize individual attribute links, select **Edit>Links**. Attribute links are listed in the *Links* tab in the Links dialog box, as shown in Figure 5–51. However, links cannot be modified via the Links dialog box.

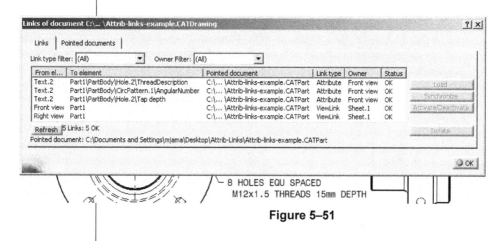

Figure 5–51

Part parameter modifications are included in the update of the drawing, as shown Figure 5–52.

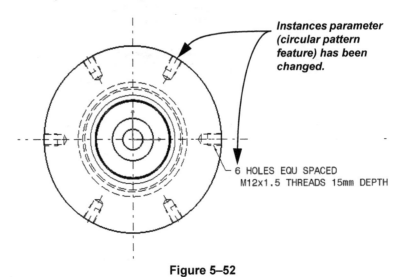

Instances parameter (circular pattern feature) has been changed.

6 HOLES EQU SPACED
M12x1.5 THREADS 15mm DEPTH

Figure 5–52

5.12 Dimension and Annotation Settings

Various options can be set to control how dimension generation and annotations are created.

Geometry and Dimension Generation

To change options, select **Tools>Options>Mechanical Design>Drafting** and select the *View* tab. The options are shown in Figure 5–53.

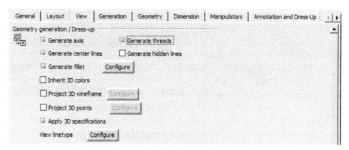

Figure 5–53

The options are described as follows:

- **Geometry Generation/Dress up:** Enables you to generate axes, threads, center lines, hidden lines, and fillets in the drawing. When generating fillets, you can click **Configure** and select the required type of representation for the fillets.

- **Inherit 3D colors:** Enables you to generate the colors of the 3D part.

- **Project 3D wireframe** or **Project 3D points:** Enable you to project wireframe elements or points from the 3D part. You can click **Configure** and specify options for the selection of wireframe or point elements.

- **Apply 3D specification:** Enables you to customize the look of a view to show/hide the sections, breakout views, or broken views.

- You can set the line types that you want to use for the section, detail, broken, and breakout views. Click **Configure** next to the View linetype.

Additional options are available in the *Generation* tab, as shown in Figure 5–54.

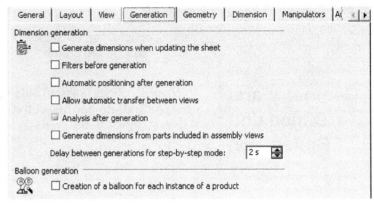

Figure 5–54

Dimension Generation settings enable you to perform the following tasks:

- Update the drawing.

- Apply filters to select which dimensions to change.

- Automatically position the created dimensions.

- Automatically transfer dimensions between views.

- Display the Dimension Analysis box after dimension creation.

- Generate dimensions from parts in an assembly.

- Set the time delay between the creation of dimensions using step by step mode.

The **Balloon generation** option enables you to create a balloon for each instance of a part used in the assembly.

Dimension Creation Settings

Select the *Dimension* tab. The options are shown in Figure 5–55.

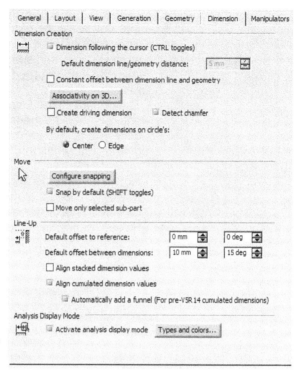

Figure 5–55

The options are described as follows:

- **Dimension following the cursor:** Enables you to have the dimension line follow the cursor as you create a dimension. If you hold <Ctrl> while creating a dimension, this option is toggled off temporarily.

- **Constant offset between dimension line and geometry:** Enables you to specify a constant offset at which all dimensions are created. When the option is toggled on, you can enter the distance in a field.

- Clicking **Associativity on 3D** enables you to create non-associative dimensions.

- **Create Driving dimensions:** Enables you to create dimensions that drive (change) the geometry.

- **Detect Chamfer:** Detects chamfers, enabling chamfer dimensions to be created with a single click.

- **Center** and **Edge:** Enable you to dimension to the center or edge of a circle.

- The options in the *Move* area enable you to toggle the **Snapping** function on or off, configure how you want the snap to occur, and specify whether you want to move only the selected sub-part (text, line, etc.).

- The options in the *Line-Up* area enable you to align stacked and cumulated dimensions, and automatically add funnels to dimensions. You can specify the distance to offset the dimensions when this option is selected.

- **Activate analysis display mode:** Enables you to display any dimensions that might have been changed on the drawing. This option is useful if you are checking drawings for Fake dimensions, out of date dimensions, etc. You can check or change the default types and colors of dimensions in the dialog box, as shown in Figure 5–56.

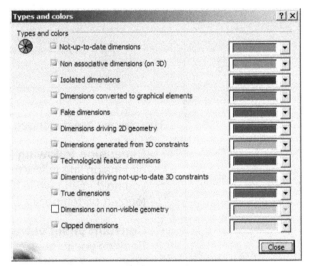

Figure 5–56

Manipulator Settings

Select the *Manipulators* tab. The options are shown in Figure 5–57.

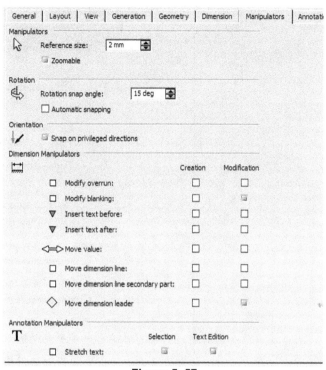

Figure 5–57

The options are described as follows:

- The options in the *Manipulators* area enable you to set the size of the dimensions and determine whether or not they can be zoomed.

- The options in the *Dimension Manipulators* area enable you to modify the overrun and blanking of dimensions. The overrun specifies the distance that the extension line passes the dimension line, and blanking is the amount of space from the selected object and the start of the extension line. You can add symbols (that are selectable) to add text before and after the dimension number, and add manipulator arrows that make it easier to move the dimensions.

Annotation Settings

Select the *Annotation and Dress-Up* tab. The options are shown in Figure 5–58.

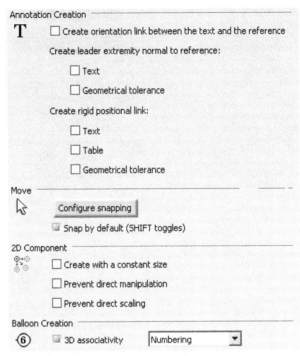

Figure 5–58

The options are described as follows:

- **Annotation Creation:** Enable you to snap text, text with leader, and Geometric Tolerances.

- **Snap by default (SHIFT toggles):** Activates snapping while moving elements in the drawing.

- The options in the *2D Component* area enable you to verify that all 2D components (such as symbols) are the same size and cannot be manipulated or scaled.

- **3D associativity:** Enables you to verify that the balloons displayed on the drawing match the parameter values from the 3D model. Balloons can be made associative to numbering, instance name, or part number parameters.

Practice 5a | Annotate a Drawing II

Practice Objectives

- Create annotations.
- Create symbols.

In this practice, you will add the following annotations to a drawing:

- Text

- Sketched geometry

- Geometric tolerances

- Dress-up features

- Roughness symbols

The completed drawing displays as shown in Figure 5–59.

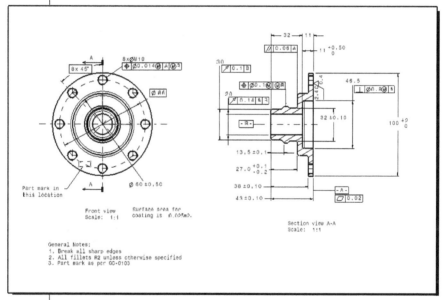

Figure 5–59

Task 1 - Open a drawing file.

1. Open **Adapter.CATDrawing**. The drawing displays as shown in Figure 5–60.

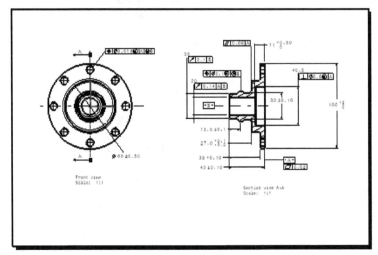

Figure 5–60

2. Select **Edit>Sheet Background** to activate Background mode.

Task 2 - Create text.

1. In the Text toolbar, click T (Text).

2. Select the location shown in Figure 5–61.

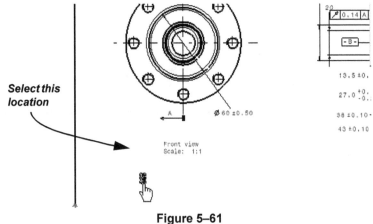

Figure 5–61

3. Enter the following text in the Text Editor, as shown in Figure 5–62. To add another line of text to the note, press <Shift> + <Enter>.

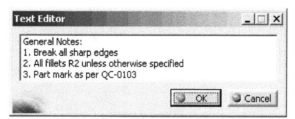

Figure 5–62

4. Click **OK**.

5. Position the text as shown in Figure 5–63.

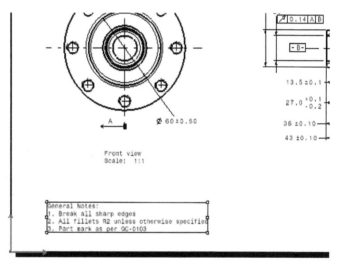

Figure 5–63

6. Select **Edit>Working Views** to activate Working views mode.

Task 3 - Create sketched geometry.

---

1. Ensure that the Front view is active. Since the view frames are hidden, the view can be activated by double-clicking it in the specification tree.

2. In the Profiles toolbar, click [ ] (Rectangle) to sketch a rectangle.

3. Sketch the rectangle in the location shown in Figure 5–64.

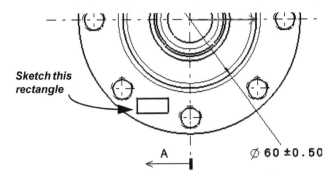

Sketch this
rectangle

$\varnothing$ 60 ±0.50

Front view
Scale: 1:1

Figure 5–64

4. Draw a selection box around the rectangle that you just created, right-click and select **Properties**.

5. Set the *Linetype* to **2** and the *Thickness* to **1**, as shown in Figure 5–65.

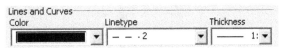

Figure 5–65

The rectangle displays as shown in Figure 5–66.

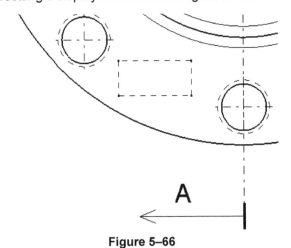

A

Figure 5–66

6. In the Text toolbar, click 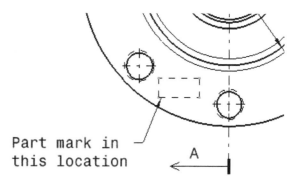 (Text with Leader) to create text with a leader, and select the rectangle you just created.

7. Enter the text shown in Figure 5–67. Position the text as required.

Part mark in
this location

A

Front view
Scale: 1:1

Figure 5–67

8. In the Circle and Ellipse toolbar, click 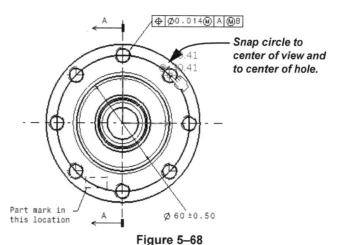 (Circle) and snap the center of the circle to the center of the view. Drag the circle out and snap it to one of the holes, as shown in Figure 5–68.

⌖ Ø0.014Ⓜ A ⓂB

Snap circle to
center of view and
to center of hole.

Part mark in
this location

A

Ø 60 ±0.50

Figure 5–68

9. Change the sketched circle properties to the following:

- *Linetype* to **2**
- *Thickness* to **1**

10. Create a dimension from the sketched circle, as shown in Figure 5–69.

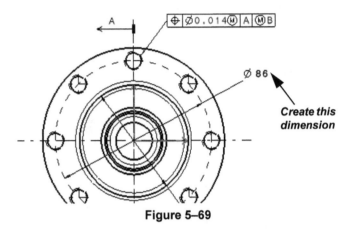

Figure 5–69

11. Select the **diameter 86 dimension**. In the Text Properties toolbar, expand ⌐A¬ None ∨ and click ☐ Rectangle ∨ . The value is now displayed as a basic dimension, as shown in Figure 5–70.

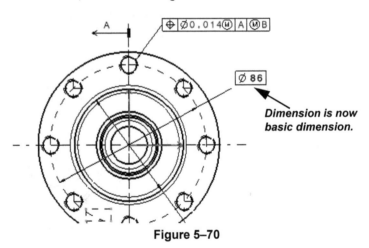

Figure 5–70

Task 4 - Add text to a geometrical tolerance.

1. Double-click on the geometrical tolerance of the hole, as shown in Figure 5–71.

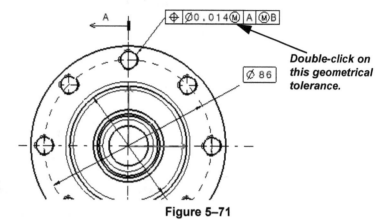

Double-click on this geometrical tolerance.

Figure 5–71

2. The Geometrical Tolerance dialog box opens. Enter the text and symbols shown in Figure 5–72.

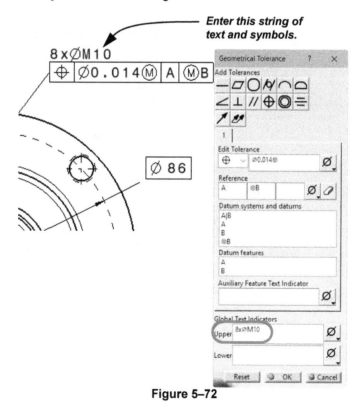

Enter this string of text and symbols.

Figure 5–72

Task 5 - Create a dress-up feature.

1. In the Axis and Threads toolbar, click 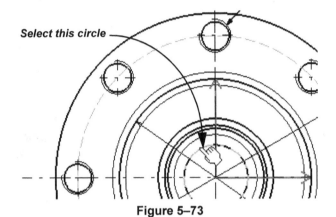 (Axis line and Center line).

2. Select the inner-most circle of the view, as shown in Figure 5–73.

Select this circle

Figure 5–73

3. Select the hole shown in Figure 5–74.

Select the edge of this hole

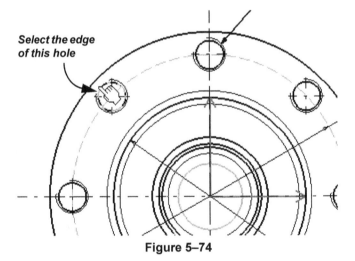

Figure 5–74

The axis displays as shown in Figure 5–75.

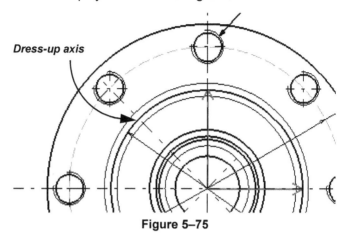

Dress-up axis

Figure 5–75

4. Create an angled basic dimension using the dress-up axis, as shown in Figure 5–76.

If the displayed angle is 90 degrees, disable the **Half Dimension** *option in the shortcut menu while creating the dimension. The menu is not available once the dimension has been placed.*

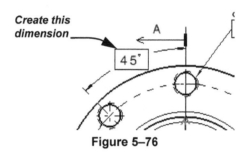

Create this dimension

45°

A

Figure 5–76

5. Select the angled basic dimension that you just created and press <Alt> + <Enter> to edit the properties of the dimension.

6. In the *Dimension Texts* tab, add a *prefix* of **8x** as shown in Figure 5–77.

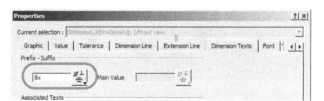

Figure 5–77

The dimension displays as shown in Figure 5–78.

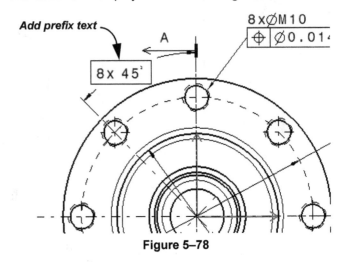

Figure 5–78

Task 6 - Create an attribute link.

1. Select **Edit>Links**.

2. In the Links dialog box, select the *Pointed documents* tab and open the **Cover.CATPart** file, as shown in Figure 5–79.

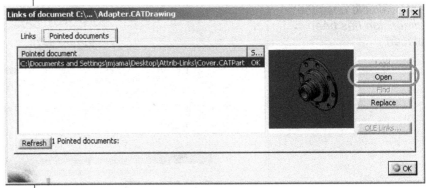

Figure 5–79

The Cover.CATPart window opens as shown in Figure 5–80.

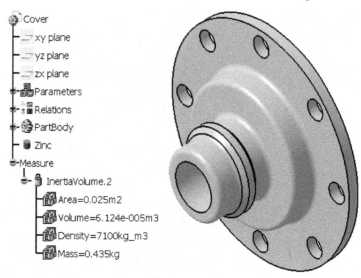

Figure 5–80

3. Activate the drawing window.

4. Click **T.** (Text). Place a new text box beneath the Front view, as shown in Figure 5–81.

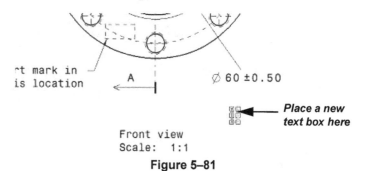

Figure 5–81

5. In the Text Editor dialog box, enter the text shown in Figure 5–82.

Press <Shift> and <Enter> to add the second line of text.

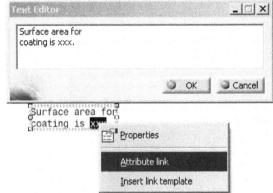

Figure 5–82

6. In the Text Editor dialog box, highlight the **xxx** text. Right-click on the highlighted text in the drawing view and select **Attribute link**, as shown in Figure 5–82.

7. Activate the Cover.CATPart window. In the specification tree, under the **Measure>InertiaVolume.2** node, select the **Area** parameter. The Attribute Links Panel opens as shown in Figure 5–83.

*If the value does not display as shown in Figure 5–83, select **Tools>Options>Param eters and Measure**, and select the Units tab. Select **Area** in the Units list and change the value for the **Decimal places for read/write numbers** to 3.*

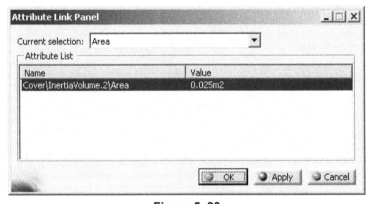

Figure 5–83

8. In the Attribute List, select the **Cover\InteriaVolume.2\Area** parameter.

9. In the Attribute Link Panel and Text Editor dialog boxes, click **OK**. The completed text box and attribute link display as shown in Figure 5–84.

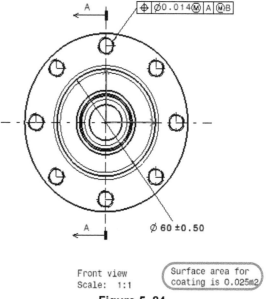

Figure 5–84

Task 7 - Create a roughness symbol.

1. In the Symbols toolbar, click (Roughness Symbol).

2. Select a location at which to place the symbol, as shown in Figure 5–85.

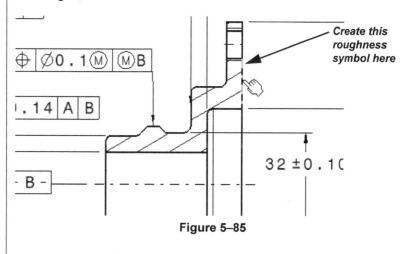

Figure 5–85

3. Define the roughness symbol, as shown in Figure 5–86. You might need to click 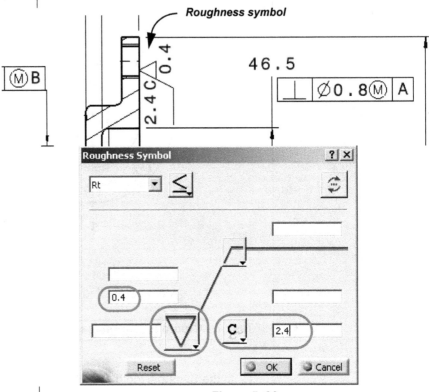 (Invert) to change the side of the entity on which the roughness symbol is created.

Figure 5–86

4. Save the drawing and close all of the files.

Practice 5b

Create a Table

Practice Objective

- Create a table from CSV.

In this practice, you will modify a drawing to display design table data for a part model. A drawing has already been started and displays as shown in Figure 5–87.

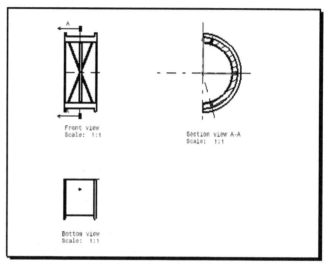

Figure 5–87

The Excel spreadsheet containing the design table data has been modified to use a .CSV extension (filename **B121463_Bushing.csv**). This is required to read the table data into the drawing. The table data is shown in Figure 5–88.

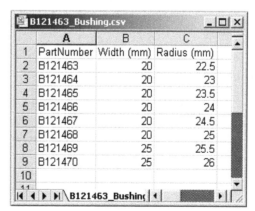

	A	B	C
1	PartNumber	Width (mm)	Radius (mm)
2	B121463	20	22.5
3	B121464	20	23
4	B121465	20	23.5
5	B121466	20	24
6	B121467	20	24.5
7	B121468	20	25
8	B121469	25	25.5
9	B121470	25	26
10			

Figure 5–88

The table refers to two model parameters: **Width** and **Radius**. Fake dimensions are used to display these parameters on the drawing to link the table data to the drawing geometry. The completed drawing displays as shown in Figure 5–89.

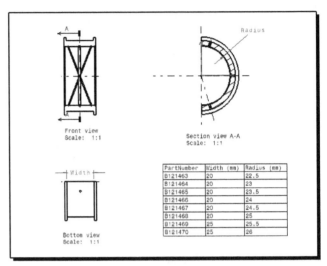

PartNumber	Width (mm)	Radius (mm)
B121463	20	22.5
B121464	20	23
B121465	20	23.5
B121466	20	24
B121467	20	24.5
B121468	20	25
B121469	25	25.5
B121470	25	26

Figure 5–89

Task 1 - Open a CATDrawing.

1. Open **B121463_Bushing.CATDrawing**. The drawing displays as shown in Figure 5–90.

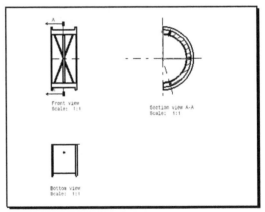

Figure 5–90

Task 2 - Create a dimension.

1. Zoom in on the Section view and create a radius dimension for the inside of the bushing, as shown in Figure 5–91.

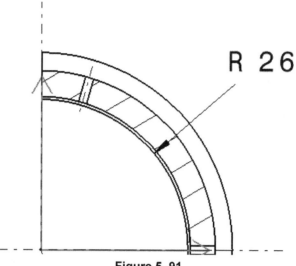

R 26

Figure 5–91

You can also select the arrow to reverse its direction.

2. Right-click on the dimension and select **Properties**.

3. Select the *Dimension Line* tab and change the *Thickness* to **2**, as shown in Figure 5–92. Change the **Reversal** option to **Outside**.

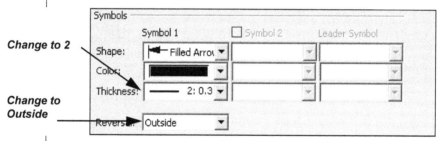

Change to 2

Change to Outside

Figure 5–92

4. Click **OK**. The radius dimension displays as shown in Figure 5–93.

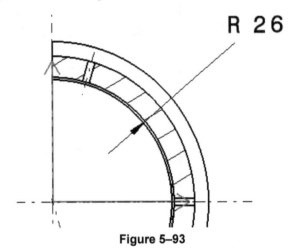

R 26

Figure 5–93

5. Zoom in on the Bottom view and create the 25 dimension shown in Figure 5–94.

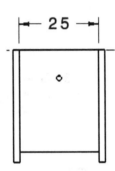

25

```
Bottom view
Scale:  1:1
```

Figure 5–94

Task 3 - Create a fake dimension.

1. Open the Properties dialog box for the 25 dimension and select the *Value* tab.

2. Select the **Fake Dimension** option. In the *Main Value* field, under the **Alphanumerical** option, enter **Width** as shown in Figure 5–95.

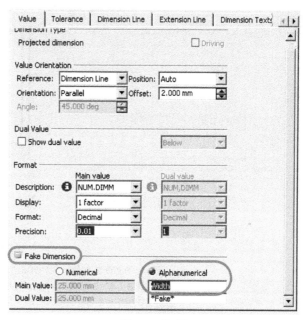

Figure 5–95

The fake dimension displays as shown in Figure 5–96.

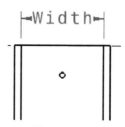

Figure 5–96

1. Open the Properties dialog box for the Width dimension. Select the *Dimension Line* tab and set the **Reversal** option to **Outside**, as shown in Figure 5–97.

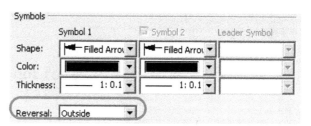

Figure 5–97

2. Click **OK**. The fake dimension displays as shown in Figure 5–98.

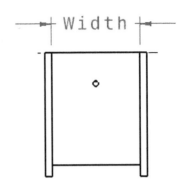

Bottom view
Scale: 1:1

Figure 5–98

3. Create a fake dimension for the R26 value. You need to use the *Dimension Texts* tab to remove the R prefix. The view displays as shown in Figure 5–99.

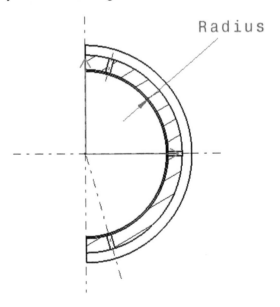

Section view A-A
Scale: 1:1

Figure 5–99

Task 4 - Create a dimension table from a .CSV file.

1. Activate the background by selecting **Edit>Sheet Background**.

2. In the Annotations toolbar, click 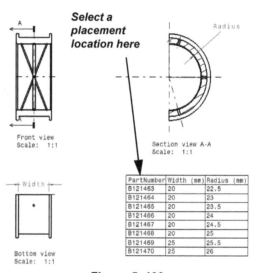 (Table From CSV).

3. Select **B121463_Bushing.csv**.

*To ensure that the table does not split on several sheets, select **Tools> Options>Mechanical Design>Drafting**, select the Annotation and Dress-Up tab, and toggle on the **Do not split table on several sheets** checkbox.*

4. Select a location for the table, as shown in Figure 5–100. If you select a location too close to the edge of the sheet, the system creates a second sheet and continues the table on the second sheet.

Figure 5–100

Task 5 - Add an attribute link to the drawing.

In this task, you will display the value of a part model parameter in the drawing. This value is associative to the part and therefore updates when modified in the model. The parameter value is added to the table. The string parameter is named **MasterPart** and the value is the filename of the part model.

1. Open **B121463_Bushing.CATPart**.

2. Select **Window>Tile Horizontally** to display the part and drawing.

3. Double-click on the table to edit it.

4. Right-click on the left cell of the **PartNumber** cell, and select **Insert row**, as shown in Figure 5–101.

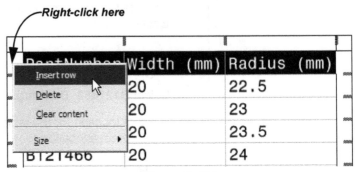

Figure 5–101

5. Right-click on the highlighted new row and select **Merge**. The table displays as shown in Figure 5–102.

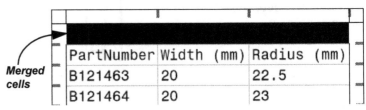

Figure 5–102

6. Double-click on the new merged cell and enter **Master:**. Do not close the Text Editor dialog box.

7. Right-click next to the text in the table and select **Attribute Link**, as shown in Figure 5–103. This operation cannot be performed in the Text Editor dialog box.

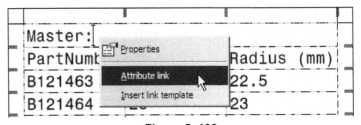

Figure 5–103

8. In the specification tree in the part model window, select
   B121463. This opens the Attribute Link Panel dialog box, as
   shown in Figure 5–104.

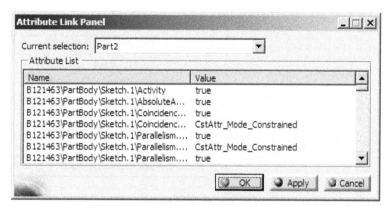

Figure 5–104

9. Scroll to the bottom of the Attribute List and select the
   MasterPart parameter, as shown in Figure 5–105.

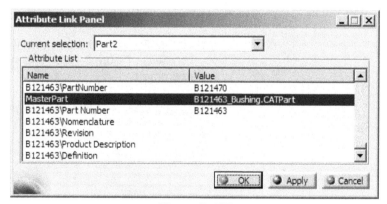

Figure 5–105

10. Click **OK**. The system places the value of the selected
    parameter into the Text Editor, as shown in Figure 5–106.

Figure 5–106

11. Click **OK** in the Text Editor and clear the table selection. The table displays as shown in Figure 5–107.

Master:B121463_Bushing.CATPart		
PartNumber	Width (mm)	Radius (mm)
B121463	20	22.5
B121464	20	23
B121465	20	23.5

Figure 5–107

12. Save the drawing and close the file.

Task 6 - (Optional) Modify the parameter.

Complete this task if time permits. In this task, you will modify the value of the MasterPart parameter and update the change in the drawing.

1. Activate the part model window.

1. Select **Tools>Formula**. The Formulas dialog box opens.

2. In the Filter Type drop-down list, select **User parameters** as shown in Figure 5–108. The system displays the **MasterPart** parameter.

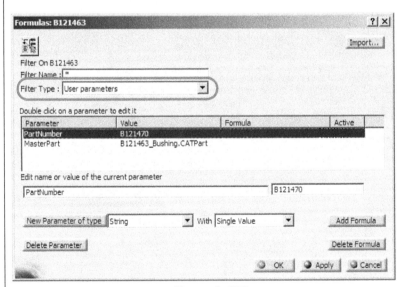

Figure 5–108

3. In the list, select **MasterPart**. The system places the parameter and value in the fields as shown in Figure 5–109.

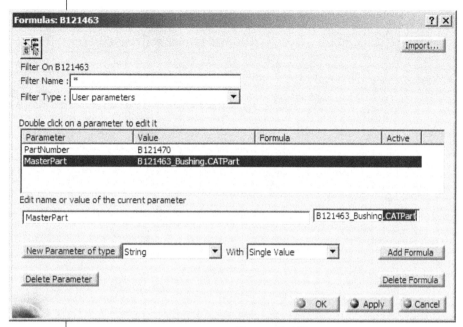

Figure 5–109

4. Modify the value of *MasterPart* to **B121463_Bushing** and press <Enter> to register the change.

5. Click **OK** to complete the operation.

6. Open **B121463 Bushing.CATDrawing**.

7. To update the drawing, you must force an update. This is done by entering **c:force update** in the *Power Input* field in the bottom right corner of the CATIA window, as shown in Figure 5–110.

Figure 5–110

Once the drawing has updated, the table displays as shown in Figure 5–111.

Master:B121463_Bushing		
PartNumber	Width (mm)	Radius (mm)
B121463	20	22.5
B121464	20	23
B121465	20	23.5

Figure 5–111

8. Save all of the files and close all of the windows.

Practice 5c

Add Weld Symbols

Practice Objective

- Create weld symbols.

In this practice, you will practice the weld symbol functionality by creating two weld symbols on the **ExhaustManifold** assembly.

Task 1 - Open an assembly drawing.

1. Open **ExhaustManifold_Detail.CATDrawing** from the *ExhaustManifold* directory. The drawing displays as shown in Figure 5–112.

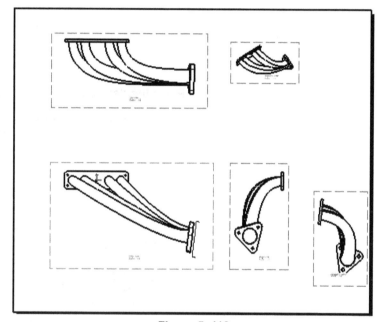

Figure 5–112

Task 2 - Create a detail view.

1. Create a detail view of the Front view, as shown in Figure 5–113.

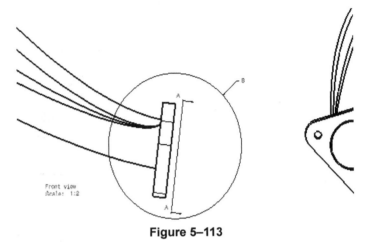

Figure 5–113

2. Place the detailed view, as shown in Figure 5–114.

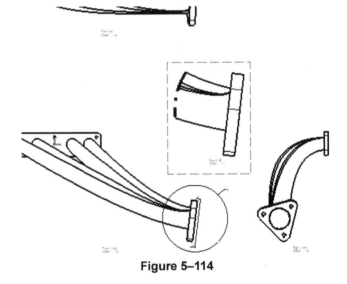

Figure 5–114

Task 3 - Create a new drawing sheet.

1. Create a new drawing sheet.

2. Cut and paste the detail view from *Sheet.1* to **Sheet.2**. The detail view displays on **Sheet.2**, as shown in Figure 5–115. Change the *Scale* of the detail view to **2:1**.

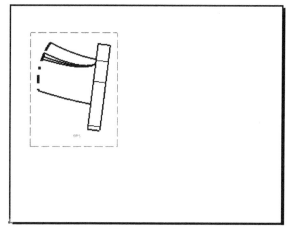

Figure 5–115

Task 4 - Create a weld symbol.

1. In the Symbols toolbar, click 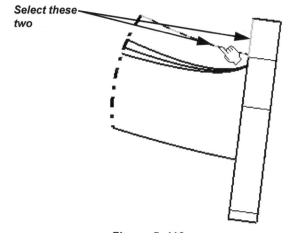 (Welding Symbol) and select the two references, as shown in Figure 5–116.

Select these two

Figure 5–116

2. Select a location at which to place the weld symbol, as shown in Figure 5–117.

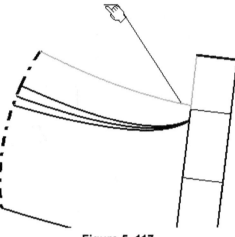

Figure 5–117

3. Specify the information for the weld symbol, as shown in Figure 5–118.

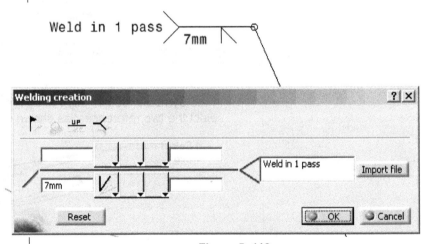

Figure 5–118

4. Click **OK** to complete the creation of the weld symbol. The weld symbol displays, as shown in Figure 5–119.

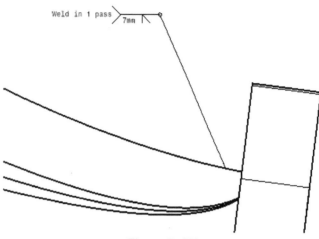

Figure 5–119

5. Copy and paste the Top view from *Sheet.1* to **Sheet.2**. Position the view as shown in Figure 5–120.

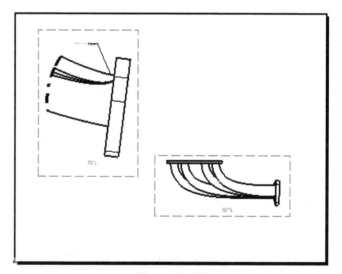

Figure 5–120

6. Click 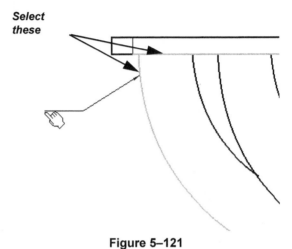 (Welding Symbol) to create a weld symbol and select the references shown in Figure 5–121.

Figure 5–121

7. Define the weld symbol, as shown in Figure 5–122.

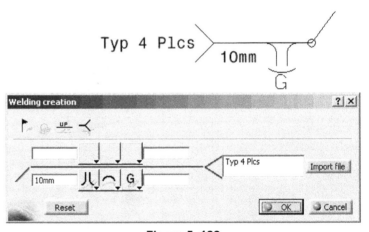

Figure 5–122

8. Click **OK** to complete the weld symbol definition.

9. You can change the attachment point for the leader by selecting the weld symbol to make it active and moving the yellow handle, as shown in Figure 5–123.

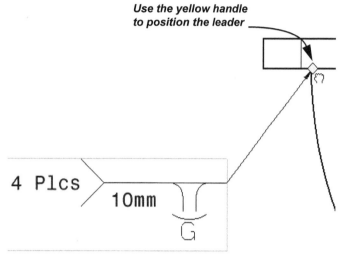

Use the yellow handle to position the leader

Figure 5–123

10. Save the drawing and close all of the files.

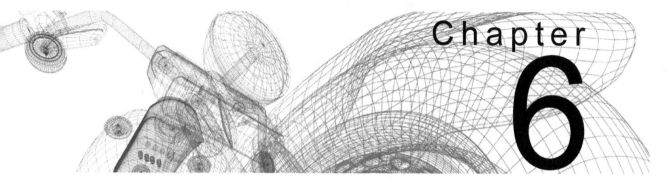

C h a p t e r

6

2D Components

2D components consist of sketched elements, text, leaders, and other geometry created in the Drafting workbench. These 2D components can be instantiated from a drawing or catalog. This chapter also introduces sketching functionality in the Drafting workbench that can be used to add geometry to imported drawing views.

Learning Objectives in this Chapter

- Create 2D sketches in drawings.
- Analyze sketches.
- Create 2D components.
- Instantiate a 2D Component.
- Instantiate components from catalogs.
- Modify an instantiated 2D component.

6.1 2D Sketching

2D draft entities are used to manually add geometry and detail to a drawing. You can create points, closed profiles, and open profiles independent of the view geometry. The sketched 2D draft entities can also be constrained. The process for creating and modifying 2D draft entities is similar to the Sketcher workbench. 2D draft entities can be used to do the following:

- Create 2D components

- Create symbols

- Create formats and titleblocks

- Update and maintain legacy data of drawings imported from other CAD systems

Tools for creating 2D draft entities can be found in the Geometry Creation toolbar, as shown in Figure 6–1.

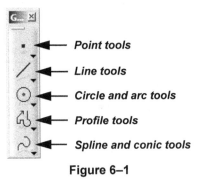

Point tools

Line tools

Circle and arc tools

Profile tools

Spline and conic tools

Figure 6–1

Draft entities can be manipulated using the tools in the Geometry Modification toolbar, as shown in Figure 6–2.

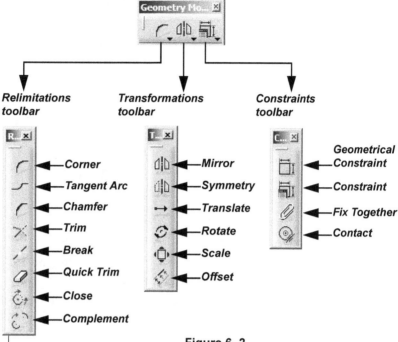

Figure 6–2

General Steps

Use the following general steps to sketch 2D drafting entities:

1. Activate a view.
2. Sketch the 2D entities.
3. Modify the properties of the 2D entities.
4. Constrain the 2D entities.

Step 1 - Activate a view.

The drawing view shown in Figure 6–3 is a legacy drawing. It was created by importing a DXF file into CATIA's Drafting workbench. Since no 3D model is associated with the view, modifications must be sketched directly on the drawing (such as the addition of a hole).

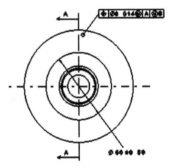

Figure 6–3

Activate the drawing view onto which the 2D sketched elements are going to be added by double-clicking on either the view's border or its name in the specification tree.

Step 2 - Sketch the 2D entities.

Using the tools available in the Geometry Creation toolbar, sketch new geometry. Two circles have been sketched in the example shown in Figure 6–4. The first circle represents a hole that is going to be cut in the resulting part. The second circle is going to be used to locate the radial distance of the hole from the center of the part.

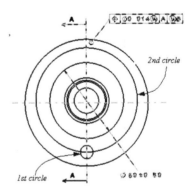

Figure 6–4

The current placement of the two holes is approximate and not important. Constraints are going to be used to position and constrain the sketched geometry.

Step 3 - Modify the properties of the 2D entities.

To modify the style or color of the 2D geometry, right-click on it and select **Properties**. The Properties dialog box provides options for controlling the color and linestyle of the selected geometry, as shown in Figure 6–5.

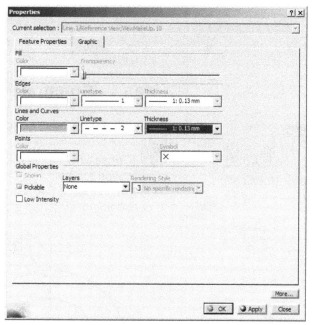

Figure 6–5

These options can also be accessed in the Graphic Properties toolbar, as shown in Figure 6–6.

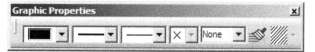

Figure 6–6

For example, the color and line font of the diameter circle can be assigned the appearance of a construction element, as shown in Figure 6–7.

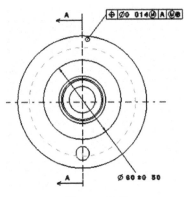

Figure 6–7

Step 4 - Constrain the 2D entities..

To create a constraint, select the entities to constrain and click

Geometry Modification toolbar

(Constraints Defined in Dialog Box) in the Geometry Modification toolbar. The Constraint Definition dialog box opens as shown in Figure 6–8. Constraining 2D draft entities is identical to constraining sketched entities in the Sketcher workbench.

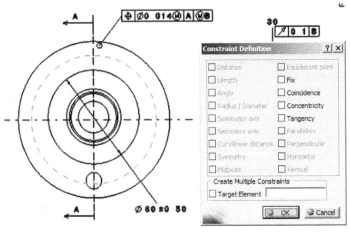

Figure 6–8

The constraints placed on 2D draft entities can be hidden/shown

by clicking (Show Constraints) in the Visualization toolbar.

6.2 Sketch Analysis

After the 2D draft entities have been created and constrained, you can analyze them by clicking 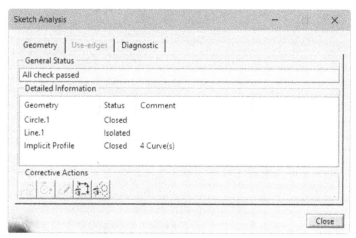 (Sketch Analysis) or selecting **Tools>Sketch Analysis**. The Sketch Analysis dialog box opens as shown in Figure 6–9.

Figure 6–9

Geometry Tab

The *Geometry* tab is used to analyze individual elements in the active view. It displays the general status of the elements being analyzed. The different values available in the *Status* column are described as follows:

Status	Description
Opened	A collection of 2D entities that form an open loop. Open loops can occur when the start and end points of a loop appear to be touching, but actually have a gap between them.
Closed	A collection of 2D entities that form a closed loop.
Isolated	A single 2D entity that is not touching or connected to any other 2D geometry.

The *Geometry* tab also displays detailed information about each selected element type and general comments, as shown in Figure 6–10.

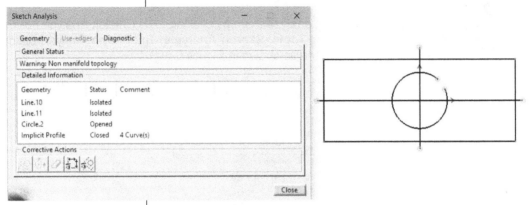

Figure 6–10

The entities shown in Figure 6–10 have several problems. The detailed information indicates that the circle is not closed (which is not the design intent), and that two line entities in the profile should be construction lines. The icons in the *Corrective Actions* area in the dialog box enable you to correct problems. These icons are described as follows:

Icon	Description
	Changes the selected entity to a construction entity.
	Closes the selected circle.
	Deletes the selected entity.
	Toggles the display of constraints on and off in the view and in the *Diagnostic* tab in the Sketch Analysis dialog box.
	Toggles the display of construction geometry on and off in the view and in the *Diagnostic* tab in the Sketch Analysis dialog box.

The icons in the *Corrective Actions* area correct the problem, as shown in Figure 6–11. Line.5 and Line.6 were converted to construction entities using . **Circle.1** was closed using .

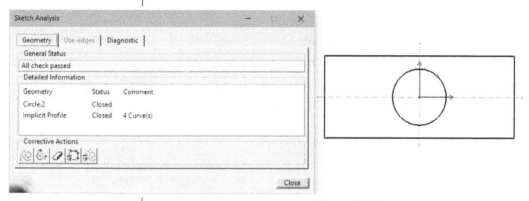

Figure 6–11

Diagnostic Tab

The *Diagnostic* tab gives a detailed summary of each 2D entity in the active view and its solving status. A 2D entity can have one of the following three status values:

- **Under-Constrained:** Additional dimensions or constraints must be applied to the entity.

- **Over-Constrained:** Too many dimensions or constraints have been applied to the element.

- **ISO-Constrained:** The entity is fully constrained.

The *Detailed Information* area lists all of the 2D entities in the active view, their current constraint status, and the type of entity (e.g., geometry, constraint, construction geometry, etc.), as shown in Figure 6–12.

Use-edges is not available in the Drafting workbench.

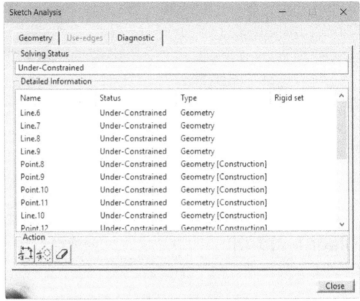

Figure 6–12

Sketch Solving Status

The Sketch Solving Status dialog box is used to determine the constraint status of the 2D entities in the active view. 2D entities can be under-constrained, over-constrained, or fully constrained (ISO-constrained). If the section is over- or under-constrained, the system highlights the affected entities on the sketch.

Click ⬚ (Sketch Solving Status) in the Tools toolbar to open the Sketch Solving Status dialog box, as shown in Figure 6–13.

Figure 6–13

You can launch the **Sketch Analysis** tool from the Sketch

Solving Status dialog box by clicking ⬚ (Sketch Analysis).

6.3 Creating 2D Components

2D components are 2D geometry and annotations that can be reused in drawings. You can instantiate a 2D component in the same drawing or in other drawings. You can also add the components to a catalog to further control standardized 2D components.

General Steps

Use the following general steps to create a 2D component:

1. Create a detail sheet.
2. Create the 2D component.
3. Save the file.

Step 1 - Create a detail sheet.

2D components are created on detail sheets that house the 2D components to be instantiated. You can create as many detail sheets as required. They can be added to an existing drawing or instantiated as a new drawing.

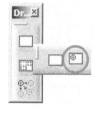

Click  (New Detail Sheet) in the Drawing toolbar to create a detail sheet. The system adds a new sheet containing a blank 2D component to the drawing, as shown in Figure 6–14.

WineOpener
Sheet.1
Sheet.2 (Detail)
2D Component.1

Figure 6–14

Each view contains a separate 2D component. To create multiple 2D components on a single detail sheet, click (New View) and select a location at which to place a new view.

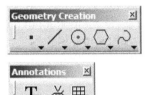

Step 2 - Create the 2D component.

2D components are created in the active view. The active view is denoted by a red border. To activate a view, double-click on the view border or view name in the specification tree.

Create the 2D component in the view by sketching 2D draft entities in the Geometry Creation toolbar or annotation entities in the Annotation toolbar. A 2D component with a sketched profile and text is shown in Figure 6–15.

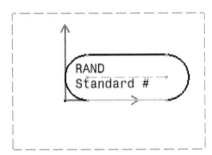

Figure 6–15

Modifiable Text

By default, text created in a 2D component cannot be modified inside the destination document. Once instantiated, text links to the original detail view and only updates if changes are made in the original 2D component. If you want the text in your 2D component to be editable once instantiated, use the **Modifiable Text** option.

Attribute links can also be added to the text.

To create modifiable text, right-click on the original text and select **Modifiable in instance**. The Text Editor dialog box then opens when you double-click on the component instantiated in the destination drawing.

Step 3 - Save the file.

Once you are satisfied with the 2D component, save the drawing.

6.4 Instantiating a 2D Component

Once you have created a 2D component, you can insert it as many times as required in the same (or an external) drawing.

General Steps

Use the following general steps to instantiate a 2D component:

1. Start the instantiation process.
2. Place the instance.

Step 1 - Start the instantiation process.

How To: Start the Installation Process

1. Activate the view into which you want to instantiate the 2D component.
2. Click  (Instantiate 2D component).
3. Activate the detail sheet containing the 2D component to be inserted.
4. Select the 2D component in the detail sheet or specification tree.

Step 2 - Place the instance.

Once the 2D component has been selected, CATIA returns to the active view to place the instance. The Tools Palette toolbars display. Use the Position toolbar as shown in Figure 6–16, to orient the component.

Tools Palette

| | | | | | | Angle: 0deg | | Scale: 1 |

Figure 6–16

The positioning tools are described as follows:

Icon	Description
![origin icon]	Changes the origin of the component. Click the icon and select a new point to act as the origin of the component.
![angle icon]	Changes the angle of the component. Click the icon. An angle vector displays. Use the mouse to change the angle. Left-click to confirm the new angle.
![horizontal mirror icon]	Mirrors the component about the horizontal axis.
![vertical mirror icon]	Mirrors the component about the vertical axis.

Scale and angle values can be changed using the Tools Palette toolbar. After these modifications have been made, click to finalize the 2D component's placement in the drawing view.

Place Instance in Another Drawing

You can also instantiate a 2D component created in a different drawing using the **Copy** and **Paste** tools.

How To: Copy a 2D Component from a Different Drawing

1. Activate the detail view containing the 2D component to be copied. Select the Geometry and Annotations inside the detail view, as shown in Figure 6–17.

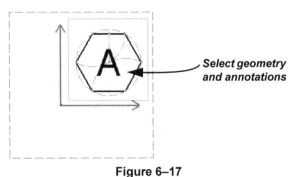

Select geometry and annotations

Figure 6–17

2. Select **Edit>Copy**.
3. Activate the target drawing.
4. Select **Edit>Paste**. The instantiated 2D component can now be moved in the drawing view.

6.5 Instantiating from Catalogs

In the Drafting workbench, a catalog is a repository of 2D components. Catalogs enable the grouping of similar components, searching, editing, and instantiation. Components that are commonly reused should be stored in a catalog.

Cataloged 2D components reference existing detail views. When instantiated into a drawing file, the cataloged 2D component is, by default, associative. However, the instantiated 2D component can be made non-associative.

Catalog Creation

To create a new catalog that contains all of the 2D components that have been created in the current drawing, select **File>Save As**. In the Save as type drop-down list, select **catalog** and enter the name of the new catalog, as shown in Figure 6–18.

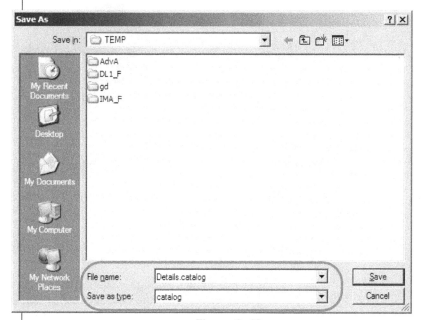

Figure 6–18

The name of the detail sheet becomes the name of the family when saved as a catalog. A family is a group of 2D components inside the catalog. For example, the catalog shown in Figure 6–19 was created from a drawing that contained two detail sheets named **Balloon Symbols** and **Datum Target**. Standard drawing sheets are not saved into the catalog.

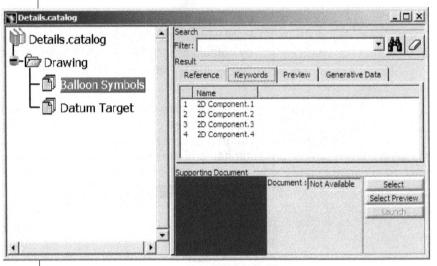

Figure 6–19

Instantiate from a Catalog

How To: Instantiate a 2D Component from a Catalog

1. Open the CATDrawing into which the 2D component is going to be instantiated.
2. Activate the view in which the 2D component is going to be placed.
3. Click (Catalog). The Catalog Browser opens.
4. In the Catalog Browser dialog box, click (Open) and browse for the catalog from which you want to instantiate. The contents of the Catalog are displayed, as shown in Figure 6–20.

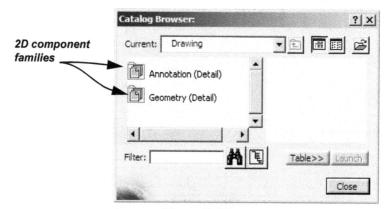

2D component families

Figure 6–20

5. Double-click on the family to display a list of 2D components grouped within it. Select a 2D component to display a preview, as shown in Figure 6–21.

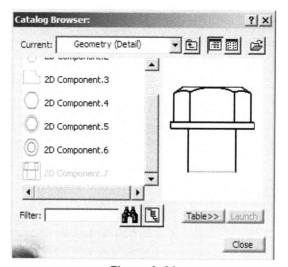

Figure 6–21

6. Double-click on the 2D component in the list to instantiate it in the active drawing view.
7. Use the Position and Tools Palette toolbars to scale, rotate, and modify the orientation of the 2D component.
8. Select a location in the view to place the 2D component. The Catalog Browser remains open until you click **Close**.

Links

When a 2D component is instantiated into a drawing, it is linked to the drawing from which it was instantiated. This link requires that the source drawing file be loaded into CATIA to be updated.

To display the links for a drawing, select **Edit>Links**. The Links dialog box lists the links for the drawing as shown in Figure 6–22.

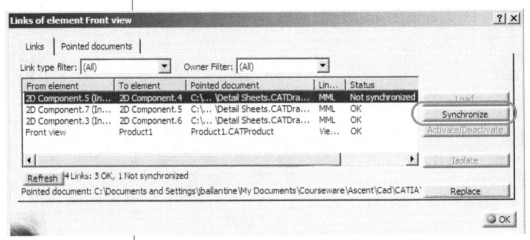

Figure 6–22

The *Status* column reports whether or not an element is synchronized. If an element is not synchronized, it uses the display of the linked element from the last synchronization.

When modifications are made to the pointed document, the instantiated 2D component can be updated through sychronization. To synchronize an element with its pointed document, select the element from the list and click **Synchronize**, as shown in Figure 6–22. The 2D component then reflects any updates that were made to the source document.

6.6 Modifying an Instantiated 2D Component

Placement

Once a component has been placed, you can modify its location and scale in the display window or use the Properties dialog box.

To modify a 2D component on the screen, select the component. Handles display at the corner of the 2D component. Drag them to resize the component. Click anywhere on the component and drag the cursor to change its location.

To define the exact placement and scale of the component, open the Properties dialog box. In the *2D component Instance* tab, as shown in Figure 6–23, you can change the position (relative to the view origin), angle, and scale of the component.

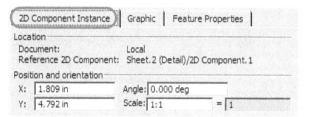

Figure 6–23

Explode the Component

Components instantiated from a catalog reference the original detail sheet used to make the 2D component. Exploding a 2D component makes it non-associative. This breaks the link between the instantiated 2D component and the source. To explode a 2D component, right-click on it and select ***.object>Explode 2D component**.

Exposing a 2D Component

Exposing a 2D component removes the link to the pointed document by copying the original 2D component into a detail sheet in the current drawing. This is an ideal method of removing the external links from a drawing, while still being able to update changes to a multi-instantiated 2D component from a single location.

For example, the datum target shown in Figure 6–24 was instantiated from a catalog. This 2D component is linked to the drawing file in which the original sketched geometry was created.

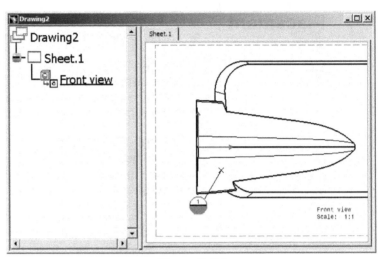

Figure 6–24

Expose the 2D component to break the link between the two drawings. The 2D component is copied into a new detail sheet that is automatically created in the drawing, as shown in Figure 6–25.

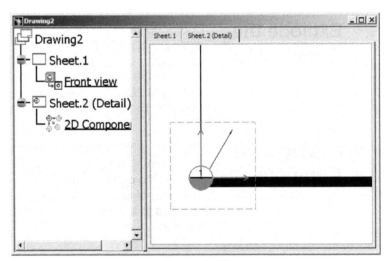

Figure 6–25

How To: Expose an Instantiated 2D Component

1. Right-click on the 2D component and select
    *.object>Expose 2D component. The Expose 2D
    component dialog box opens as shown in Figure 6–26.

Figure 6–26

2. Select an option in the dialog box:
    *   **In a new detail sheet:** Adds the exposed component to a
        new detail sheet
    *   **In an existing detail sheet:** Adds the exposed
        component to the detail sheet selected from the list. If no
        detail sheet exists in the current drawing, this option is not
        available.

Replacing

How To: Replace a 2D Component

1. If required, instantiate the replacing 2D component into the
    drawing.
2. Right-click on the 2D component to be replaced and select
    *.Object>Replace Reference.
3. Select the replacing 2D component.

    2D components that have been pasted from a different
    drawing cannot be exploded, exposed, or replaced. They
    also cannot be scaled, rotated, or translated using the
    Properties dialog box.

Practice 6a

Creating 2D Components

Practice Objectives

- Create 2D components.
- Reuse a 2D component in the same drawing.

In this practice, you will create 2D components consisting of sketched geometry and annotations. The 2D components will be added to a new detail sheet in the drawing. They will then be instantiated into a drawing view. The completed drawing view displays as shown in Figure 6–27.

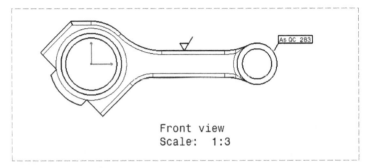

Front view
Scale: 1:3

Figure 6–27

Task 1 - Open a drawing file.

1. Open **ConnectingRod.CATDrawing** and **ConnectingRod.CATPart**. The drawing displays as shown in Figure 6–28.

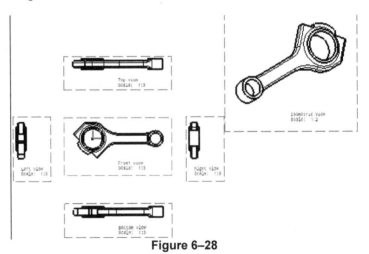

Figure 6–28

Task 2 - Create a new detail sheet.

1. In the Sheets sub-toolbar, click 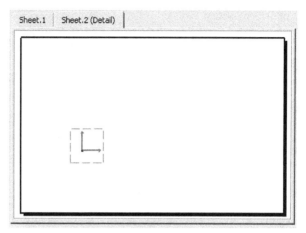 (New Detail Sheet). The newly created detail sheet displays and a view is automatically created at the bottom left corner of the sheet, as shown in Figure 6–29.

Sheet.1 | Sheet.2 (Detail)

Figure 6–29

Task 3 - Create a 2D component inside the new view.

1. In the Geometry Creation toolbar, use (Line) to create the 2D sketch (three lines), as shown in Figure 6–30. 2D geometry and annotations are created in the active view.

The view frame of an active view displays in red.

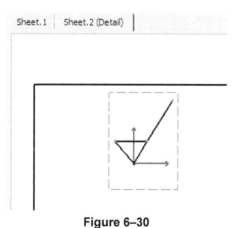

Sheet.1 | Sheet.2 (Detail)

Figure 6–30

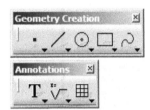

Task 4 - Create another 2D component.

In this task, you will create another 2D component. This component will consist of geometry and text. It will represent a quality control symbol.

1. In the Drawing toolbar, click 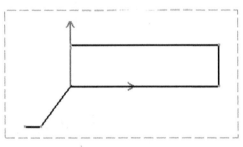 (New View).

2. A new view will display attached to the cursor. Click to place the view on the sheet. The new view is not active.

3. Double-click on the border of the view you just created to make it active.

4. Using tools from the Geometry Creation toolbar, create the shape shown in Figure 6–31.

Figure 6–31

5. In the Annotations toolbar, click **T** (Text).

6. Click in the active view to define where to place the text.

7. The Text Editor dialog box opens. Enter the text shown in Figure 6–32. Click **OK** when you are finished.

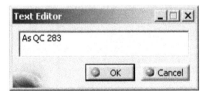

Figure 6–32

The completed 2D component displays as shown in Figure 6–33.

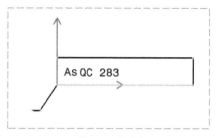

Figure 6–33

8. Right-click on the text and select **Modifiable in instance**. This enables you to modify the text in the instance.

Task 5 - Create a 2D component instance in the drawing.

In this task, you will instantiate 2D components. Instantiated 2D components are always placed in the active view.

1. Double-click on the Front View in Sheet 1 to make it active.

2. In the Drawing toolbar, click ⊞ (Instantiate 2D component).

3. In the specification tree or by directly clicking on the view in the detail sheet, select **2D component.1**.

Design Considerations

The 2D component will follow the cursor inside the Front View. The position, scaling, and angle can be changed using the Position and the Tools Palette toolbars.

4. Click to place the 2D component in the view. Position it as shown in Figure 6–34.

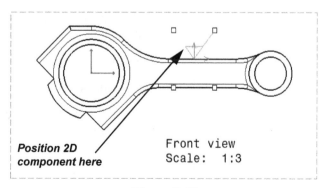

Position 2D component here   Front view
                                    Scale: 1:3

Figure 6–34

5. Click anywhere in the background of the drawing to complete the action.

Design Considerations

Consider the scale of the views and the scale of the 2D component required to obtain predictable results. The size of the sketched elements in the 2D component will be scaled by the view in which it is placed.

6. Instantiate **2D component.2** in the Front View, as shown in Figure 6–35.

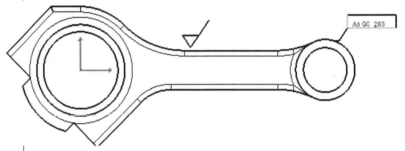

AS QC 283

Figure 6–35

Task 6 - Apply a scale to the 2D component text.

Design Considerations

The 2D component is scaled according to the scale of the front view. However, the text size will always remain identical to the size defined on the detail sheet. Text can be adjusted using the Text Properties toolbar.

Alternatively, you can apply a scale to the text in the detail sheet. When you apply a scale, the text is scaled according to the scale of the view in which it is placed.

1. Activate **Sheet.2** (Detail).

2. Right-click on the text in the 2D Component.2 view and select **Properties**.

3. Select the *Text* tab.

4. Enable the **Apply Scale** option and close the dialog box.

5. Activate **Sheet.1.** Similar to the geometry in the 2D component, the text is now scaled according to the Front view.

6. Save and close the drawing.

Practice 6b

Reusing 2D Components from a Catalog

Practice Objectives

- Create a 2D component.
- Add a 2D component to a catalog.
- Insert a 2D component from a catalog.

In this practice, you will continue working with 2D components. A catalog will be created consisting of 2D components. Instead of sketching the 2D component, you will copy and paste from a DXF file. The created catalog will then be used to instantiate 2D components into a drawing.

Task 1 - Create a new drawing.

1. Select **File>New**. In the New dialog box, select **Drawing**.

2. Create a B-sized ANSI drawing.

Task 2 - Create a new detail sheet.

1. In the Drawing toolbar, click (New Detail Sheet). A new view is automatically created.

Task 3 - Create a 2D component.

In this task, you will copy and paste geometry from a DXF file into the newly created detail sheet.

1. Open **2DComponent.dxf**. The imported drawing displays as shown in Figure 6–36.

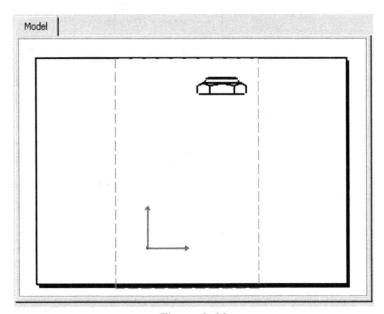

Model

Figure 6–36

2. Select the geometry from the view in the imported drawing by dragging a box around it. Do not select the view in the specification tree.

3. Select **Edit>Copy**. Alternatively, you can right-click and select **Copy**.

4. Activate the empty drawing file and ensure that **Sheet.2** (Detail) is active.

5. Select **Edit>Paste**. The geometry from the DXF file pastes into the view on the detail sheet.

*Toggle off the **Duplicate mode** checkbox when repositioning the geometry.*

6. Reposition the component using ➡ (Translate) in the Geometry Modification toolbar (Transformations sub-toolbar). The view displays as shown in Figure 6–37.

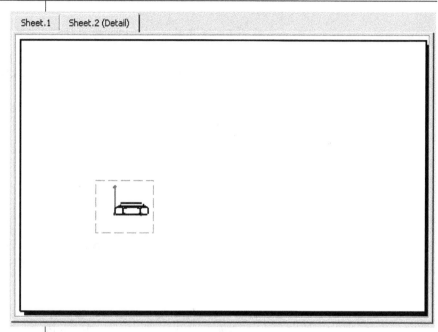

Figure 6–37

7. Close the **2DComponent DXF** file without saving.

Task 4 - Create more 2D components.

1. In the Drawing toolbar, click (New View).

2. Click on the detail sheet to place the new view. The placement location is not important.

3. Double-click on the newly placed view to make it active.

4. Sketch a circle in the active view, as shown in Figure 6–38.

Figure 6–38

5. In the Dress Up toolbar, click (Area Fill). The Tools Palette dialog box opens.

6. Ensure that 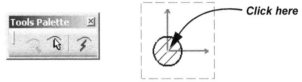 (Automatic Detection) is highlighted.

7. Click inside the circle to indicate where to apply the fill. The drawing displays as shown in Figure 6–39.

Figure 6–39

8. Click directly on the cross-hatching, not the circle.

9. Right-click and select **Properties.** You will change the properties of the fill added to the inside of the circle.

10. Select the *Pattern* tab.

11. In the Type drop-down list, select **Coloring**. Change the fill *Color* to **black**, as shown in Figure 6–40.

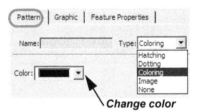

Figure 6–40

12. Click **OK** when you have finished adjusting the Fill properties. The model displays as shown in Figure 6–41.

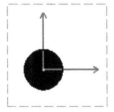

Figure 6–41

13. In the Annotations toolbar, click [T] (Text).

14. Click in the view to place the text. The Text editor dialog box opens.

15. Enter the text shown in Figure 6–42.

To add the second line of text press <Shift>+<Enter>.

Figure 6–42

16. Click **OK** when you have finished. The 2D component displays as shown in Figure 6–43.

Figure 6–43

To position an element freely on the drawing, press <Shift> while dragging the element

17. Right-click on the text and select **Modifiable in Instance**. This will enable you to edit the text when the 2D component is instantiated into another drawing. If this option is not set, the text cannot be changed upon instantiation.

Task 5 - Save the 2D components to a catalog.

In this task, you will save the drawing files as a catalog. Before this can be done, the drawing must be saved.

1. Save the drawing. For the *Drawing name*, enter **2DComp**.

2. Select **File>Save As** to create a catalog. For the *File name*, enter **2DComp**.

3. In the Save as type drop-down list, change *CATDrawing* to **catalog** as shown in Figure 6–44.

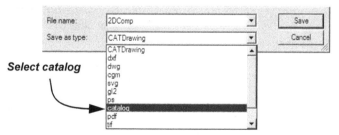

Figure 6–44

4. Save the catalog and close the drawing window.

Task 6 - Open a drawing.

1. Open **Adapter_Comp.CATDrawing**. The drawing displays as shown in Figure 6–45.

    If you completed **Practice 5a**, you can continue to use **Adapter.CATDrawing** instead.

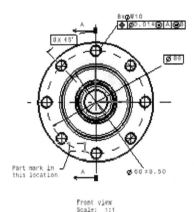

Front view
Scale: 1:1

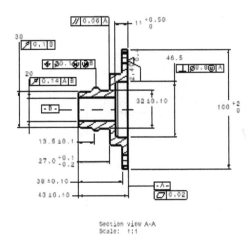

Section view A-A
Scale: 1:1

General Notes:
1. Break all sharp edges
2. All fillets R2 unless otherwise specified
3. Part mark as per QC-0103

Figure 6–45

Task 7 - Instantiate a 2D component from a catalog.

1. Ensure that the Front view is active by double-clicking on it in the specification tree. This step is required because the 2D component will instantiate into the active view.

2. Click ⬙ (Catalog Browser). This icon can become hidden at the right side of the bottom toolbar.

3. In the Catalog Browser dialog box, click 🗁 (Browse another catalog).

4. Locate **2DComp.catalog** and click **Open**. The Catalog Browser opens as shown in Figure 6–46.

Figure 6–46

5. Double-click on **Sheet.2** (Detail).

6. In the list, select **2D component.2**. A preview of the component displays, as shown in Figure 6–47.

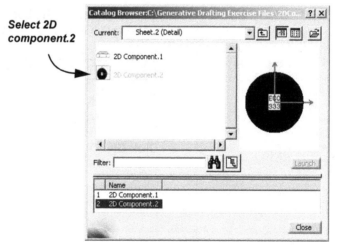

Figure 6–47

7. Double-click on **2D component.2** to instantiate it into the drawing.

8. The 2D component displays, attached to the cursor. Click to place the component in a location similar to that shown in Figure 6–48. You can click and drag the component to adjust its placement after instantiation.

Place the 2D component here

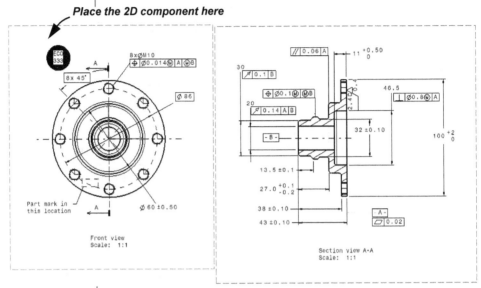

Figure 6–48

9. Click anywhere in the background to complete the instantiation and close the Catalog Browser.

Task 8 - Modify the instantiated 2D component.

1. Double-click on the text in the instantiated 2D component.

2. In the Text Editor, change *333* to **123**.

3. Click **OK**. The drawing displays as shown in Figure 6–49.

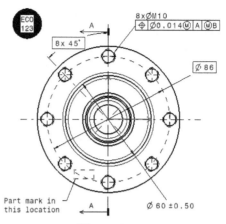

Figure 6–49

Task 9 - Investigate the model links.

In this task, you will review the links that have been created when instantiating the 2D component.

*If the Status indicates
Not synchronized,
click **Synchronize** to
update the link.*

1. Select the Front View.

2. Select **Edit>Links.** The Links dialog box opens as shown in Figure 6–50.

Instantiated 2D component from catalog   **2D component is updated**

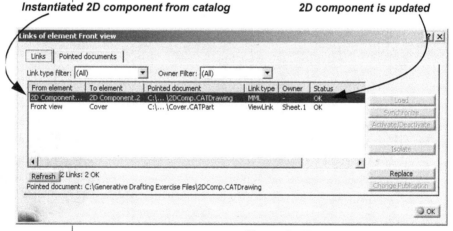

Figure 6–50

**Design
Considerations**

The instantiated 2D component (**2D component.2**) references **2DComp.CATDrawing**. The 2D component was originally created in this document. The 2D component is now up to date.

3. Click **OK** to exit the Links dialog box.

Task 10 - Expose a 2D component.

In this task, you will break the link between the instantiated 2D component and the drawing in which it was created. This is done by exposing the 2D component.

*Since there is no existing detail sheet in the drawing, only the **In a new detail sheet** option is available.*

1. Right-click on the instantiated 2D component and select **2D component.x (Instance) object>Expose 2D component.** The Expose 2D Component dialog box opens as shown in Figure 6–51.

Figure 6–51

2. Click **OK**. Note the changes after the 2D component is exposed. The model and specification tree are shown in Figure 6–52.

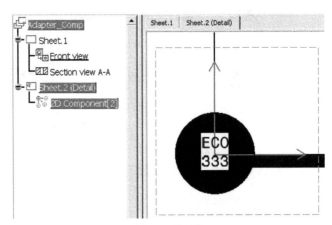

Figure 6–52

3. Activate **Sheet.1**.

4. Select the 2D component in the Front view.

5. Select **Edit>Links**. The 2D component no longer references **2DComp.CATDrawing**. It now points to the newly created detail sheet.

6. Click **OK** in the Links message.

Task 11 - Insert a second 2D component.

In this task, you will instantiate the quality control symbol a second time in the same drawing.

1. Activate Section view A-A.

2. Click ⬚ (Instantiate 2D component). On the detail sheet in the specification tree, select the 2D component.

3. Place the symbol in the location shown in Figure 6–53.

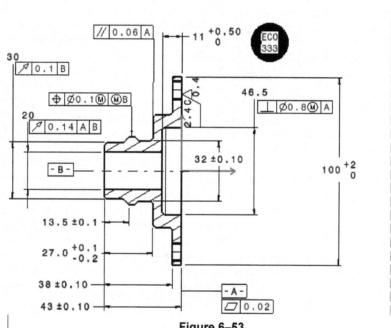

Figure 6–53

4. Modify the text in the symbol to read **ECO 124**.

Task 12 - Modify the 2D component.

Modifying the 2D component must be done using the detail sheet.

1. Activate **Sheet.2** (Detail).

2. Change the color of the fill from *black* to **red**. This can be done by double-clicking on the fill and selecting a new color in the Properties dialog box.

3. Activate **Sheet.1**. The instantiated 2D components have updated associatively with the changes to the detail sheet, as shown in Figure 6–54.

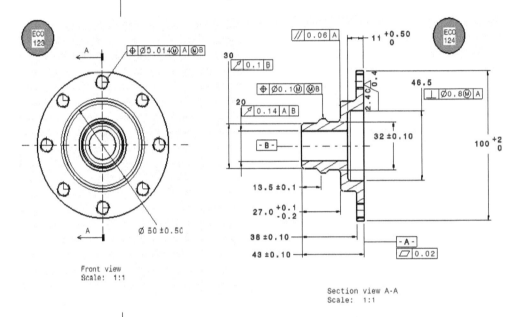

Figure 6–54

4. Save the drawing.

Task 13 - (Optional) Replace a 2D component.

In this task, you will add a new 2D component to the detail sheet and replace one of the symbols added to **Sheet.1**.

1. Activate **Sheet.2** (Detail) and add a new detail view.

2. Create the symbol shown in Figure 6–55. Ensure that the text is modifiable in the instance.

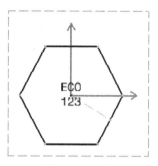

Figure 6–55

Hide the two construction circles before filling the hexagon.

3. Click 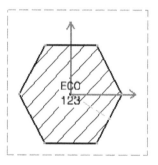 (Area Fill), and click anywhere inside the hexagon. The system will apply a default hatch to the view, as shown in Figure 6–56.

Figure 6–56

4. Modify the hatching properties to use a *Coloring* type of **Black**. The completed 2D component displays as shown in Figure 6–57.

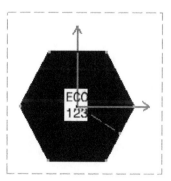

Figure 6–57

5. Activate **Sheet.1.**

6. Right-click on one of the instantiated 2D components and select **2D Component.# (Instance) object>Replace Reference**.

7. In the specification tree, select the new 2D component. The system will replace the circular symbol with the new hexagonal one, as shown in Figure 6–58.

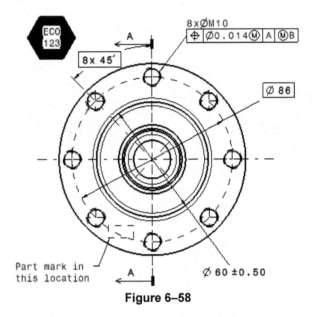

Figure 6–58

8. Save the drawing and close all of the windows.

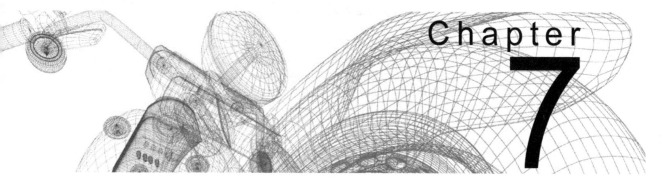

7

Product Drawings

Most assembly drawings use the same techniques and functionality to create views, notes, and dimensions. This chapter focuses on functionality specific to assembly drawing creation.

Learning Objectives in this Chapter

- Generate a Bill of Materials.
- Display Balloons on a Drawing.
- Create scenes to simplify the display of the assembly.
- Create a view from a scene.
- Use overload properties.
- Use Modify Links to permit components to be excluded from an assembly drawing view for illustrative purposes.
- Recognize and apply component drafting properties.
- Recognize and apply various view generation modes.

7.1 Generate Bill of Materials

The Bill of Material (BOM) report can be displayed on the assembly drawing to report the component names and the quantities used in the assembly. It is recommended that you position the BOM report in Background mode.

In the assembly, the BOM format can be defined to display a variety of parameters and model information. The drawing report reflects the customization performed in the product file.

General Steps

Use the following general steps to display the BOM report:

1. Check the format of the BOM report.
2. Add the BOM report to the drawing.

> ### Step 1 - Check the format of the BOM report.

Activate the .CATProduct window and select **Analyze>Bill of Material** to display the Bill of Material report. The report displays as shown in Figure 7–1. By default, the system uses the AP203 format, which displays the **Quantity**, **Part Number**, **Type**, **Nomenclature**, and **Revision** parameters for the current assembly.

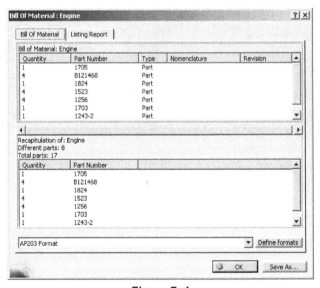

Figure 7–1

To customize the display of the report, click **Define Formats** and configure the items in the *Displayed properties* columns, as shown in Figure 7–2. The drawing report reflects the customization performed in the product file.

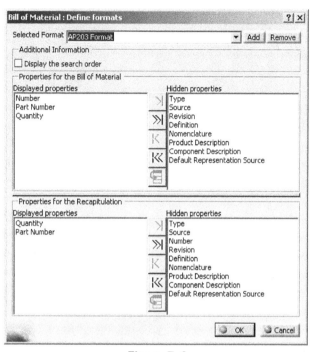

Figure 7–2

Step 2 - Add the BOM report to the drawing.

Inserting a Bill of Material report in Background mode places the report in the background. Inserting a Bill of Material report in Working Views mode places the report in the active view.

Activate the drawing and select **Edit>Sheet Background** to set the *Drawing* to Background mode. Select **Insert>Drawing>Bill of Material** or click (Bill of Material) in the Drawing toolbar.

Activate the assembly window and select the product in the specification tree to specify the source model for the BOM report.

Activate the drawing and select a location to place the report. The report is added to the drawing, as shown in Figure 7–3.

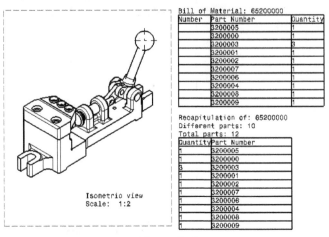

Figure 7–3

Inserting Into a View

Alternatively, you can set the *Edit mode* to **Working Views** in Step 2. This enables you to add the BOM report to a view instead of to the background by selecting **Insert>Generation>Bill of Material** and selecting a location in the active view, as shown in Figure 7–4.

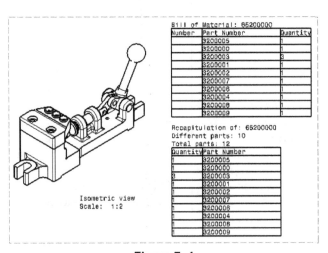

Figure 7–4

When this is done, the BOM report becomes associated to the active view. If the view is deleted or moved, the report is also deleted or moved. However, if the report is inserted in Background mode, it is copied into new drawings when you select **Insert Background View** in the Page Setup dialog box.

7.2 Display Balloons on a Drawing

Balloons provide a correlation between the geometry of a drawing view and the Bill of Materials report. The index number for each component is displayed in a balloon with a leader pointing to the component geometry in the active drawing view. Assembly components can be located in a view or on a Bill of Materials report using the index number.

General Steps

Use the following general steps to display the balloons on a drawing:

1. Assign index numbers to the assembly.
2. Add balloons to the drawing.

Step 1 - Assign index numbers to the assembly.

Activate the assembly window. Generate numbering by clicking

(Generate Numbering) and selecting the product in the specification tree. Select a numbering mode in the Generate Numbering dialog box shown in Figure 7–5 and click **OK**.

Figure 7–5

Step 2 - Add balloons to the drawing.

Activate the drawing and a drawing view to which the balloons are going to be attached.

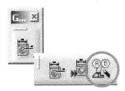

Click 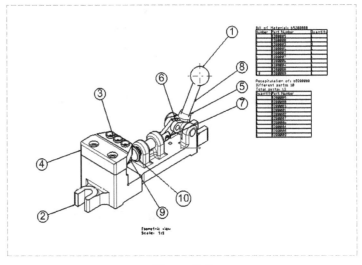 (Generate Balloons) in the Dimension Generation toolbar. The balloons are added to the active view in a random arrangement. Rearrange the balloons and customize the font and size as required. An example is shown in Figure 7–6.

Figure 7–6

Draft Balloons

Balloons can also be created in a drawing instead of being generated from the product.

How To: Create a Balloon

1. In the Text toolbar, click (Balloon) or select **Insert>Annotation>Text>Balloon**.
2. Select a component from any view to attach and identify the balloon.
3. Enter a number for the balloon. If numbering has already been generated for the product, the system defaults to the assigned instance number for the component. A unique number can be entered. However, try to avoid using numbering that does not correlate to the BOM report.

Draft balloons display and behave identically to generated balloons. However, since the balloon number must be entered manually for a draft balloon, they are less likely to correspond to the number convention that was applied to the product and displayed in the BOM.

7.3 Scenes

Product drawings differ from part drawings in that they need to display manufacturing and assembly information for multiple parts that are included in the product. Due to the complexity of product models, visualizing specific details of the assembly becomes difficult. Scenes can be used to simplify the display of the assembly in a product drawing and reduce the system requirements required to manipulate and update the drawing.

Scenes enable a designer to store the display settings of components in an assembly. Scenes can be used in the following ways:

- Hide/Show components to simplify the display.

- Activate/Deactivate components to display the model at a specific stage in assembly.

- Explode the assembly to visualize all components in the assembly in a single view.

- Use viewpoints to display critical orientations of the model.

You can use scenes to configure the display of the model in the product drawing. When a scene is applied to the model and a drawing view is created, the state of the model in the scene is used to generate the drawing view geometry.

Scenes in a product model can be found in **Applications** in the specification tree or as an icon in the bottom left corner of the main window, as shown in Figure 7–7.

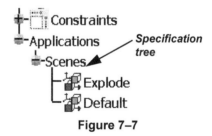

Figure 7–7

7.4 Create a View From a Scene

General Steps

Use the following general steps to create a view of an assembly scene in your drawing:

1. Create a new drawing view.
2. Select a scene from the assembly.
3. Select a reference from the assembly.

Step 1 - Create a new drawing view.

Click ▢ (Front View) or ▢ (Isometric View) to create a new drawing view.

Step 2 - Select a scene from the assembly.

Activate the assembly window. Select the required scene from **Applications** in the specification tree, as shown in Figure 7–8.

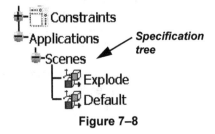

Figure 7–8

Step 3 - Select a reference from the assembly.

Select a reference from the model. The reference has to be a planar face or surface for a Front view, or any model surface for the Isometric view. The view of the selected scene displays in the drawing as shown in Figure 7–9.

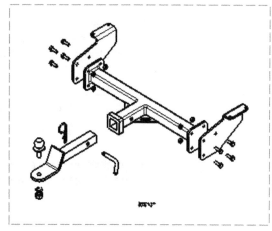

Figure 7–9

7.5 Use Overload Properties

Overload Properties enables you to change the graphics properties of the components that are displayed in a selected drawing view.

General Steps

Use the following general steps to configure an assembly view using overload properties:

1. Activate the **Overload Properties** tool.
2. Select the components to manipulate.
3. Edit the properties of the selected components.

Step 1 - Activate the Overload Properties tool.

Right-click on the view in the specification tree and select *
object>Overload Properties, as shown in Figure 7–10.

Figure 7–10

The Characteristics dialog box opens as shown in Figure 7–11.

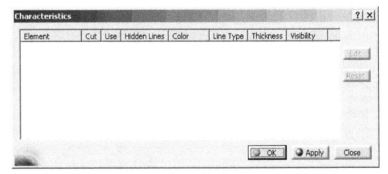

Figure 7–11

Step 2 - Select the components to manipulate.

Select the parts of the assembly that you want to control in the view. The part numbers of the selected components are listed in the Characteristics dialog box, as shown in Figure 7–12.

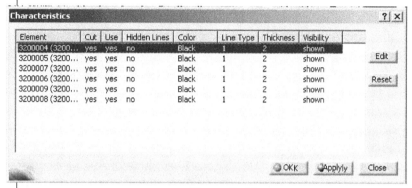

Figure 7–12

Step 3 - Edit the properties of the selected components.

Select one or more of the parts and click **Edit**. The Editor dialog box opens as shown in Figure 7–13.

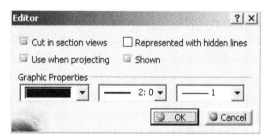

Figure 7–13

You can change the following properties for selected components:

- **Cut in section views:** Turns the part into a solid part again if a section view is being manipulated.

- **Represented with hidden lines:** Displays the part with hidden lines.

- **Use when projecting:** Toggle off to prevent the part from being displayed in a projected view.

- **Shown:** Toggle off to hide the part in the view.

Figure 7–14 shows a partial cross-section view.

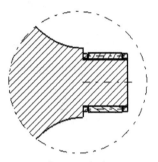

Figure 7–14

Figure 7–15 shows the same view with the **Cut in section views** option cleared for the indicated part.

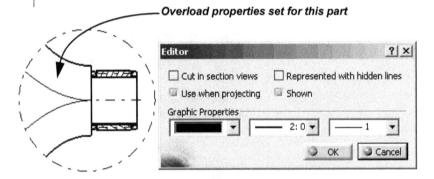

Figure 7–15

Figure 7–16 shows the same view with the **Shown** option cleared for the same component.

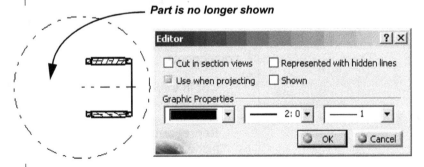

Figure 7–16

7.6 Modify Links

The **Modify Links** option permits components to be excluded from an assembly drawing view for illustrative purposes. Drawing views created from an assembly automatically display all of the parts in the product. By breaking the link between the part and drawing view, the part is no longer represented in the product drawing view.

General Steps

Use the following general steps to modify the components shown in a product drawing view:

1. Open the Modify Links dialog box.
2. Select the components to display in the product model.
3. Add the selected components.
4. Update the drawing view to display the link modifications.

Step 1 - Open the Modify Links dialog box.

A drawing view is shown in Figure 7–17 with all parts displayed. This view is linked to every component of the product.

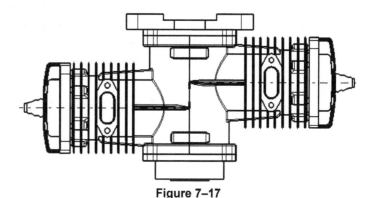

Figure 7–17

To remove parts from the view, tile the drawing and product windows so that they are both displayed by selecting **Window>Tile Horizontally** or **Window>Tile Vertically**. Then right-click on the product drawing view and select ***.object>Modify Links**, as shown in Figure 7–18.

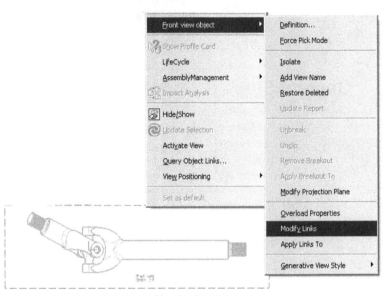

Figure 7–18

The Links Modification dialog box opens as shown in Figure 7–19. Note that the pointed document is the assembly CATProduct file. The *Pointed elements* field indicates that the drawing is linked to the Whole assembly.

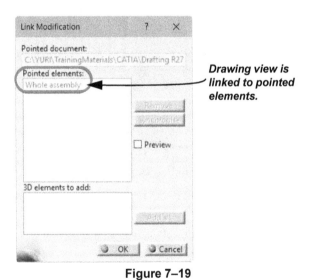

Drawing view is linked to pointed elements.

Figure 7–19

Step 2 - Select the components to display in the product model.

With the Links Modification dialog box open, activate the product window. In the specification tree, select the components to display in the drawing view. Multiple components can be selected by pressing <Ctrl>.

When you have finished selecting components, activate the drawing window. The components selected in the product window are listed in the *3D elements to add* area in the Link Modification dialog box, as shown in Figure 7–20.

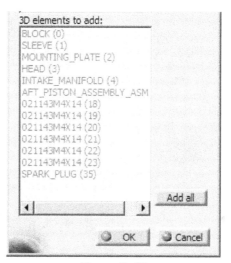

Figure 7–20

Step 3 - Add the selected components.

Click **Add all** in the Links Modification dialog box. The dialog box updates, as shown in Figure 7–21. The preview window displays the newly added pointed elements.

Figure 7–21

Click **OK** to complete the link modification.

Step 4 - Update the drawing view to display the link modifications.

Update the drawing view by clicking [icon]. The view updates to display the modified links, as shown in Figure 7–22.

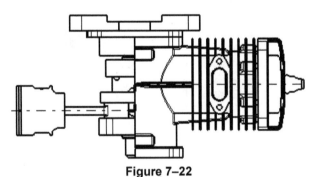

Figure 7–22

The drawing view is now only linked to the specified components, rather than to the entire assembly.

7.7 Component Drafting Properties

When creating drafting views of a product assembly, you might need to modify the display properties of individual components to display hidden lines, exclude from a section cut, or completely exclude from all views. Individual component drafting properties accommodate individual part display requirements.

To access the component drafting properties, open the product in the Assembly Design workbench. Select the part containing the drafting properties to be modified. Right-click on the part's main node, select **Properties** and select the *Drafting* tab. The dialog box opens as shown in Figure 7–23.

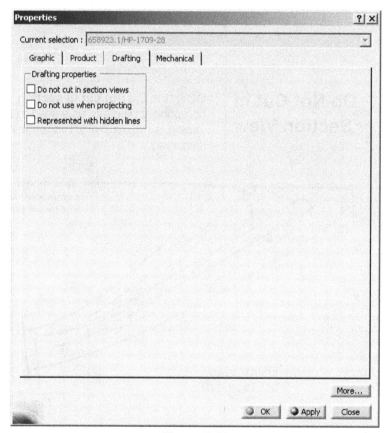

Figure 7–23

A product assembly with default component drafting properties is shown in Figure 7–24. In the following examples, the head mount component properties are going to be modified.

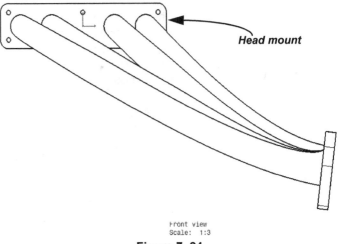

Head mount

Front view
Scale: 1:3

Figure 7–24

Do Not Cut in Section View

When the **Do not cut in section view** option is enabled, the component displays as a solid in any views that intersect it, as shown in Figure 7–25. Hidden lines are not automatically displayed.

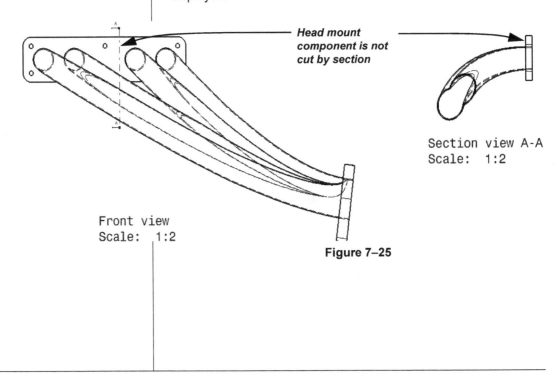

Head mount
component is not
cut by section

Section view A-A
Scale: 1:2

Front view
Scale: 1:2

Figure 7–25

Do Not Use when Projecting

When this option is enabled, the component is not included in any drawing views, as shown in Figure 7–26.

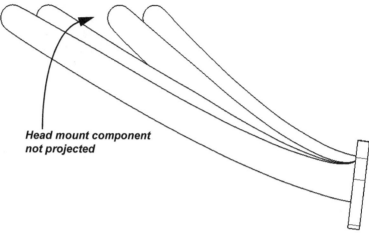

Head mount component not projected

Figure 7–26

Represented With Hidden Lines

When this option is enabled, the component displays hidden lines in all views, as shown in Figure 7–27. This option cannot be disabled in the individual view properties.

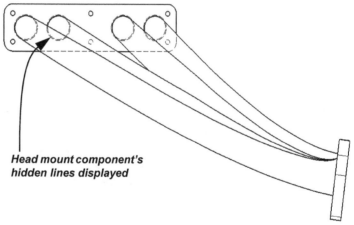

Head mount component's hidden lines displayed

Figure 7–27

To apply component drafting property changes to a drawing, update the drawing file.

7.8 View Generation Modes

CGR

You can use a CGR representation to enhance the performance of CATIA when updating the display of model geometry in drawing views. A CGR (CATIA Graphical Representation) file loads faster than a standard CATProduct because it is tessellated data. Therefore, only the external appearance of the model is used and displayed. It is the same concept that is used in DMU (Digital Mockup) to keep the file sizes small and make the model load and move faster on the screen.

You can replace the view geometry with a CGR representation using one of two methods:

View Setting

Open the Properties dialog box for the selected view. Select CGR in the View Generation mode drop-down list (at the bottom of the dialog box), as shown in Figure 7–28.

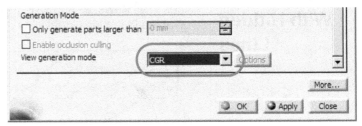

Figure 7–28

Global Setting

Select **Tools>Options>Mechanical Design>Drafting>View** and select **CGR** in the View generation mode drop-down list, as shown in Figure 7–29. All of the created views are displayed using a CGR representation.

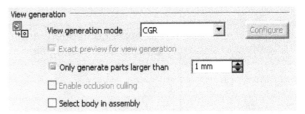

Figure 7–29

Additionally, a size filter can be established by entering a minimum part size in the field next to the **Only generate parts larger than** option. In this example, all models that are smaller than 1mm are removed from the drawing views.

Approximate

For large assemblies, the approximate view generation mode is beneficial. It is similar to CGR mode in that it improves CATIA's performance. However, Approximate mode is able to further reduce memory usage at the expense of view detail and quality.

Approximate view generation mode has the following restrictions:

- You cannot create detail views.

- Dress-up features (threads, arrows, fill, and center lines) can be created.

- Auxiliary view profiles are non-associative.

- Annotations are non-associative.

- Not all radius/diameter dimensions can be created.

To change the *View generation mode* to **Approximate**, open the Properties dialog box for the selected view. In the *View* tab, scroll down to Generation Mode. Select **Approximate** in the drop-down list, as shown in Figure 7–30.

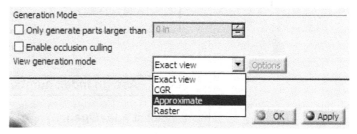

Figure 7–30

Practice 7a

BOM, Balloons, and CGR Views

Practice Objectives

- Generate a BOM and add it to the drawing.
- Use Balloons to reference the BOM index.
- Create views from CGRs.

In this practice, you will generate a drawing with views, a Bill of Materials (BOM), and balloons. The completed drawing displays as shown in Figure 7–31.

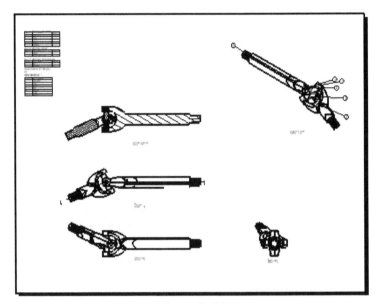

Figure 7–31

Task 1 - Assign index numbers to the assembly file.

1. Select **File>Open**.

2. Hold <Ctrl> and select **DriveShaft.CATDrawing** and **DriveShaft.CATProduct** from the *DriveShaft* directory.

3. Click **Open**.

4. Activate the DriveShaft.CATProduct window.

5. At the top of the specification tree, select **HP-1709-28**. In the Product Structure Tools toolbar, click  (Generate Numbering).

6. In the Generate Numbering dialog box, set the *mode* to **Integer: 1,2,3...** as shown in Figure 7–32.

Figure 7–32

7. Click **OK**.

Task 2 - Define the Bill of Material (BOM) report.

---

1. Select **Analyze>Bill of Material** while in the Product window. The default report window opens as shown in Figure 7–33.

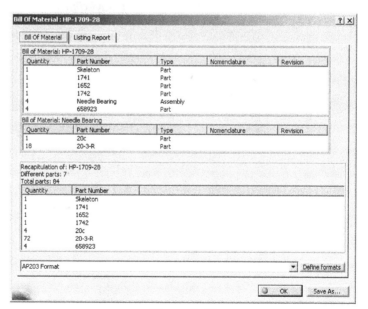

Figure 7–33

2. Click **Define Formats** to customize the report display. The Define Formats dialog box opens as shown in Figure 7–34.

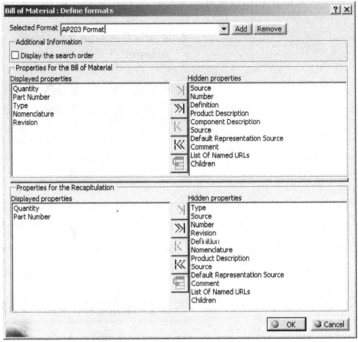

Figure 7–34

3. In the *Displayed properties* column, select **Type** and click

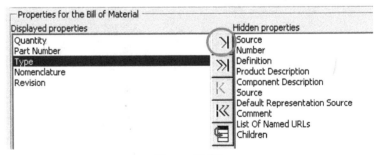

to move it to the *Hidden properties* column, as shown in Figure 7–35.

Figure 7–35

4. Repeat Step 5 for the **Nomenclature** and **Revision** properties. The dialog box opens as shown in Figure 7–36.

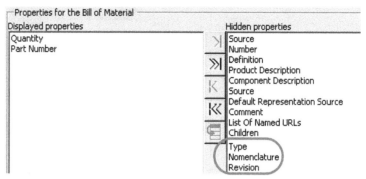

Figure 7–36

5. In the *Hidden properties* column, select **Number** and click

   K to move it to the *Displayed properties* column.

6. In the *Displayed properties* column, select **Number** and click

   (Change order).

7. Select **Quantity** to move the Number property to the top of the list, as shown in Figure 7–37.

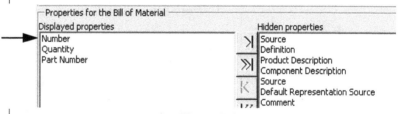

Figure 7–37

8. Move the Part Number property to the middle of the list, as shown in Figure 7–38.

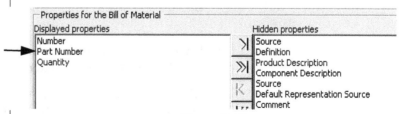

Figure 7–38

9. Click **OK** in the Define formats dialog box. The Bill of Material dialog box opens as shown in Figure 7–39.

| Bill Of Material : HP-1709-28 | | ? x |

Bill Of Material | Listing Report

Bill of Material: HP-1709-28

Number	Part Number	Quantity
1	Skeleton	1
2	1741	1
3	1652	1
4	1742	1
	Needle Bearing	4
5	658923	4

Bill of Material: Needle Bearing

Number	Part Number	Quantity
6	20c	1
7	20-3-R	18

Recapitulation of: HP-1709-28
Different parts: 7
Total parts: 84

Quantity	Part Number	
1	Skeleton	
1	1741	
1	1652	
1	1742	
4	20c	
72	20-3-R	
4	658923	

AP203 Format ▼ | Define formats

OK | Save As...

Figure 7–39

10. Click **OK** in the Bill of Material dialog box.

Task 3 - Add the BOM report to the drawing.

1. Activate the drawing window.

2. Select **Edit>Update Current Sheet**, if the option is available (if the views do not need to be updated, this option will not be available).

3. Select **Edit>Sheet Background** to change to the Background mode.

4. In the Drawing toolbar, click (Bill of Material) or select **Insert>Drawing>Bill of Material**.

5. Activate the product window. At the top of the specification tree, select **HP-1709-28**. This automatically reactivates the drawing window.

6. Select the upper left corner of the drawing to place the BOM in the Background of the drawing, as shown in Figure 7–40.

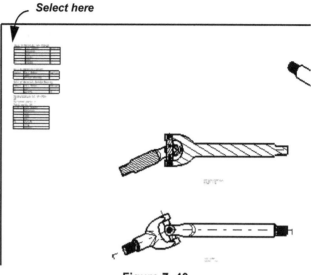

Figure 7–40

Task 4 - Add balloons to a view.

1. Select **Edit>Working Views** to return to the Drawing View mode.

2. Activate the Isometric view.

3. In the Generation toolbar, click ⬚ (Generate Balloons). The view displays as shown in Figure 7–41.

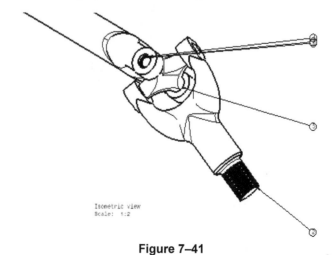

Figure 7–41

4. Rearrange the balloons to make them more visible (as shown in Figure 7–42) by dragging a box around all the balloons to select them. Then, select **7mm** from the *font size* menu.

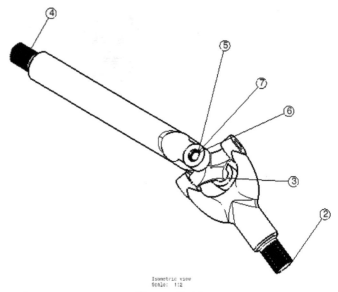

Figure 7–42

Task 5 - Replace view geometry with a CGR representation.

1. Right-click on Front view and select **Properties**.

2. Select the *View* tab and scroll to the bottom in the Properties dialog box.

3. In the View generation mode drop-down list, select **CGR** as shown in Figure 7–43.

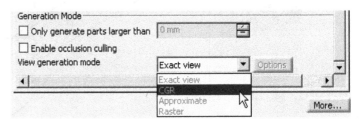

Figure 7–43

4. Click **OK** to close the Drawing Warning dialog box as shown in Figure 7–44.

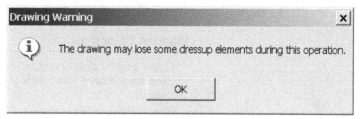

Figure 7–44

5. Toggle off the **Display View Frame** option for this view by clearing it at the top of the Properties dialog box.

6. Click **OK** in the Properties dialog box.

7. Toggle off the view frames of the remaining views.

8. Save the drawing. The drawing displays as shown in Figure 7–45.

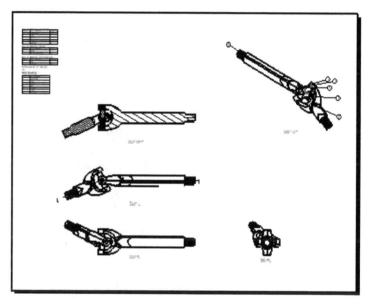

Figure 7–45

9. Close all open files.

Practice 7b

Drawing Views and Overload Properties

Practice Objectives

- Create a scene of an assembly file.
- Generate a drawing view from a scene view using two different methods.
- Change the overload properties of existing views.

In this practice, you will generate a drawing with views from scenes. You will also change the display properties of parts in existing views by defining their Overload Properties. The completed drawing displays as shown in Figure 7–46.

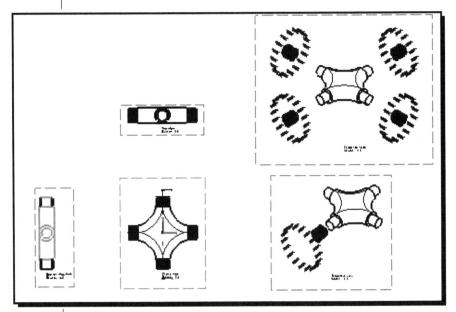

Figure 7–46

Task 1 - Create a scene in the assembly file.

1. Select **File>Open**.

2. Press <Ctrl> and select **SpiderScenes.CATProduct** and **SpiderScenes.CATDrawing** from the *DriveShaft* directory.

3. Click **Open**.

4. Activate the SpiderScenes.CATProduct window.

5. In the specification tree, expand the **Applications** node by selecting the plus (+) symbol. Expand the **Scenes** branch in the same way.

6. In the Scenes toolbar, click (Enhanced Scene). The Enhanced Scene dialog box opens.

7. Clear the **Automatic naming** option and enter **Explode_1** as the name of the scene, as shown in Figure 7–47.

Enhanced Scene ? ✕

Definition

Name:

Explode_1

☐ Automatic naming

Overload Mode:
   ● Partial   ○ Full

   OK   Cancel

Figure 7–47

8. Click **OK**.

9. The assembly changes to **Scene** mode. The specification tree lists the scene name under the **Applications** node, as shown in Figure 7–48.

Applications

Scenes

Explode_1

Explode_2

Figure 7–48

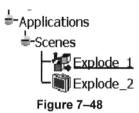
Task 2 - Create an exploded view for the scene.

1. In the Enhanced Scenes toolbar, click (Explode) to explode the scene of the assembly.

*If a Warning dialog box displays regarding moves performed in scene context, enable the **Do not display this message again** option, and click **Close**.*

2. In the Explode dialog box, select the *Fixed product* field, In the specification tree, select the **1652** part number. This fixes the main part in space and explodes all of the other components. The dialog box opens as shown in Figure 7–49.

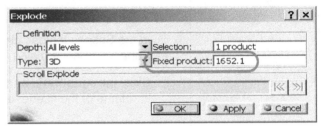

Figure 7–49

3. Leave the *Depth* set to **All levels** and the *Type* set to **3D**.

4. Click **OK**.

5. In the View toolbar, click ⬛ (Isometric View) to change the geometry viewpoint to an Isometric orientation.

6. Click 📷 (Save Viewpoint) to store the viewpoint of the scene. The scene displays as shown in Figure 7–50. Do not exit the scene.

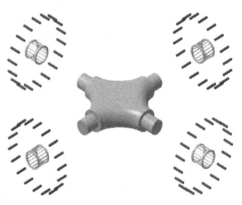

Figure 7–50

Task 3 - Generate a drawing view from the scene just created.

1. With the **Explode_1** scene still open, activate the SpiderScenes.CATDrawing window.

2. In the Projections toolbar, click 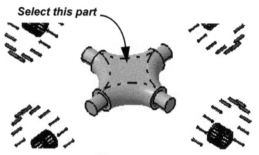 (Isometric View).

3. Activate the product window.

4. In the specification tree, select **Explode_1** to specify that the drawing view is created from the scene.

5. Select from the part, as shown in Figure 7–51.

Select this part

Figure 7–51

6. The drawing window activates automatically. Place the view in the upper right corner of the drawing, as shown in Figure 7–52.

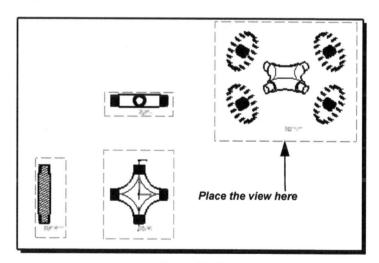

Place the view here

Figure 7–52

7. Activate the product window.

8. Click  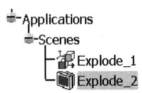 (Exit Scene) to exit the scene.

Task 4 - Create a drawing view from a previously saved scene.

1. Activate the drawing window.

2. If required, select **Edit>Update Current Sheet** (if the views do not need to be updated, this option will not be available).

3. In the Projections toolbar, click  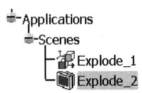 (Isometric View).

4. Activate the product window.

5. In the specification tree, in the **Scenes** branch, select **Explode_2** as shown in Figure 7–53.

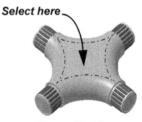

Figure 7–53

6. Select the part, as shown in Figure 7–54, to create the view.

Select here

Figure 7–54

7. The drawing window automatically activates. Place the view below the one you previously created, as shown in Figure 7–55.

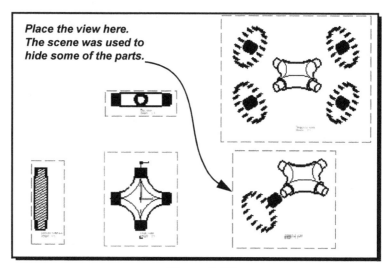

Place the view here. The scene was used to hide some of the parts.

Figure 7–55

Task 5 - Change the Overload Properties of an existing view.

1. Zoom in to Section view A-A to display the geometry in the view more clearly.

2. In the specification tree, right-click on Section view A-A and select **Section view A-A object>Overload Properties**. The Characteristics dialog box opens as shown in Figure 7–56.

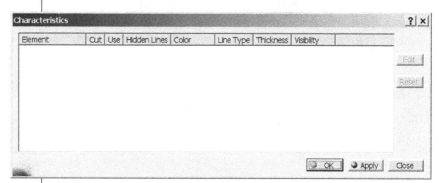

Figure 7–56

3. In the Section view, select **1652 (1652.1)** as shown in Figure 7–57.

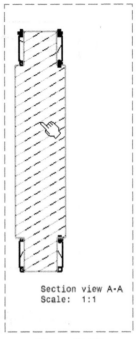

Section view A-A
Scale: 1:1

Figure 7–57

4. Select **1652 (1652.1)** and click **Edit** in the Characteristics dialog box, as shown in Figure 7–58.

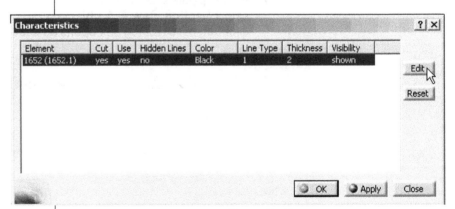

Element	Cut	Use	Hidden Lines	Color	Line Type	Thickness	Visibility	
1652 (1652.1)	yes	yes	no	Black	1	2	shown	

Figure 7–58

5. The Editor dialog box opens. Clear the **Cut in section views** option to display the part as not affected by the section cut.

6. In the Graphic Properties drop-down list, change the *color* to **red** as shown in Figure 7–59.

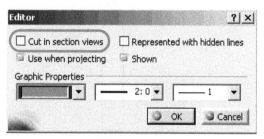

Figure 7–59

7. Click **OK** to close the Editor.

8. In the Characteristics dialog box, click **Apply** to complete the changes to the view. The view displays as shown in Figure 7–60.

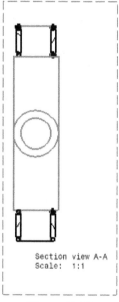

Figure 7–60

9. In the Section view, select **20c (20c.1)** as shown in Figure 7–61.

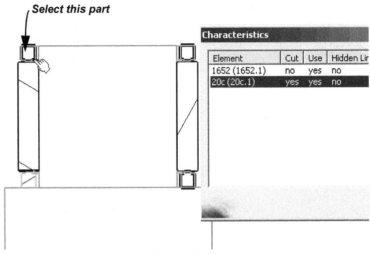

Select this part

Figure 7–61

10. Click **Edit** in the Characteristics dialog box.

11. Clear the **Shown** option, as shown in Figure 7–62.

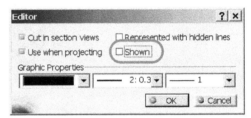

Figure 7–62

12. Click **OK** to close the Editor and then click **OK** to close the Characteristics dialog box. The view displays as shown in Figure 7–63.

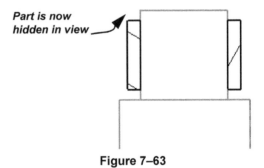

Part is now hidden in view

Figure 7–63

The drawing displays as shown in Figure 7–64.

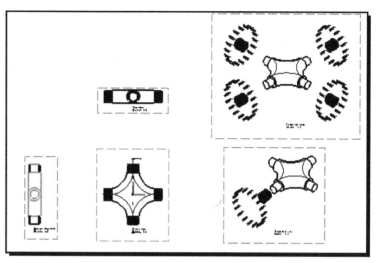

Figure 7–64

13. Save the drawing and close all of the files.

Practice 7c | Wine Opener

Practice Objectives

- Use Modify Links to control component display.
- Superpose two views.
- Use the Area Fill tool.

In this practice, you will create drawing views for the upper and lower limits of the wine opener. To accomplish this, you will create views using assembly scenes. The scenes have been created for you. Drawing views will then be superposed on top of one another. You will also use the **Modify Links** tool to remove components from an isometric view. The completed drawing displays as shown in Figure 7–65.

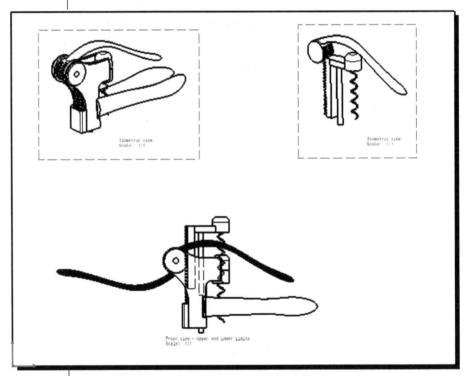

Figure 7–65

Task 1 - Open an assembly model and create a new drawing.

1. Open **WineOpener_scenes.CATProduct**.

2. Create a new drawing file. For the *sheet style*, select **C ANSI**.

Task 2 - Create two isometric views.

1. Place two isometric views, as shown in Figure 7–66. Ensure that you rotate the product to the correct orientation before selecting it to place the views.

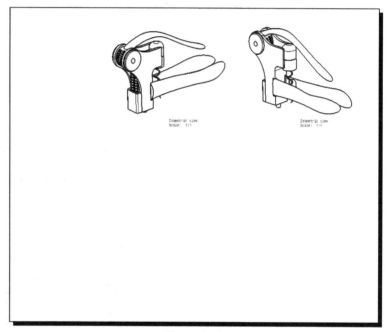

Figure 7–66

2. Right-click on the isometric view on the right side of the sheet and select **Isometric View Object>Modify Links**.

3. With the Links Modification dialog box open, select **Window> Tile Horizontally**.

4. In the product window, in the specification tree, select **Pinion Handle** and **Rack Corkscrew**. Ensure that both components are selected by pressing <Ctrl> during selection.

5. Return to the drawing window.

6. In the Link Modification dialog box, click **Add all**, as shown in Figure 7–67.

Figure 7–67

7. Click **OK** to close the Link Modification dialog box.

8. Update the drawing view. The isometric view displays as shown in Figure 7–68.

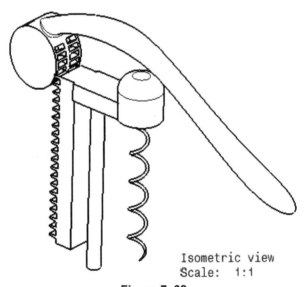

Isometric view
Scale: 1:1

Figure 7–68

Task 3 - Create view from scenes.

1. Click ![icon] (Front View).

2. Activate the assembly window. In the **Applications>Scenes** node, select the **Upper Lim** scene.

3. Select an appropriate planar surface on the model and place the scene.

4. Create a second front view using the **Lower Lim** scene.

5. Position the two front views as shown in Figure 7–69.

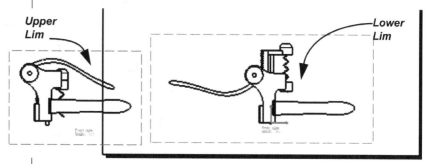

Figure 7–69

6. Right-click on the front view on the left side and select **View Positioning>Superpose**.

7. Select the front view on the right side. The two views immediately become superposed on the origin of the second view, as shown in Figure 7–70.

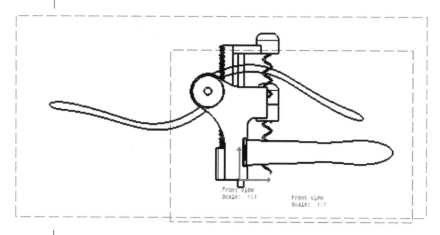

Figure 7–70

Task 4 - Change the overload properties of an existing view.

1. Using the overload properties, change the **Rack Corkscrew.CAT- Part** display to hidden lines, as shown in Figure 7–71.

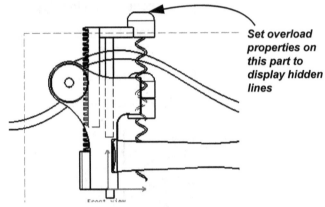

Set overload properties on this part to display hidden lines

Figure 7–71

Task 5 - Add dress-up elements

1. In the Dress-up toolbar, click ![Area Fill] (Area Fill) to place a fill on the parts shown in Figure 7–72.

2. Change the properties of the fill from a *hatch* to **solid black**.

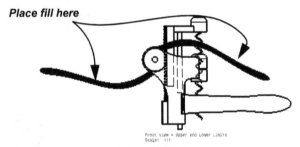

Place fill here

Figure 7–72

Task 6 - Adjust view properties.

1. Modify the front view properties so that the view frames are not displayed.

2. Save the drawing and close the file.

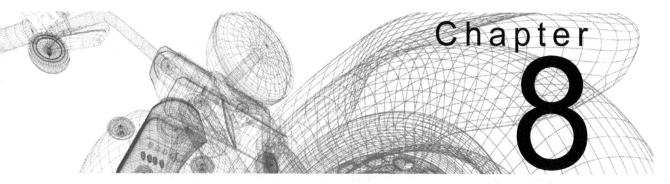

Chapter 8

Complete the Drawing

Once all of the manufacturing information has been added to a drawing, general information and borders can be added by inserting a frame and title block.

Learning Objectives in this Chapter

- Create 2D frame and title block.
- Insert a frame and title block.
- Insert a background view.
- Print a drawing.
- Import and export 2D data.
- Insert an image.
- Understand large drawing management techniques.

8.1 Frame and Title Block

You can use two methods to add a title block to a drafting sheet:

- Insert a frame and title block created by VBScript.

- Create a frame and title block from 2D geometry creation tools.

Insert Frame and Title Block

A frame and title block can be created using the VB Script functionality. A frame and title block created in this way can be saved in a title block directory. The standard installation of CATIA V5 includes example frame and title blocks located at: **\<install directory>\<current_release>\win_b64\VBScript\FrameTitle Block**. Obtain the location of your company's custom frame and title block directory from your CATIA system administrator.

2D Drafting Functionality

2D drafting tools can be used to create a frame and title block geometry and text.

8.2 Create 2D Frame and Title Block

General Steps

Use the following general steps to create 2D frame and title block geometry:

1. Create a new drawing file.
2. Define frame and title block.
3. Save the drawing.
4. (Optional) Reuse the sheet template.

Step 1 - Create a new drawing file.

Create a drawing file using the required sheet size.

Step 2 - Define frame and title block.

Use the tools in the Geometry Creation toolbar shown in Figure 8–1 to create frame geometry.

Figure 8–1

Figure 8–2 shows an example of a sketched frame.

*You can use the grid with the **Snap to point** option to aid in frame creation.*

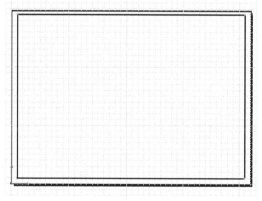

Figure 8–2

You can sketch tables using geometry creation tools or by clicking ⊞ (Table). An example of a table with text is shown in Figure 8–3.

	By	Date
Drawn		
Checker		
Designer		
Approved		

Figure 8–3

Step 3 - Save the drawing.

Save the drawing to a shared directory on a server to permit everyone to have access to the company standard title blocks.

Step 4 - (Optional) Reuse the sheet template.

This 2D frame and title block drawing file can be used as a template for future drawing files. You can easily open the template, create drawing views, and save the completed drawing as a new file.

To create a new drawing using a template file, select **File>New from**. The **Show Preview** option located at the bottom of the File Selection dialog box can be used to confirm your selection. Navigate to the custom frame and title block directory. Select the required frame and title block template and click **Open**.

To save the file, select **File>Save**. Because the file was opened using **New from**, the Save As dialog box automatically opens to ensure that the new drawing file is saved independent of the frame and title block template file.

8.3 Insert a Frame and Title Block

Customizing the example frame and title block macro files using Visual Basic Script is discussed in detail in Appendix A.

The standard CATIA installation contains several examples of frame and title block styles. The frame and title block geometry is drawn automatically by macro scripts. These macros also provide actions to customize and maintain the sheet background.

General Steps

Use the following general steps to insert and modify a frame and title block:

1. Create a frame and title block.
2. Add review and revision information.
3. Modify the title block (as required).

Step 1 - Create a frame and title block.

To add a frame and title block from the VBScript examples, select **Edit>Sheet Background** and **Insert>Drawing>Frame and Title Block**. The Manage Frame and title block dialog box opens as shown in Figure 8–4.

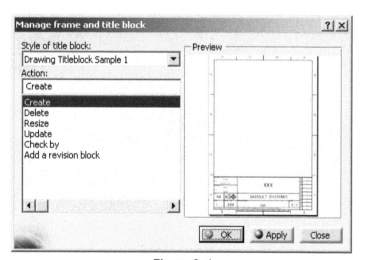

Figure 8–4

Select the required title block in the Style of title block drop-down list. Ensure that **Create** is selected in the list of actions. Click **Apply** to create the frame and title block.

Step 2 - Add review and revision information.

CheckedBy

Select the **Check by** action and click **Apply**. The Controller's name text input box opens, as shown in Figure 8–5.

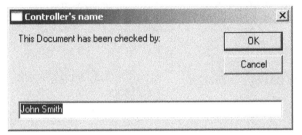

Figure 8–5

Enter the name of the controller and click **OK**. The controller's name and verification date sections of the title block update automatically, as shown in Figure 8–6.

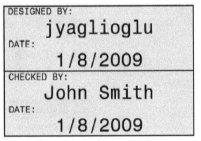

Figure 8–6

Add Revision Block

To add revision information, select the **Add a revision block** action and click **Apply**. The Reviewer's name text input box opens as shown in Figure 8–7. Enter the name of the reviewer and click **OK**.

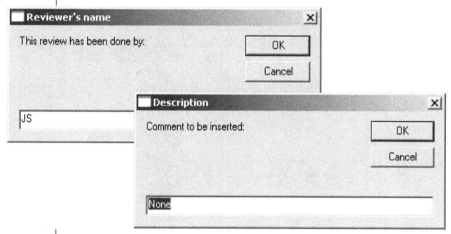

Figure 8–7

The Description dialog box opens next, as shown in Figure 8–7. Enter a comment (optional) and click **OK**. The completed revision block displays as shown in Figure 8–8.

REV	DATE	DESCRIPTION	INIT
A	2/26/2007	None	JS

Figure 8–8

Step 3 - Modify the title block (as required).

Once a title block has been added to a drawing, you might need to modify it based on changes to the drawing. The following operations can be performed using the Insert Frame and Title Block dialog box:

- Resize the title block

- Delete the title block

Resize the Title Block

Frame and title block positioning and rulers do not update automatically when the sheet format is changed, as shown in Figure 8–9.

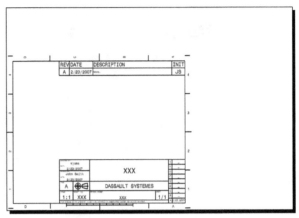

Figure 8–9

To update a frame and title block to fit the new sheet format, select **Resize** in the list of actions and click **Apply**. The background is automatically fitted to the new sheet format, as shown in Figure 8–10.

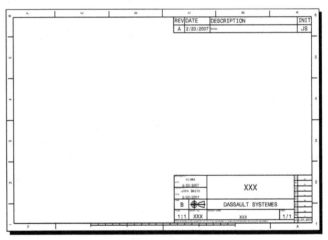

Figure 8–10

Delete the Title Block

To replace the current background style, the original frame and title block must be deleted.

Select the current background style in the Style of Titleblock drop-down list. Select **Delete** in the list of actions and click **Apply**.

8.4 Insert a Background View

The Page Setup dialog box can be used to resize an existing drawing sheet. It can also be used to insert a drawing of a frame and title block into the background view.

General Steps

Use the following general steps to insert a sketched frame and title block:

1. Open a drawing file.
2. Activate Page Setup.
3. Insert a background view.

Step 1 - Open a drawing file.

Open the drawing file to add a sketched title block.

Step 2 - Activate Page Setup.

Select **File>Page Setup**. The Page Setup dialog box opens as shown in Figure 8–11.

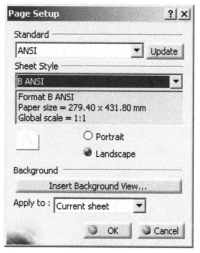

Figure 8–11

To change the sheet size or drawing standard, select new options in the Standard and Sheet Style drop-down lists and click **OK**.

Step 3 - Insert a background view.

Click **Insert Background View** in the Page Setup dialog box, browse to the directory containing title block drawings, and select the appropriate size. Click **OK** to complete the operation.

Settings

Select **Tools>Options>Mechanical Design>Drafting** and select the *Layout* tab to display the options that control new sheet creation and title block file location.

If the **Copy background view** option has been enabled, any new sheets that are created display the First sheet or a sheet from another drawing, as shown in Figure 8–12.

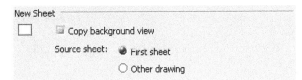

Figure 8–12

Enter the file path to a shared directory in which the company title block VBScripts are stored, as shown in Figure 8–13.

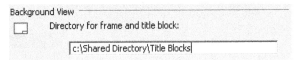

Figure 8–13

8.5 Print a Drawing

Select **File>Print** to print a drawing. The Print dialog box opens as shown in Figure 8–14.

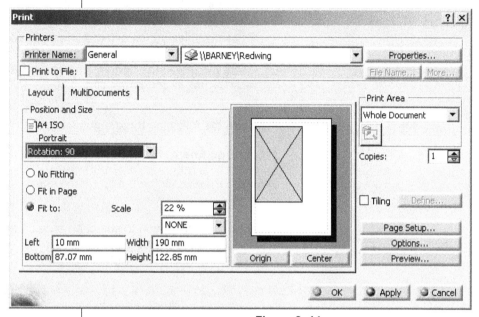

Figure 8–14

Use the *Layout* tab to control the position, orientation, size, and portion of the drawing to be printed.

Position and Size

How To: Control the Position, Orientation, and Size of the Print

1. Set the orientation of the drawing by selecting an option in the drop-down list, as shown in Figure 8–15.

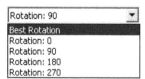

Figure 8–15

2. Select a fitting option to control the size of the plot. The following options are available:

- **No Fitting:** Generates the print using its original size. No scaling is performed.
- **Fit in Page:** Scales the print to fit the size of the page, including margins.
- **Fit to:** Enables you to select a scaling percentage or new sheet size to which to scale the print. Click **Origin** to locate the plot in the bottom left corner of the page, or click **Center** to center the plot.

Print Area

You can use the following three options to adjust the print area:

- **Whole Document:** Prints the entire drawing sheet.

- **Display:** Prints only the portion of the sheet displayed in the main window.

- **Selection:** Enables you to select an area on the drawing sheet to print. Click (Select mode).

If the drawing contains more than one sheet, the options in the *Multi Documents* tab enable you to control which sheets are printed, as shown in Figure 8–16.

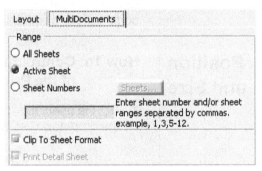

Figure 8–16

Quick Print

If you click 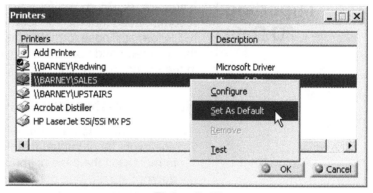 (Print) in the Standard toolbar, the system automatically prints a copy of the drawing to the default printer using the default settings in the Print dialog box. Select **File>Printer Setup** to select the default printer.

Right-click on the printer in the list in the Printers dialog box and select **Set as Default**, as shown in Figure 8–17.

Printers		_ □ ×
Printers	**Description**	
🖨 Add Printer		
🖨 \\BARNEY\Redwing	Microsoft Driver	
🖨 \\BARNEY\SALES		
🖨 \\BARNEY\UPSTAIRS		
🖨 Acrobat Distiller		
🖨 HP LaserJet 5Si/5Si MX PS		

Configure
Set As Default
Remove
Test

OK   Cancel

Figure 8–17

8.6 Import and Export 2D Data

An intermediate file format is required when sending or receiving data from another CAD software package. CATIA can import and export 2D data in the Generative Drafting workbench in a variety of file formats. CGM, DXF, and IGES are the most commonly used formats and provide the most successful results.

Importing 2D Data

If you are receiving data from another CAD system, it is recommended that the sender provide the data in the DXF or IGES format. These formats preserve the vector properties of the geometry and text, enabling you to select individual entities in the imported drawing.

How To: Create a New Drawing Using Interface Data

1. Select **File>Open** and browse for the interface file.
2. You might be prompted to select a drawing standard and format, as in the case of importing a DXF file. Select the appropriate drawing parameters in the New Drawing dialog box and click **OK**. The interface data is imported into a new drawing file.
3. If you require the interface data to be added as a new or existing sheet on a drawing, you can select the items and cut or copy them from the new drawing. The items can then be pasted into the existing drawing.

Try some of the following workarounds if you encounter any errors when importing a 2D file into CATIA:

- The path length and name can cause problems when reading files into CATIA. Copy the file to a location with a simplified path name, such as **C:\Temp** on a Windows system, or copy it to your home directory on a UNIX system.

- Rename the file to remove any extra characters or spaces (e.g., **test.dxf**).

- If the file was sent by email or ftp, have the sender zip or compress the file to protect it against corruption.

- Request that the file be sent in another file format.

Exporting 2D Data

You might want to export a 2D file from the Generative Drafting workbench to send a drawing to another CAD system, or to remove the file association from the 3D model when sending a drawing to another CATIA user.

How To: Export a 2D File from CATIA

1. With the drawing open in CATIA, select **File>Save As**.
2. In the Save as type drop-down list, select a file format as shown in Figure 8–18.

Figure 8–18

3. Enter a unique name for the file and click **Save**.

The following table lists the different types of 2D file formats available and the applications where they can be used. If the format supports multi-sheets, a separate export file is automatically generated for each sheet in the drawing. Otherwise, only the current sheet is exported.

File Format	Multi-Sheet Support	Result
DXF	Yes	DXF (Drawing eXchange Format). Can be imported into most CAD systems.
DWG	Yes	Native AutoCAD format.
CGM	No	Computer Graphics Metafile. When imported, entities cannot be individually selected. Can be imported into most CAD systems.
GL2	No	Hewlett Packard Graphics Language 2 format. A plot file that can be sent directly to a HP-GL2 capable printer.
PS	No	Postscript file. Can be sent directly to a postscript capable printer.
CATALOG	Yes (Detail Sheets only)	Creates a catalog file of 2D Components that can be added to other CATIA drawings.
PDF	Yes	Creates an image of the drawing that can be viewed using Adobe Acrobat.
TIF	No	Creates a TIFF image of the drawing that can be viewed using a graphics package or Internet Explorer.
JPG	No	Creates a JPEG image of the drawing that can be viewed using a graphics package or Internet Explorer.
IG2	No	Creates an IGES file. The filename should be renamed to .IGS to be recognized by other CAD systems. Can be imported into most CAD systems.

8.7 Insert an Image

Select **Insert>Object** to add an exact image of a logo or any other object to the title block or drawing. If you add it to the title block, ensure that Background mode has been activated.

The Insert Object dialog box opens as shown in Figure 8–19.

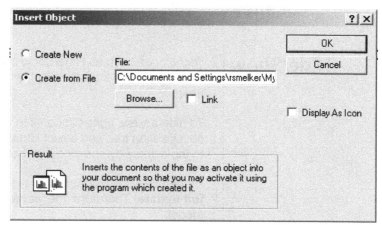

Figure 8–19

Click **Browse** and browse to the bitmap image that you want to use. Click **OK** to place the image in the drawing, as shown in Figure 8–20.

Typically, the image displays in the lower left corner of the drawing.

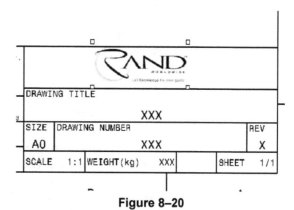

Figure 8–20

You can also select **Create New** to launch a default editor and create a new object, if the required object does not exist.

Alternatively, you can use **Insert>Picture** to import an existing image file. Many formats are supported, such as Bitmap, PNG, JPEG, and so on.

8.8 Large Drawing Management Techniques

Use the following techniques to help manage a drawing with a large number of views and sheets.

Scenes

Scenes simplify assembly geometry. Deactivate components that are not required in a specific view.

Hide/Show

Techniques such as Hide/Show can simplify a drawing by removing views from the display that are not currently being used.

To hide a view, right-click on it in the drawing window or specification tree and select **Hide/Show**. You can return the view to the display by showing it in the specification tree.

Hidden views still update with the drawing when you perform a **full update**. Therefore, the views remain associative to the model.

View Generation Mode

Two view generation modes improve drawing performance when working with large models: CGR and Approximate.

CGR

CGR representations in drawing views decrease the update time of the drawing. The CGR representation only considers the external surfaces of the part or assembly model, which speeds up view generation.

Approximate

When working with large and complex drawings, such as component assemblies, use the Approximate view generation mode to reduce drawing update time during drawing creation. In the View Properties dialog box, select **Approximate** in the View generation mode drop-down list and click **Options**.

The **Level Of Detail** coefficient dictates how accurately the small geometric elements (surfaces, edges, etc.) will display in the view. A low level of detail coefficient simplifies the display of small features and resembles the CGR mode. A high level of detail includes all part features and resembles the Exact mode.

Local Update

A drawing can be updated in a variety of ways in the Drafting workbench. Depending on what is selected in the specification tree, you can localize the update to specific drawing views. You can update a drawing in the following ways:

- All views of the drawing update if you update the drawing from the specification tree. As well, all views on all sheets update if there are multiple sheets.

- All views on a sheet update when it is selected. Other drawing sheets are not included in the update. The update symbol remains displayed in the specification tree on other sheets and in their views until you perform an update.

- To update specific views of a drawing, select them individually in the specification tree, right-click, and select **Update Selection**. All other views are not included in the update.

These methods help you to manage a complicated drawing during view generation and detailing, by ensuring that only required elements are updated. Be sure to update the entire drawing before you save or store a drawing.

Practice 8a

Create a Title Block

Practice Objectives

- Create a Title Block.
- Insert an image.

In this practice, you will build a title block for a B-size drawing. The title block includes a border, tables, and an image. You will apply this title block to a drawing in a later practice. The completed title block displays as shown in Figure 8–21.

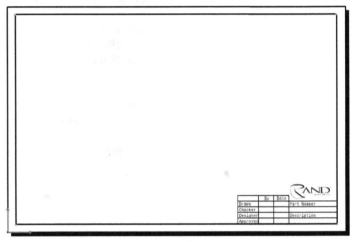

Figure 8–21

Task 1 - Set option settings.

1. Select **Tools>Options>Mechanical Design>Drafting** and select the *General* tab. Enable the **Display** and **Snap to point** options. Ensure that the *Primary spacing* is set to **100** and the *Graduations* are set to **10**, as shown in Figure 8–22.

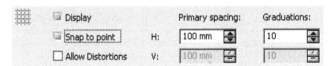

Figure 8–22

2. Click **OK**.

Task 2 - Create a drawing.

1. Create a **B ANSI** drawing. The drawing displays as shown in Figure 8–23.

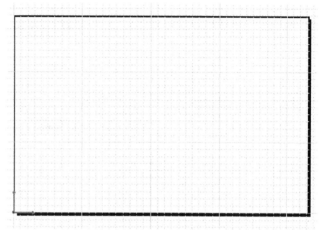

Figure 8–23

Task 3 - Activate the Background View.

1. Select **Edit>Sheet Background** to create geometry for the background.

Task 4 - Create 2D geometry.

1. In the Geometry Creation toolbar, click 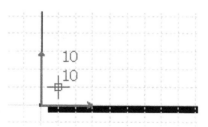 (Rectangle) and sketch a rectangle.

2. Begin sketching the rectangle from the **10, 10** position, as shown in Figure 8–24.

Figure 8–24

3. Drag the rectangle to the **420, 270** position, as shown in Figure 8–25.

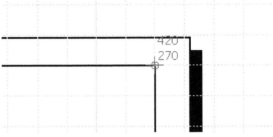

Figure 8–25

The completed rectangle displays as shown in Figure 8–26.

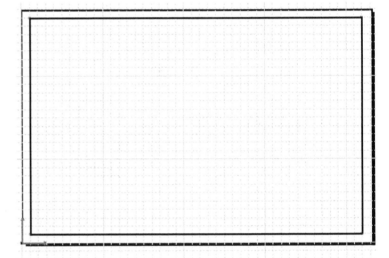

Figure 8–26

Task 5 - Create a table.

1. Click ⊞ (Table). Enter **3** *columns* and **5** *rows* using the Table Editor, as shown in Figure 8–27.

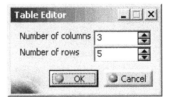

Figure 8–27

2. Click **OK**.

3. Select a location for the table in the lower right corner of the sheet, as shown in Figure 8–28.

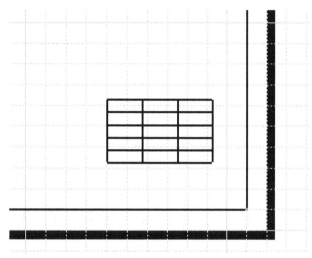

Figure 8–28

Task 6 - Enter text.

1. Double-click on the table to make it active.

2. Double-click on the cell shown in Figure 8–29. The Text Editor opens.

Double-click this cell

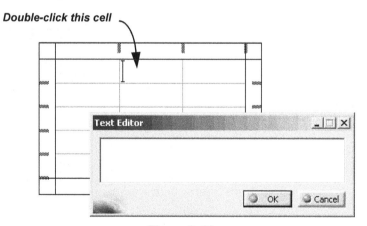

Figure 8–29

3. In the Text Editor, enter **By** as shown in Figure 8–30.

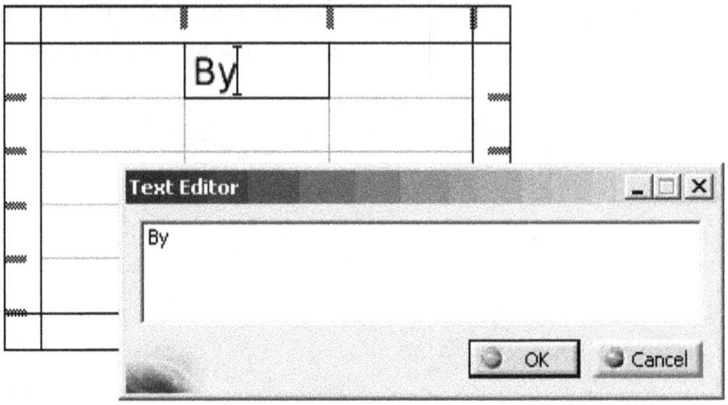

Figure 8–30

4. Click **OK** in the Text Editor.

Task 7 - Change the anchor point of text.

1. Select the cell. In the Text Properties toolbar, click

   A (Anchor Point) as shown in Figure 8–31.

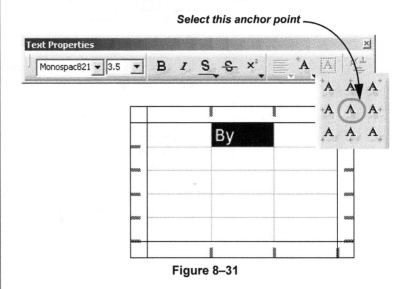

Figure 8–31

2. Enter the text shown in Figure 8–32 in the appropriate cells. Ensure that the **Date** text is centered.

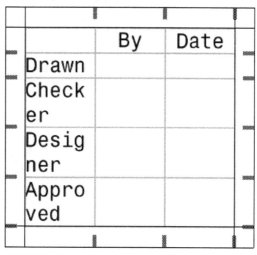

Figure 8–32

3. Place the cursor in the margin above the column, as shown in Figure 8–33.

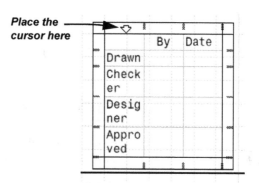

Figure 8–33

If the table is not active, double-click on it to make it active again.

4. Resize the left text column by placing the cursor in the margin area above the first column. Right-click and select **Size>Autofit**, as shown in Figure 8–34.

Insert column
Delete
Clear content
Size
Set size
Autofit
Date
Desig
ner
Appro
ved

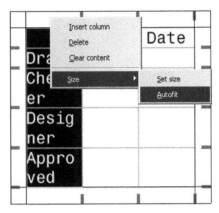

Figure 8–34

The table updates as shown in Figure 8–35.

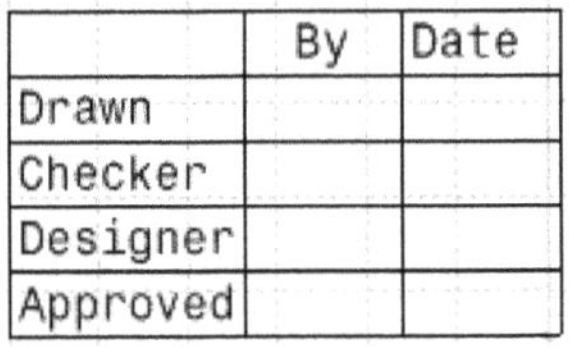

By
Date
Drawn
Checker
Designer
Approved

Figure 8–35

Task 8 - Place a CSV table.

Click *to place a table from CSV.*

1. Place a table from CSV named **TitleBlock.csv**. Browse to the training files directory to select the *.CSV file.

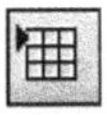

2. Place the table from CSV at the location shown in Figure 8–36.

Part Number
Description
By
Date
Drawn
Checker
Designer
Approved

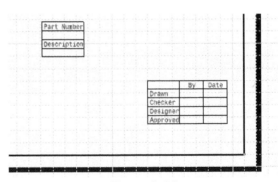

Figure 8–36

3. Double-click on the table and place the cursor in the margin above the column, as shown in Figure 8–37.

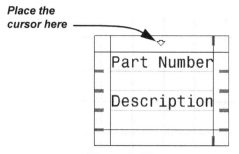

Figure 8–37

4. Right-click and select **Size>Set size**, as shown in Figure 8–38.

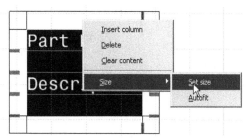

Figure 8–38

5. In the Size dialog box, enter **60mm** as shown in Figure 8–39.

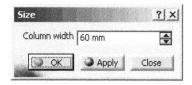

Figure 8–39

6. Click **OK**. The table updates as shown in Figure 8–40.

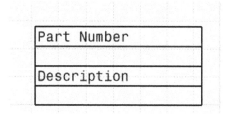

Figure 8–40

7. Select both tables (do not double-click).

8. In the Graphic Properties toolbar, select a *line size* of **2** as shown in Figure 8–41.

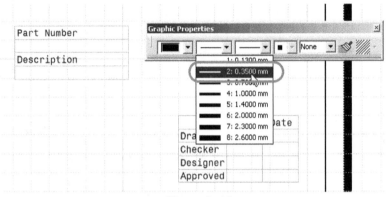

Figure 8–41

9. Zoom in to the tables and drag them to the positions shown in Figure 8–42. To temporarily disable the **Snap to Point** option, press <Shift> while dragging the table to a new location.

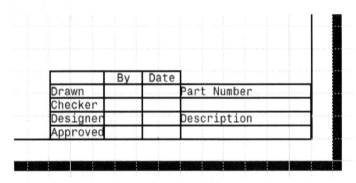

Figure 8–42

Task 9 - Import a picture.

1. Select **Insert>Picture**.

2. Select **RAND_worldwide.bmp** from the practice files.

3. Place the picture, as shown in Figure 8–43.

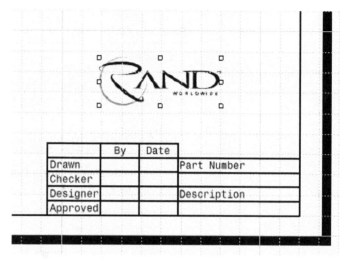

Figure 8–43

4. Zoom in as required and move the picture to the location shown in Figure 8–44. Use the handles to resize the picture as required.

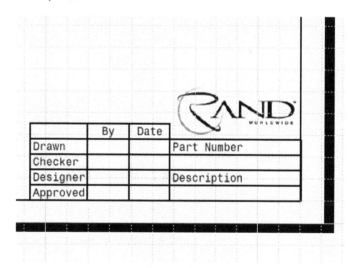

Figure 8–44

5. Save the drawing as **B TitleBlock** and close the file.

Practice 8b | Insert a Title Block

Practice Objective

- Insert a Title Block.

In this practice, you will insert previously created title blocks into **Adapter.CATDrawing** and **ExhaustManifold.CATDrawing**.

Task 1 - Open a drawing file.

1. Open **Adapter_Tblock.CATDrawing**. The drawing displays as shown in Figure 8–45.

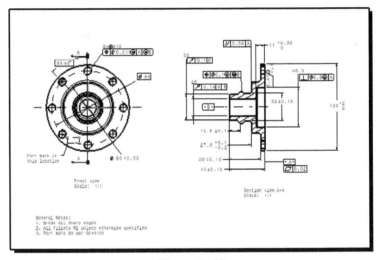

Figure 8–45

Task 2 - Move a note.

The General Notes of this drawing are placed in the background view. If you insert a title block, it overwrites the background view and erases the General Notes.

1. Select **Edit>Sheet Background**.

2. Right-click on the General Note and select **Cut**.

3. Select **Edit>Working Views**.

4. In the specification tree, double-click on **Sheet.1.** Note that none of the views are currently active.

5. In the specification tree, right-click on Sheet.1, and select **Paste**.

6. Move the notes to the location shown in Figure 8–46.

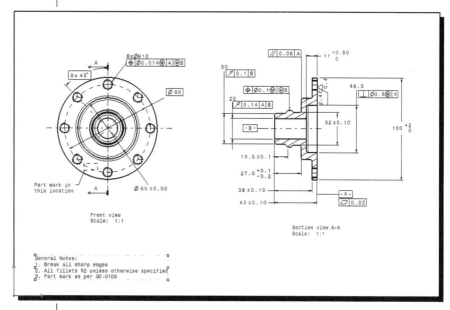

Figure 8–46

Task 3 - Insert a background view.

1. Select **File>Page Setup**. The Page Setup dialog box opens as shown in Figure 8–47.

Figure 8–47

---

2. Click **Insert Background View**. The Insert elements into sheet dialog box opens as shown in Figure 8–48.

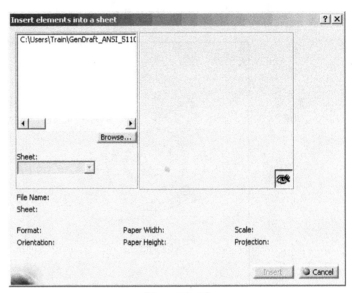

Figure 8–48

3. Click **Browse**, and browse to **B_TitleBlock_ Complete.CATDrawing**, as shown in Figure 8–49.

   If you completed the previous practice you can continue to use **B TitleBlock.CATDrawing** instead.

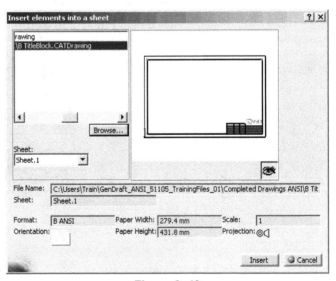

Figure 8–49

4. Click **Insert** and **OK** in the Page Setup dialog box. The drawing updates as shown in Figure 8–50.

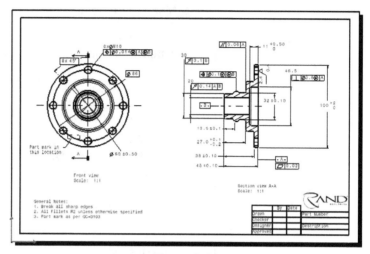

Figure 8–50

5. Save the drawing and close the file.

Task 4 - Insert a VBScript title block.

1. Open **ExhaustManifold_ Com.CATDrawing** from the *ExhaustManifold* directory. The drawing displays as shown in Figure 8–51.

   If you completed the previous practice you can continue to use **ExhaustManifold.CATDrawing** instead.

2. Ensure that Sheet.1 is displayed, as shown in Figure 8–51.

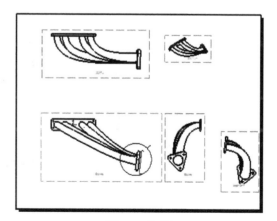

Figure 8–51

3. Activate Background mode.

4. Select **Insert>Drawing>Frame and Title Block.** The Manage frame and title block dialog box opens.

5. In the Style of Titleblock drop-down list, select **Drawing Titleblock Sample 1** as shown in Figure 8–52.

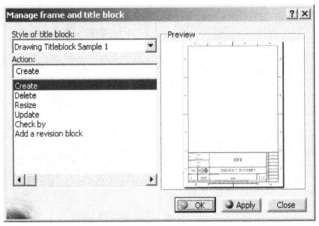

Figure 8–52

6. Click **Apply**. The drawing updates with the selected title block, as shown in Figure 8–53.

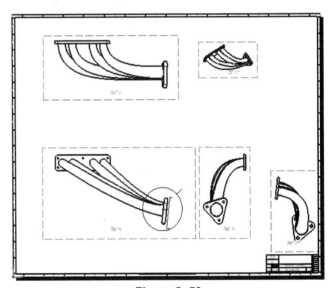

Figure 8–53

7. Click **OK**.

8. Zoom in to the title block and note that the VBScript has entered the current parameter values in the appropriate fields, as shown in Figure 8–54.

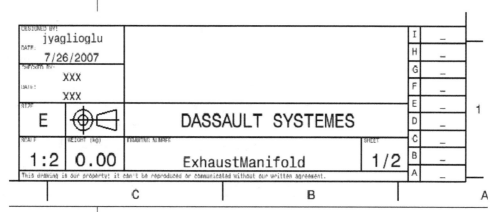

Figure 8–54

9. Save the drawing and close all of the files.

Practice 8c

Insert Parameters into a Table

Practice Objectives

- Create center of gravity parameters.
- Insert the parameters into a drawing table.
- Modify and update the parameters.

In this practice, you will create a table on a drawing that is linked to the center of gravity parameters of the part.

Task 1 - Open files.

1. Open **Cover-2.CATPart** and **Cover-2.CATDrawing**.

Task 2 - Create a table in the drawing.

1. Activate the drawing window. The drawing displays as shown in Figure 8–55.

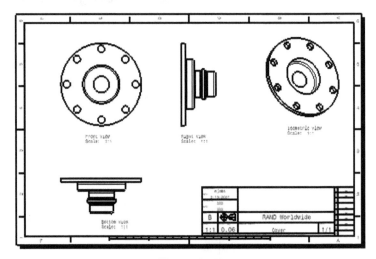

Figure 8–55

Tables are traditionally placed in the sheet background. The working view is reserved for part views and 2D geometry.

2. Activate the sheet background.

3. In the Annotations toolbar, click ▦▾ (Table).

4. In the Table Editor dialog box, for the *Number of columns*, enter **3** and for the *Number of rows*, enter **2** as shown in Figure 8–56.

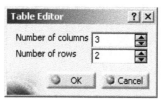

Figure 8–56

To move a table, select it and drag it to the new position.

5. Click **OK**.

6. Move the cursor to the area above the title block and click to place the table, as shown in Figure 8–57.

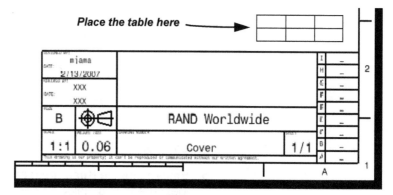

Figure 8–57

Task 3 - Create center of gravity parameters in the part file.

1. Activate the part window.

2. In the specification tree, select the **PartBody** and click (Measure Inertia) to begin measuring the model inertia.

3. In the Measure Inertia dialog box, click **Customize**. Only select the options shown in Figure 8–58.

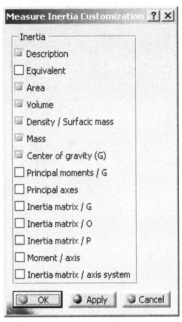

Figure 8–58

4. Click **OK**.

5. Ensure that the **Keep measure** option is enabled in the Measure Inertia dialog box and click **OK** again to complete the feature. The inertia volume and center of gravity parameters are displayed in the specification tree under the Measure node.

Task 4 - Fill in the drawing table with inertia data.

1. Activate the drawing window.

2. Double-click on the table to make it active.

3. Double-click on the cell shown in Figure 8–59. The Text Editor dialog box opens.

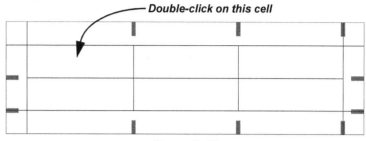

Double-click on this cell

Figure 8–59

4. Configure the top row of the table, as shown in Figure 8–60.

COGx	COGy	COGz

Figure 8–60

5. Select the top row of cells. In the Text Properties toolbar, click

Ā▾ (Anchor Point) to center the text in each cell. The table displays as shown in Figure 8–61.

COGx	COGy	COGz

Figure 8–61

Task 5 - Use attribute links to fill in the second row of the table.

1. Tile the windows horizontally by selecting **Window>Tile Horizontally**.

2. Double-click on the first cell of the second row in the table. When the Text Editor dialog box opens, right-click on the cell and select **Attribute link**, as shown in Figure 8–62. Note that the text cannot be right-clicked in the Text Editor.

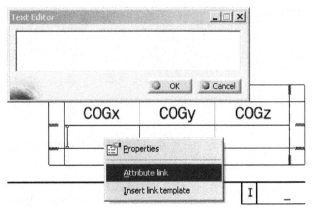

Figure 8–62

3. In the cover part specification tree, select the **Gx** parameter as shown in Figure 8–63.

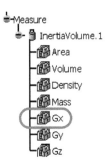

Figure 8–63

4. The Attribute Link Panel dialog box opens as shown in Figure 8–64. Select the parameter in the Attribute List.

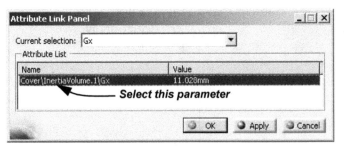

Figure 8–64

5. In the Attribute Link Panel and Text Editor dialog boxes, click **OK** to complete the feature.

6. Create attribute links for the remaining two cells at the center of gravity table.

7. To fit the cell widths to the center of gravity values, move the cursor to the square cell at the top left of the table. Right-click on it and select **Autofit** as shown in Figure 8–65.

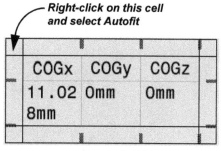

Right-click on this cell and select Autofit

Figure 8–65

The completed table displays as shown in Figure 8–66.

COGx	COGy	COGz
11.028mm	0mm	0mm

Figure 8–66

Task 6 - Modify the parameters.

1. Activate the part window.

2. In the specification tree, double-click on the **Shaft.1** feature.

3. Modify the *100mm dimension*, as shown in Figure 8–67, to **150mm**.

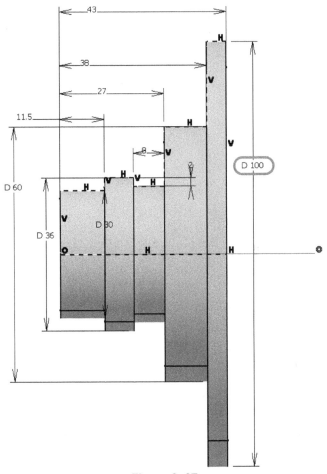

Figure 8–67

4. The inertia measurement node displays as shown in Figure 8–68, indicating that the data is out of date.

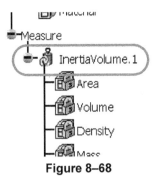

Figure 8–68

5. In the specification tree, right-click on the inertia measurement node and select **Local Update**.

6. Activate the drawing window and click ⟳ (Update current sheet). You might need to force an update on the drawing by entering **c:force update** in the *Power Input* field.

7. The parameters displayed in the COG table have updated with the new center of gravity parameters, as shown in Figure 8–69. The values displayed in the table cells are linked to the parameters in the **Cover-2.CATPart** file.

COGx	COGy	COGz
7.233mm	0mm	0mm

Figure 8–69

8. Save and close all of the files.

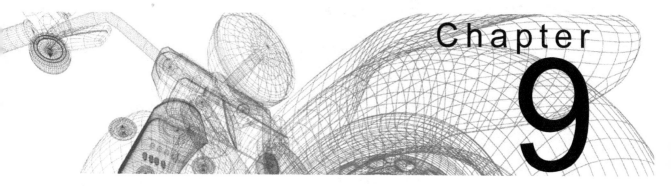

Chapter

9

Projects

This chapter provides drawing projects that can be completed throughout the duration of the course.

Learning Objectives in this Chapter

- Project A - Handle
- Project B - Mounting Plate
- Project C - Product Drawing

Practice 9a

Project A - Handle

Practice Objectives

- Create a part drawing with minimal instruction.
- Create drawing views using the View Creation Wizard.
- Create additional Projection, Section, Clipping, Detail, and Isometric views.
- Create a title block.

This project can be completed anytime after Chapters 1 and 2 have been completed.

In this project, you will create two drawing sheets for a power drill handle. The first sheet will contain projection and detail views and the second sheet will contain cross-section views.

Task 1 - Open a part model.

1. Open **Handle.CATPart**. The model displays as shown in Figure 9–1.

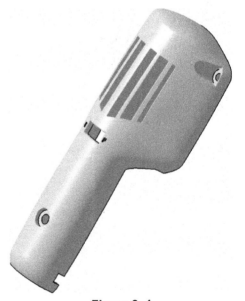

Figure 9–1

2. Select **File>New**. In the New dialog box, in the *List of Types*, select **Drawing**.

3. Click **OK**. The new Drawing dialog box opens.

4. For the *Standard*, enter **ANSI** and for the *Sheet Style*, select **C ANSI** as shown in Figure 9–2.

Figure 9–2

5. Add views and a title block as shown in Figure 9–3. Ensure that the Front, Bottom, and Right views are linked. In addition, ensure that Section view A-A is a half section.

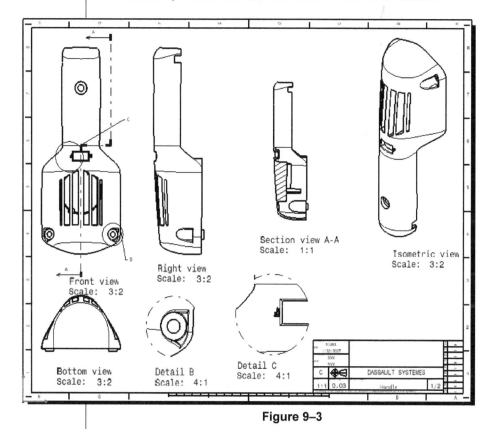

Figure 9–3

6. Add a new sheet and create the views shown in Figure 9–4.

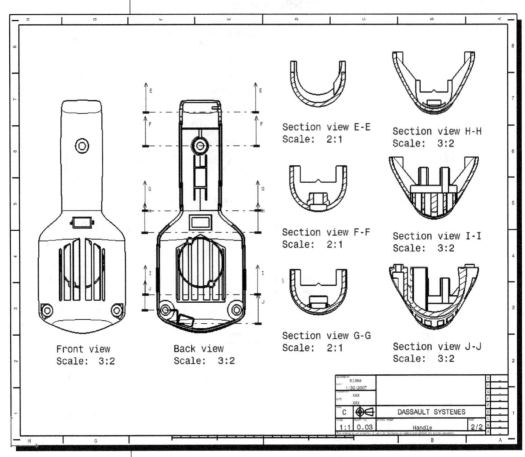

Figure 9–4

7. Save and close all of the files.

Practice 9b

Project B - Mounting Plate

Practice Objective

- Create a part drawing.

This project can be done anytime after Chapters 1 through 6 have been completed.

Task 1 - Create a drawing.

1. Open **MOUNTING_PLATE.CATPart**.

2. Create the C ANSI size drawing shown in Figure 9–5.

Design Considerations

The dimensions are in inches for this practice. The units of a dimension can be changed after it has been created using the Numerical Properties toolbar options. Note that changing the default units of dimensions must be done by a CAD Administrator from the Drawing Standards file.

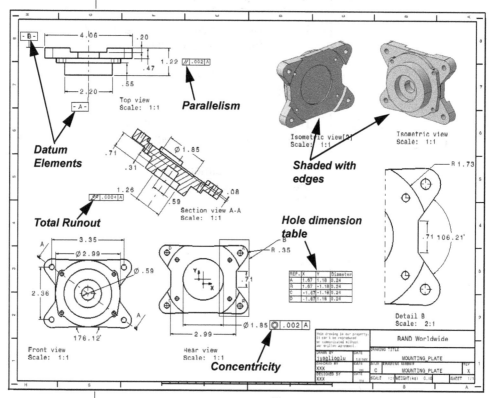

Figure 9–5

Practice 9c

Project C - Product Drawing

Practice Objective

• Create a product drawing.

This project can be done anytime after Chapters 1 through 7 have been completed.

In this project, you will create a product drawing for an aircraft engine. An assortment of views ranging from standard projection views, isometric, section, and clipping views will be included in this drawing. You will create a bill of materials and balloons. Scenes have been created for you in the CATProduct file. You will use them to create some of the views required in this project. Four sheets will be required for the drawing. The last sheet will be reserved for creating 2D components, shown in Figure 9–9. The final product drawing will display as shown in Figure 9–6, Figure 9–7, Figure 9–8, and Figure 9–9.

Task 1 - Open an assembly model.

1. Open **aft_engine_section_asm_with_scenes.CATProduct** from the *ProjectC* directory.

2. Create the D ANSI size drawing shown in Figure 9–6 through Figure 9–9.

Design Considerations

The dimensions are in inches for this practice. The units of a dimension can be changed after it has been created using the Numerical Properties toolbar options. Note that changing the default units of dimensions must be done in the Drawing Standards file by a CAD Administrator.

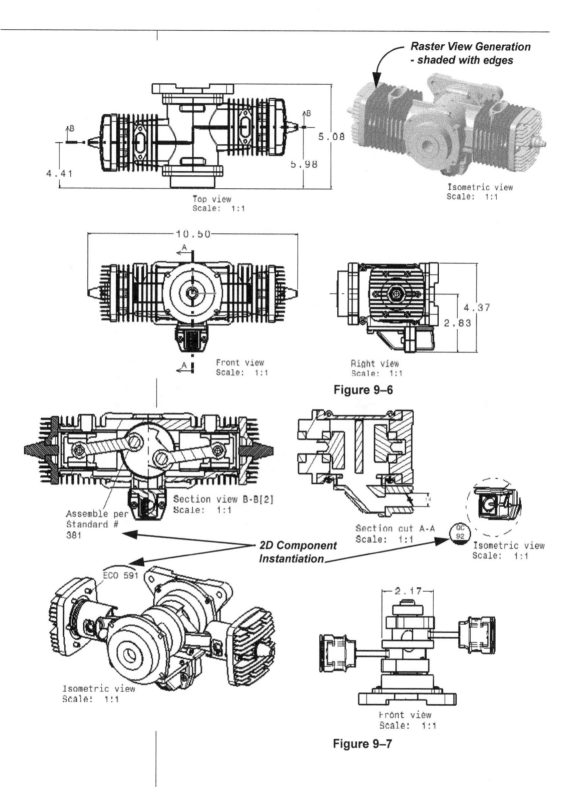

Raster View Generation - shaded with edges

Isometric view
Scale: 1:1

5.08

5.98

4.41

Top view
Scale: 1:1

10.50

A

Front view
Scale: 1:1

Right view
Scale: 1:1

4.37

2.83

Figure 9–6

Section view B-B[2]
Scale: 1:1

Assemble per
Standard #
381

Section cut A-A
Scale: 1:1

QC
92

Isometric view
Scale: 1:1

**2D Component
Instantiation**

ECO 591

Isometric view
Scale: 1:1

2.17

Front view
Scale: 1:1

Figure 9–7

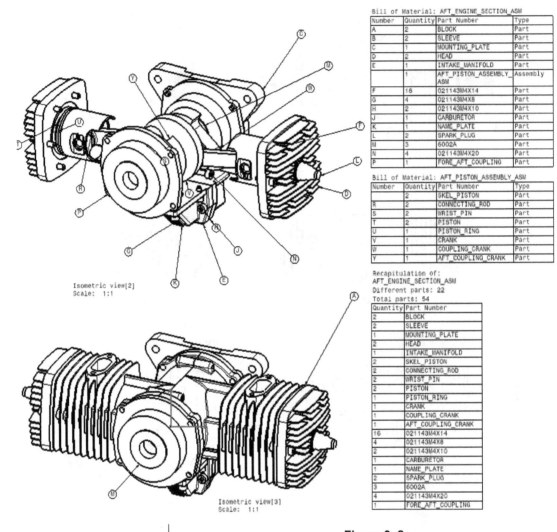

Isometric view[2]
Scale: 1:1

Isometric view[3]
Scale: 1:1

Bill of Material: AFT_ENGINE_SECTION_ASM

Number	Quantity	Part Number	Type
A	2	BLOCK	Part
B	2	SLEEVE	Part
C	1	MOUNTING_PLATE	Part
D	2	HEAD	Part
E	1	INTAKE_MANIFOLD	Part
	1	AFT_PISTON_ASSEMBLY_ASM	Assembly
F	16	021143M4X14	Part
G	4	021143M4X8	Part
H	2	021143M4X10	Part
J	1	CARBURETOR	Part
K	1	NAME_PLATE	Part
L	2	SPARK_PLUG	Part
M	3	6002A	Part
N	4	021143M4X20	Part
P	1	FORE_AFT_COUPLING	Part

Bill of Material: AFT_PISTON_ASSEMBLY_ASM

Number	Quantity	Part Number	Type
	2	SKEL_PISTON	Part
R	2	CONNECTING_ROD	Part
S	2	WRIST_PIN	Part
T	2	PISTON	Part
U	1	PISTON_RING	Part
V	1	CRANK	Part
W	1	COUPLING_CRANK	Part
Y	1	AFT_COUPLING_CRANK	Part

Recapitulation of:
AFT_ENGINE_SECTION_ASM
Different parts: 22
Total parts: 54

Quantity	Part Number
2	BLOCK
2	SLEEVE
1	MOUNTING_PLATE
2	HEAD
1	INTAKE_MANIFOLD
2	SKEL_PISTON
2	CONNECTING_ROD
2	WRIST_PIN
2	PISTON
1	PISTON_RING
1	CRANK
1	COUPLING_CRANK
1	AFT_COUPLING_CRANK
16	021143M4X14
4	021143M4X8
2	021143M4X10
1	CARBURETOR
1	NAME_PLATE
2	SPARK_PLUG
3	6002A
4	021143M4X20
1	FORE_AFT_COUPLING

Figure 9–8

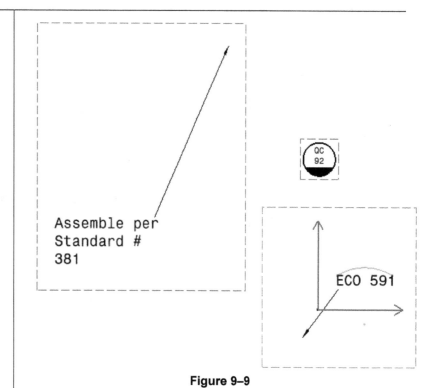

Figure 9–9

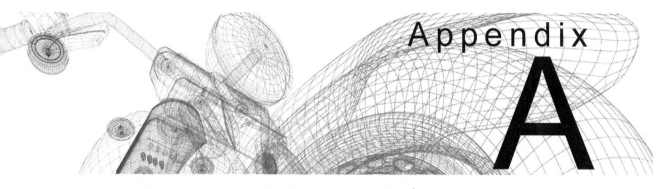

Appendix A

Drawing Frame and Title Block Customization

This appendix provides instruction regarding the customization of a frame and title block script. It does not teach how to create a script from scratch, but shows how some common modifications can be performed. Basic programming skills and experience with the Visual Basic programming language are a required prerequisite.

Learning Objectives in this Chapter

- Customizing a script.
- Understand the anatomy of a sample macro.
- Make basic and advanced modifications to macros.
- Add graphics via macros.

A.1 Customizing a Script

General Steps

Use the following general steps to configure a custom frame and title block:

1. Open and edit the macro.
2. Save the changes.
3. Test the macro.

Step 1 - Open and edit the macro.

The standard installation of CATIA V5 includes examples of frame and title block macros. These files are located in the **<install_directory>\ <current_release>\win_b64\VBScript\ FrameTitleBlock** directory.

Macro CATScript files can be edited using a plain text editor (such as Notepad for Windows) or CATIA's integrated Visual Basic Editor. The CATIA VB Editor is used in this appendix.

To open the VB Editor, select **Tools>Macro>Visual Basic Editor**. The Launch VBA dialog box opens, as shown in Figure A–1, if a Visual Basic for Application (VBA) project is not already open.

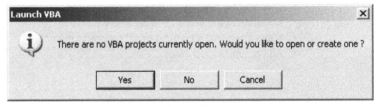

Figure A–1

Loading a VBA Project

Select **Yes** in the Launch VBA dialog box. The Macro libraries dialog box opens as shown in Figure A–2.

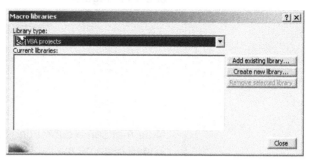

Figure A–2

To add an existing library, select **Add existing library** and open the VBA file. To create a new library, select **Create new library**. Enter the address of the frame and title block macro directory in the Create a new VBA project dialog box, as shown in Figure A–3. Click **OK** to create the new script file.

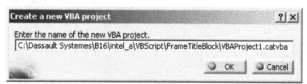

Figure A–3

Importing a CATScript

Select **File>Import File**. In the Import File dialog box, select **All Files** in the Files of type drop-down list. Navigate to the default frame and title block directory, select a CATScript file, and click **Open**, as shown in Figure A–4.

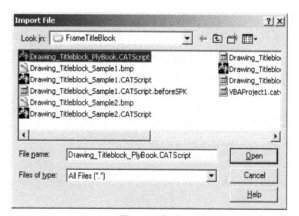

Figure A–4

In the project browser, double-click on the **Modules** node to expand it and double-click on **Module1** to open the script file, as shown in Figure A–5. Examine the source code.

Figure A–5

Note that some subroutines start with the **CATDrw_** prefix. These become available actions in the Manage frame and title block dialog box, as shown in Figure A–6.

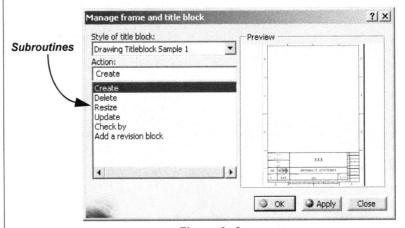

Figure A–6

Note the use of comments (green text) in the source code. Documentation improves code readability and promotes concurrent engineering. It is good programming practice to document the purpose of each segment of code, and any changes and updates that are made. Comments are denoted by a single quotation mark at the beginning of the comment.

Step 2 - Save the changes.

If using a plain text editor, save the file with a unique filename and a .CATScript extension.

Select **File>Export File...** and select **All Files** in the Save as type drop-down list. Save the file in the default frame and title block macro folder with a unique filename and a .CATScript extension, as shown in Figure A–7.

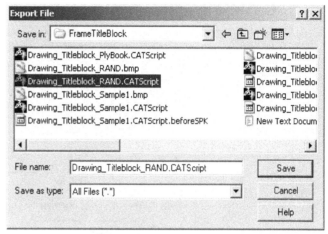

Figure A–7

Before a macro can be applied to a drawing, all instances of the pound (#) symbol must be removed from the file.

The new frame and title block macro can be applied to the sheet background in the same CATIA session.

Step 3 - Test the macro.

Once modified, the functionality of a macro should be tested. In the Drafting workbench, select the modified macro in the Style of Titleblock drop-down list and apply all of the actions (**Create**, **Delete**, **Resize**, etc.) to ensure that the macro performs as intended.

A.2 Anatomy of a Sample Macro

Because the sample frame and title block macro files are very large, it is important to develop an understanding of macro layout. The Frame & Title Block Flowchart in Figure A–8 shows some of the main subroutines that are executed when a new frame and title block are applied to a sheet background.

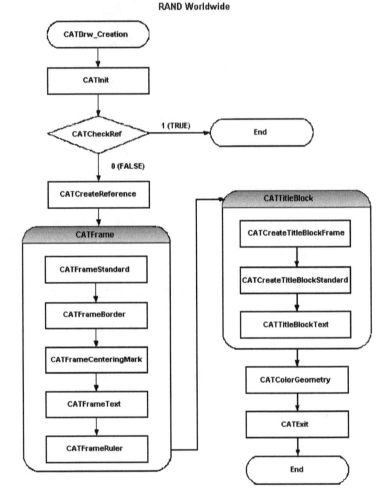

Figure A–8

CATInit

The **CATInit** subroutine initializes macro variables, and is located at the beginning of all action subroutines. **CATInit** makes objects available, such as **Sheet** (containing sheet width and height parameters) and **Fact** (2D Factory permits lines to be drawn).

CATCheckRef

The **CATCheckRef** subroutine ensures that a frame and title block have not been inserted using a different macro.

CATCreate Reference

The **CATCreateReference** subroutine adds a text entity to the sheet. The text entity is empty, although its name and location are used to store vital information for other actions. The text area is called the Reference, and the **CATCheckRef** subroutine uses it to verify which macro was used to create the frame and title block.

CATFrame

The **CATFrame** calls several smaller subroutines to draw the frame. **CATFrameStandard** is the first of these subroutines and, while it does not draw anything, it sets up important variables that are used by the rest of the **CATFrame** subroutines, shown in Figure A–9.

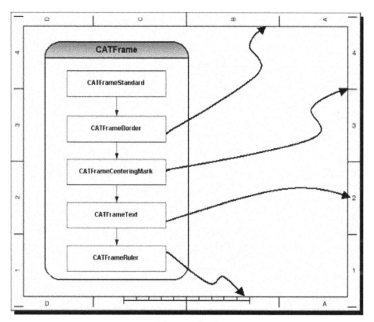

Figure A–9

CATTitleBlock

Similar to **CATFrame**, **CATTitleBlock** calls other subroutines to create the title block. There are three critical subroutine calls in **CATTitleBlock**:

- **CATTitleBlockFrame** draws the title block table.

- **CATTitleBlockStandard** draws an icon of either the 1st angle or 3rd angle.

- **CATTitleBlockText** creates text fields in the title block table. This subroutine calls another important subroutine, **CATLinks**, which fills in some of the text from the part document information.

CATExit

The final subroutine, **CATExit**, prepares an undo point so that the creation of a frame and title block can be undone.

A.3 Basic Modifications

Syntax

In the Visual Basic programming language, the pound (#) symbol is used to denote a fractional value (a value with a decimal point). However, this type indicator is not compatible with **CATScript** files, and must be removed from the macro before it can be applied to a sheet background. To remove all instances of the pound symbol, select **Edit>Replace** in the VB Editor or plain text editor menu bar and replace all pound symbols with null space.

Helper Functions

To give the macro script a unique and meaningful name, modify the **GetMacroID** function. The function is located among many other helper functions near the beginning of the script. The **GetMacroID** function is shown in Figure A–10.

```
Function GetMacroID() As String
   GetMacroID = "Drawing Titleblock RAND"
End Function
```

Figure A–10

Text Fields

The default company name and other title block table headings can be customized by modifying the **CATTitleBlockText** parameter values, as shown in Figure A–11.

```
Text_01 = "This drawing is our property."
Text_02 = "SCALE"
Text_03 = ""
Text_04 = "WEIGHT (kg)"
Text_05 = "XXX"
Text_06 = "DRAWING NUMBER"
Text_07 = "SHEET"
Text_08 = "SIZE"
Text_09 = "USER"
Text_10 = "YYY"                    ' Paper Format
Text_11 = "RAND WORLDWIDE"
Text_12 = "CHECKED BY:"
Text_13 = "DATE:"
Text_14 = "DESIGNED BY:"
Text_15 = CATIA.SystemService.Environ("LOGNAME")
```

Figure A–11

The default relative location of the text parameters listed in Figure A–11 is shown in Figure A–12.

Text_14				
Text_13		Text_05		
Text_12				
Text_13				
Text_08		Text_11		
Text_02	Text_04	Text_06		Text_07
Text_03		Text_05		

Text_01

Figure A–12

Table Cell Sizes

The default title block table cell sizes can be modified in the helper functions **Col** and **Row**, as shown in Figure A–13.

```
Function Col(idx As Integer) As Variant
  Col = Array(-190, -170, -145, -45, -25, -20)(idx - 1)
End Function

Function Row(idx As Integer) As Variant
  Row = Array(4, 17, 30, 45, 60)(idx - 1)
End Function

Function GetRulerLength() As Double
```

Figure A–13

The **Col(1)** parameter defines the boundary of the table's base cell. As it is measured from the vertical origin, it effectively sets the overall width of the table. Each consecutive column of cells *overlaps* the base cell, as shown in Figure A–14, and should have an offset value that is less than every preceding column boundary.

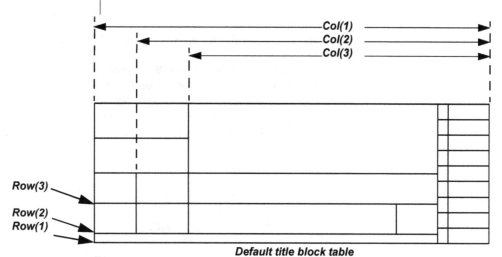

Default title block table

Figure A–14

The **Row(1)** parameter defines the boundary of the first row from the horizontal origin. Each consecutive row of cells is placed *behind* the first, as shown in Figure A–14, and should have an offset value that is greater than every preceding row boundary.

A.4 Advanced Modifications

In addition to customizing title block text fields and table structure, your input and custom graphics can also be incorporated into a sheet background.

User Input Boxes

Although there are several ways to add your input, two essential methods use the **InputBox** and **MsgBox** functions.

To create a text input box, a variable of type string must be created in the header of the script file, as shown in Figure A–15. This variable, named **CompanyName**, stores a user-entered string. Although the variable declaration can be placed anywhere in the code, it is good programming practice to group all variable declarations in the header of a file.

```
Public SheetFormat     As catPaperSize        ' Sheet for
Public sheetProjMethod As catSheetProjectionMethod
Public orientationSheet As catPaperOrientation
Public documentStd  As CatDrawingStandard
Public StartTime, EndTime
Public CompanyName     As String
```

Figure A–15

The first input box parameter, <prompt>, is the only one that is mandatory.

Placement of the input box code is critical. For an input box that prompts you the enter the company name and inserts it into the title block table, the code must be placed in the **CATTitleBlockText** subroutine. The syntax code of an **InputBox** is:

<string_variable> = InputBox("<prompt>", "<title>", "default_value")

In the example shown in Figure A–16, two lines of code have been added. The first prompts you to enter a value for the string parameter. The second assigns this value to Text_11, which the macro uses later in the code for the company name.

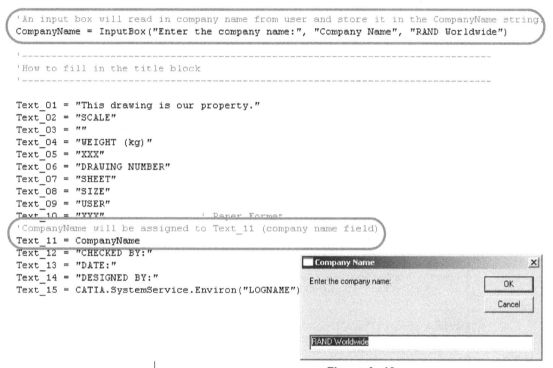

```
Sub CATTitleBlockText()

'An input box will read in company name from user and store it in the CompanyName string
CompanyName = InputBox("Enter the company name:", "Company Name", "RAND Worldwide")


'-----------------------------------------------------------------------------------
'How to fill in the title block
'-----------------------------------------------------------------------------------

    Text_01 = "This drawing is our property."
    Text_02 = "SCALE"
    Text_03 = ""
    Text_04 = "WEIGHT (kg)"
    Text_05 = "XXX"
    Text_06 = "DRAWING NUMBER"
    Text_07 = "SHEET"
    Text_08 = "SIZE"
    Text_09 = "USER"
    Text_10 = "XXX"                    ' Paper Format
    'CompanyName will be assigned to Text_11 (company name field)
    Text_11 = CompanyName
    Text_12 = "CHECKED BY:"
    Text_13 = "DATE:"
    Text_14 = "DESIGNED BY:"
    Text_15 = CATIA.SystemService.Environ("LOGNAME")
```

Figure A–16

The input box opens when its containing subroutine is executed (more generally, when the frame and title block macro is applied to a sheet background), as shown in Figure A–16.

When you enter a string into the input field and click **OK**, it is assigned to the **CompanyName** variable. The value of **CompanyName** is then called as the **Text_11** parameter value. Therefore, the company name cell of the title block table contains the value of the **CompanyName** string.

Clicking **Cancel** prevents modification of the **CompanyName** variable. Nothing is displayed in the company name cell in the title block.

Message Boxes

Message boxes are used to obtain user response, such as "Yes", "No", "Cancel", etc. by returning the value indicating which button on the dialog box was clicked. Additionally, they provide error messages and important information.

The syntax for a **MsgBox** is similar to that of an **InputBox**. The code shown in Figure A–17 produces a message box that prompts you about whether centering marks should be added to the frame during the creation of a background. Investigate the code and note its placement and documentation.

```
Sub CATFrame()
'-----------------------------------------------------------------------------
'How to create the Frame
'-----------------------------------------------------------------------------
Dim Cst_1    As Double   'Length (in cm) between 2 horinzontal marks
Dim Cst_2    As Double   'Length (in cm) between 2 vertical marks
Dim Nb_CM_H  As Integer  'Number/2 of horizontal centring marks
Dim Nb_CM_V  As Integer  'Number/2 of vertical centring marks
Dim Ruler    As Integer  'Ruler length (in cm)

CATFrameStandard Nb_CM_H, Nb_CM_V, Ruler, Cst_1, Cst_2
CATFrameBorder
'Edited by mjama, Feb19/07
'Create a message box prompting for addition of centring marks
Dim ans As VbMsgBoxResult
    ans = MsgBox("Do you want to add Centring Marks to the frame?", vbYesNo, _
          "Centering Marks")
'Begin if/else statement
'If and only if user selects YES, centring marks will be added.
If ans = vbYes Then
    MsgBox "Centring Marks will be added."
    CATFrameCentringMark Nb_CM_H, Nb_CM_V, Ruler, Cst_1, Cst_2
End If
'End modification by mjama.
CATFrameText Nb_CM_H, Nb_CM_V, Ruler, Cst_1, Cst_2
CATFrameRuler Ruler, Cst_1

End Sub
```

Indicates that the current code continues onto the next line.

Figure A–17

As noted in the code comments, centering marks are added to the frame if you select **Yes** in the Centering Marks dialog box. If you select **No**, centering marks are not added as shown in Figure A–18.

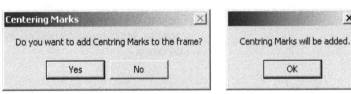

Figure A–18

The **MsgBox** function offers many different button and return data styles, as shown in the table below. The syntax for these styles is identical to the **MsgBox** syntax shown in Figure A–17, with the respective **MsgBox** style name in place of *vbYesNo*.

MsgBox Style Name	Example
vbYesNo	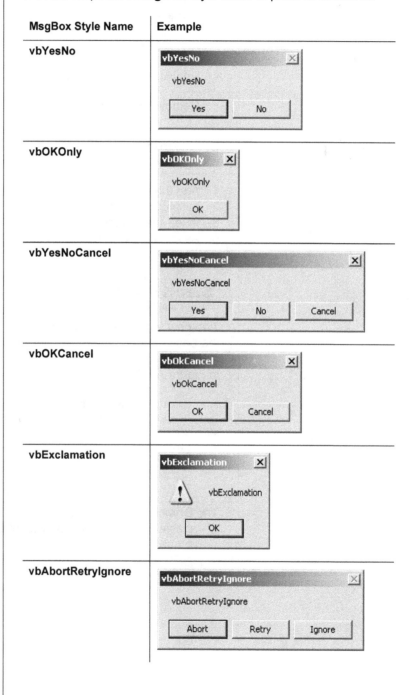
vbOKOnly	
vbYesNoCancel	
vbOKCancel	
vbExclamation	
vbAbortRetryIgnore	

A.5 Adding Graphics

Corporate logos and engineering symbols can be added automatically during background creation using a macro script. VB script can be used to perform the following tasks:

- Add a picture to the frame and title block.

- Replace/move a picture.

- Remove a picture.

General Steps

Use the following general steps to insert a graphic into the sheet background:

1. Add the required global variables.
2. Initialize the graphic object in **CATInit**.
3. Insert the graphic.
4. Associate the graphic with the sheet background.

Step 1 - Add the required global variables.

Two new variables, **DrwPictures** and **Pic**, must be created at the beginning of the **CATScript** file to enable graphic creation and manipulation. In the script header file, insert the code shown in Figure A–19.

```
Public sheetProjMethod As catSheetProjectionMethod
Public orientationSheet As catPaperOrientation
Public documentStd  As CatDrawingStandard
'USER ENTERED VARIABLES
Public DrwPictures As DrawingPictures
Public Pic As DrawingPicture
```

Figure A–19

The **DrwPictures** variable is a collection. A collection is an array of variables. In this case, an array of **DrawingPicture** objects.

Step 2 - Initialize the graphic object in CATInit.

Before the new variables can be used, they must be initialized. The **CATInit** subroutine is used to initialize variables and objects in **CATScript** macros.

To initialize the **DrwPictures** variable, insert the code into the **CATInit** subroutine, as shown in Figure A–20.

```
Function CATInit(targetSheet As CATIABase)
    '-----------------------------------------------------------
    'How to init the dialog and create main objects
    '-----------------------------------------------------------
    Set Selection = CATIA.ActiveDocument.Selection
    Set Sheet = targetSheet
    Set Sheets = Sheet.Parent
    Set ActiveDoc = Sheets.Parent
    Set Views = Sheet.Views
    Set View = Views.Item(2)          'Get the background view
    'USER INSERTED INITIALIZATION
    Set DrwPictures = View.Pictures
    Set Texts = View.Texts
    Set Fact = View.Factory2D
    Set GeomElems = View.GeometricElements
```

Figure A–20

This makes **DrwPictures** reference the collection of pictures in the active document's background view.

Step 3 - Insert the graphic.

The placement of the graphic insertion code depends on the number of pictures added.

If a single corporate logo is to be added to a cell of the title block, the code is placed in the **CATTitleBlockText** subroutine, which is responsible for filling in the title block table. If many graphics, such as symbols, are to be inserted, a new subroutine dedicated to graphic insertion should be created and named **CATInsertPictures**.

The code shown in Figure A–21 inserts and formats the size and location of a graphic. It can be added to the **CATTitleBlockText** subroutine or independently placed into a new subroutine, as shown in Figure A–21.

```
'Created by <your name>, <today's date>.
Public Sub CATInsertPictures()
  '---------------------------------------------------------------------
  'This subroutine inserts all pictures into the titleblock
  '---------------------------------------------------------------------
  Set Pic = DrwPictures.Add("[file name of graphic including path]", OH + Col(3), _
       OV + Row(3))

  With Pic
    .Name = "[Name of graphic object]"
    .Height = Row(5) - Row(3)
    .Width = .Height / .GetOriginalHeight * .GetOriginalWidth
  End With

End Sub
```

e.g., *"TitleBlock_Pic_1"*

Figure A–21

Step 4 - Associate the graphic with the sheet background.

Graphics inserted by a frame and title block macro are static. The location of a graphic does not update when the sheet format is changed and the frame and title block are resized. Furthermore, a graphic is not included in the deletion of the sheet background that inserted it. This functionality can be incorporated into a frame and title block script by associating the graphic with existing formatting subroutines.

Resizing/ Moving a Graphic

The existing **CATDrw_Resizing** subroutine, which resizes the frame and title block, calls a subroutine named **CATMoveTitleBlockText**. This subroutine replaces the title block location during frame and title block resizing. Therefore, this is a good place to insert the graphic location update code, as shown in Figure A–22.

```
'Selects then moves all picture items with name of "TitleBlock_Pic_*"
SelectAll "CATDrwSearch.DrwPicture.Name=TitleBlock_Pic_*"
Count = Selection.Count2
For ii = 1 To Count
  Set Pic = Selection.Item2(ii).Value
  Pic.X = Pic.X + Translation(0)
  Pic.Y = Pic.Y + Translation(1)
Next
```

Figure A–22

This code uses a **SelectAll** helper function that selects all of the picture names that begin with **TitleBlock_Pic_** and moves them. The search criteria, **TitleBlock_Pic_*** should be used when naming all of the inserted graphics to organize them. This organization also helps when removing them.

Deleting a Graphic

Because of the way the macro is created, if you name all of your pictures so that they begin with **TitleBlock_**, you do not have to do anything else to have them deleted. The code is shown in Figure A–23.

DeleteAll is another helper function that is used as a **Selection** tool to find, select, and delete all objects that fall under a certain criteria.

```
End Sub

Sub CATDrw_Deletion(targetSheet As CATIABase)
'-------------------------------------------------------------
'How to delete the FTB
'-------------------------------------------------------------
If Not CATInit(targetSheet) Then Exit Sub
If CATCheckRef(0) Then Exit Sub
DeleteAll "..Name=Frame_*"
DeleteAll "..Name=TitleBlock_*"
DeleteAll "..Name=RevisionBlock_*"
DeleteAll "..Name=Reference_*"
CATExit targetSheet
End Sub
```

Figure A–23

Practice A1

Modifying Macros

Practice Objectives

- Modify and export a sample macro file.
- Customize the company name and title block table.
- Obtain user input.
- Add a graphic.

Task 1 - Create a new drawing.

1. Create a new drawing file using an **ANSI** *Standard* and a **C ANSI** *sheet size*.

2. Activate the sheet background.

Task 2 - Open a macro file in the VB Editor.

Design Considerations

Although a CATScript file can be opened and edited using a plain text editor, such as Windows Notepad, CATIA's Visual Basic Editor provides enhanced readability, navigation, and editing features (e.g., key word highlighting, auto-complete function calls, and debugging).

1. Select **Tools>Macro>Visual Basic Editor**. Alternatively, you can launch the Visual Basic Editor by pressing <Alt>+<F11>. If a VBA project is not open, the Launch VBA dialog box opens as shown in Figure A–24.

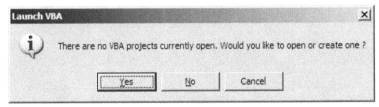

Figure A–24

2. Click **Yes** to create a new project. The Macro Library dialog box opens.

3. Click **Create new library** and accept the default name.

4. Close the Macro Libraries dialog box. The VB Editor opens.

5. To import an existing frame and title block, select **File>Import File** and navigate to the *C:\Program Files\ DassaultSystemes\B27\win_b64\VBScript\FrameTitleBlock* directory.

6. In Files of type drop-down list, select **All files** and open **Drawing_Titleblock_Sample1.CATScript**.

7. In the project browser, double-click on the **Module1** node to display the CATScript file, as shown in Figure A–25.

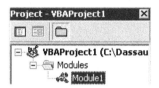

Figure A–25

Task 3 - Initialize the sample macro.

Before a macro can be applied to a drawing, all instances of the pound (#) symbol must be removed from the file.

1. Select **Edit>Replace**.

2. In the *Find What* field, enter the pound (#) symbol. Leave the *Replace With* field blank, as shown in Figure A–26.

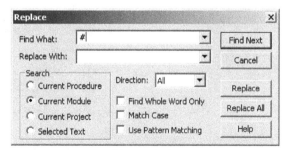

Figure A–26

3. Click **Replace All** and complete the replace feature.

4. Go to the beginning of the CATScript file. Add modification comments to the existing file documentation, as shown in Figure A–27.

```
' ***********************************************************************
' Purpose:        To draw a Frame and TitleBlock
'
' Assumptions:    A Drafting document should be active
'
' Author:         GDG\DU\PYW
' Modified by:    <your name>
' Date Modified   <today's date>
' Languages:      VBScript
' Version:        V5R20
' Reg. Settings: English (United States)
' ***********************************************************************
```

Figure A–27

Task 4 - Modify the default title block table format.

1. Activate the **CATCreateTitleBlockFrame** subroutine by selecting it in the Procedure Browser drop-down list, located at the top right of the VB Editor window, as shown in Figure A–28.

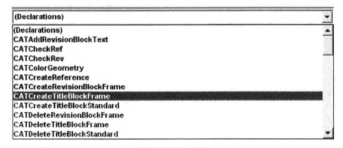

Figure A–28

2. Examine the **CATCreateTitleBlockFrame** subroutine. You will delete the line separating the sheet size and standard icons, as shown in Figure A–29.

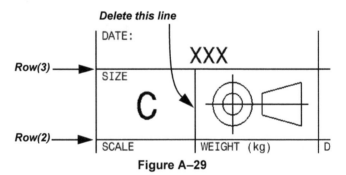

Figure A–29

3. Locate the code for **TitleBlock_Line_Column_1**, as shown in Figure A–30.

```
CreateLine GetOH() + Col(2), GetOV() + Row(1), GetOH() + Col(2), (GetOV() + Row(3)) "TitleBlock_Line_Column_1"
CreateLine GetOH() + Col(3), GetOV() + Row(1), GetOH() + Col(3), GetOV() + Row(3), "TitleBlock_Line_Column_2"
CreateLine GetOH() + Col(4), GetOV() + Row(1), GetOH() + Col(4), GetOV() + Row(2), "TitleBlock_Line_Column_3"
CreateLine GetOH() + Col(5), GetOV(), GetOH() + Col(5), GetOV() + Row(5), "TitleBlock_Line_Column_4"
CreateLine GetOH() + Col(6), GetOV(), GetOH() + Col(6), GetOV() + Row(5), "TitleBlock_Line_Column_5"
```

Figure A–30

4. Modify the *Row(3) parameter* to **Row(2)**. The boundary line for this column will now be drawn from the vertical origin up to the second row, rather than to the third.

Task 5 - Modify the MacroID and company name.

<Ctrl> + <F> can be used to find the parameter.

1. In the Procedure Browser drop-down list, select **GetMacroID** to activate the function header.

2. Locate the **GetMacroID** parameter and modify its value from *Drawing_Titleblock_Sample1* to **Drawing_Titleblock_RAND**, as shown in Figure A–31.

```
Function GetMacroID() As String
   GetMacroID = "Drawing_Titleblock_RAND"
End Function
```

Figure A–31

3. Activate the **CATTitleBlockText** subroutine.

4. Locate the **Text_11** parameter and modify its value from *DASSAULT SYSTEMES* to **RAND WORLDWIDE**, as shown in Figure A–32.

```
Text_10 = "XXX"
Text_11 = "RAND WORLDWIDE"
Text_12 = "CHECKED BY:"
```

Figure A–32

Task 6 - Export and test the macro.

Design Considerations

As with any programming project, modifications to macro script files should be saved and tested frequently. This practice simplifies the identification and resolution of bugs, which can be overwhelming if permitted to stack up.

1. In the project browser, right-click on **Module1** and select **Export File**.

2. Name the file **Drawing_Titleblock_RAND.CATScript** and save it in the *FrameTitleBlock* directory. Verify that the **Save as type** option in the Export File dialog box is set to **All Files**.

3. Switch to the CATIA Drafting workbench, and ensure the sheet background is active.

4. Select **Insert>Drawing>Frame and Title Block**.

A preview will not display in the Insert Frame and Title Block dialog box until a bitmap image is placed in the macro directory.

5. In the Style of Titleblock drop-down list, select **Drawing_Titleblock_RAND** as shown in Figure A–33. If options do not display in the *Action* field in the Insert Frame and Title Block dialog box, check the script file for syntax errors.

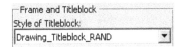

Figure A–33

Design Considerations

Common syntax errors include missing line continuation indicators (underscore), missing documentation indicators (quotation mark), and missing quotation marks surrounding string parameters (e.g., the **MacroID** value).

6. Click **Apply**. The title block displays as shown in Figure A–34.

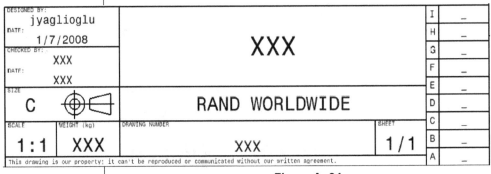

Figure A–34

7. To remove the frame and title block from the sheet background, select **Deletion** and click **Apply**.

8. Close the Manage frame and title block dialog box.

Task 7 - Obtain user input.

1. Activate the **CATFrame** subroutine in VB Editor.

2. Examine and enter the code shown in Figure A–35

```
CATFrameStandard Nb_CM_H, Nb_CM_V, Ruler, Cst_1, Cst_2
CATFrameBorder
'Modified by <your name>, <today's date>
'Create a message box prompting for centering marks
Dim ans As VbMsgBoxResult
  ans = MsgBox("Do you want to add Centering Marks to the frame?", vbYesNo, _
      "Centering Marks")
'Begin if/else statement
'If and only if the user selects YES, centering marks will be added.
If ans = vbYes Then
  MsgBox "Centering Marks will be added."
  CATFrameCentringMark Nb_CM_H, Nb_CM_V, Ruler, Cst_1, Cst_2
End If
'End modification
CATFrameText Nb_CM_H, Nb_CM_V, Ruler, Cst_1, Cst_2
CATFrameRuler Ruler, Cst 1
```

Indicates that the current code continues onto the next line.

Figure A–35

3. Export and test the macro.

Task 8 - Insert a graphic.

1. In the Procedure Browser drop-down list, select **(Declarations)** to activate the script header.

2. Enter the code shown in Figure A–36 below the existing Public variable declarations.

```
Public ActiveDoc      As Document
'USER ENTERED VARIABLES
Public DrwPictures As DrawingPictures
Public Pic As DrawingPicture
```

Figure A–36

3. Activate the **CATInit** subroutine. To initialize the **DrwPictures** object, insert the code shown in Figure A–37.

```
Set Views = Sheet.Views
Set View = Views.Item(2)        'Get the background view
Set DrwPictures = View.Pictures
Set Texts = View.Texts
Set Fact = View.Factory2D
Set GeomElems = View.GeometricElements
```

Figure A–37

Design Considerations

When implementing a procedure into a script, such as the automatic insertion and formatting of graphics, use the **Add Procedure** tool to simplify the subroutine creation process and ensure correct syntax.

4. Select **Insert>Procedure...** Enter **CATInsertPictures** as the name of the new procedure and accept all of the default options, as shown in Figure A–38.

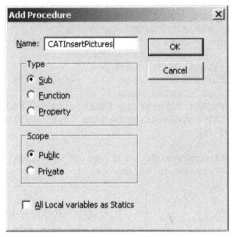

Figure A–38

5. Activate the newly created **CATInsertPictures** subroutine. Enter the code shown in Figure A–39 as the body of the subroutine.

If the location of the file is different from the one shown in Figure A–39, change the path to point to the location of the file.

```
'Created by <your name>, <today's date>
Public Sub CATInsertPictures()
'--------------------------------------------------------------------------------------
'This subroutine inserts all pictures into the titleblock
'--------------------------------------------------------------------------------------


Set Pic = DrwPictures.Add("C:\Generative Drafting Exercise Files\RAND_Worldwide.bmp",
          GetOH() + Col(3), GetOV() + Row(3))

With Pic
.Name = "TitleBlock_Pic_RAND"
.Height = Row(5) - Row(3)
.Width = .Height / .GetOriginalHeight * .GetOriginalWidth
End With
```

Indicates that the current code continues onto the next line.

Figure A–39

6. For this subroutine to be executed when the sheet background is being applied to the sheet, it must be called by a main subroutine. Enter the code shown in Figure A–40 into the **CATDrw_Creation** subroutine, after **CATTitleBlock**.

```
CATCreateReference              'To place on the drawing a reference point
CATFrame        'To draw the frame
'Modified by <your name>, <today`s date>.
CATInsertPictures 'To insert company logo into title block
CATCreateTitleBlockFrame        'To draw the geometry
CATCreateTitleBlockStandard 'To draw the standard representation
CATTitleBlockText        'To fill in the title block
CATColorGeometry 'To change the geometry color
CATExit targetSheet        'To save the sketch edition
```

Figure A–40

*Select **Edit>Find** and search a sample of the code shown in Figure A–41 to locate it easily.*

7. To prevent the default cell text from overlapping the company logo, activate the **CATTitleBlockText** subroutine and comment out the code shown in Figure A–41.

```
CreateTextAF Text_13, GetOH() + Col(1) + 1, GetOV() + 0.5 * (Row(4) + Row(5)), "TitleBlock_Text_DDate", catTopLeft, 1.5
CreateTextAF "" + Date, GetOH() + Col(3) + 2.5, GetOV() + Row(4), "TitleBlock_Text_DDate_1", catBottomCenter, 3
'CreateTextAF Text_05, GetOH() + 0.5 * (Col(3) + Col(5)), GetOV() + Row(4), "TitleBlock_Text_Title_1", catMiddleCenter, 7
For ii = 1 to GetNbOfRevision()
```

Figure A–41

8. Export and test the macro file. The title block displays as shown in Figure A–42.

Figure A–42

Task 9 - (Optional) Relocate the graphics.

1. Make the required changes to the macro to have the **Resizing** relocate the graphics.

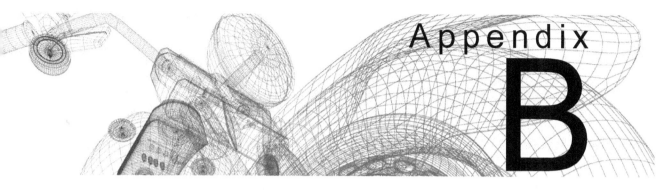

Appendix B

Extracting FT&A Views

This appendix introduces methods of displaying annotation views that have been created in the 3D model as a drawing view. A brief introduction to the Functional Tolerancing & Annotation workbench and the use of annotation sets is provided.

Learning Objectives in this Chapter

- Understand the basics of Functional Tolerancing and Annotation.
- Create a drawing.

B.1 Functional Tolerancing and Annotation

Using the Functional Tolerancing & Annotation workbench, all dimensions and annotations are stored directly in the 3D model. This eliminates the need to develop a drawing and supports a paperless design and manufacturing environment. An example of an annotated part model is shown in Figure B–1.

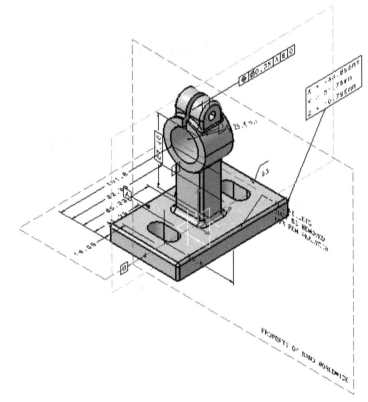

Figure B–1

Annotation Switch On/Off

Since 3D annotations add visual complexity to the model, they can be toggled on and off to simplify the display. If you receive a model that has no annotations displayed, you must toggle on the annotation set. To toggle the annotations on and off, right-click on the annotation set and select **Annotation Set Switch On/ Switch Off**. This is useful when viewing an annotated model in an assembly.

When an annotation set has been toggled off, its name displays in the specification tree, as shown in Figure B–2. However, the branch cannot be expanded and no annotations display on the model.

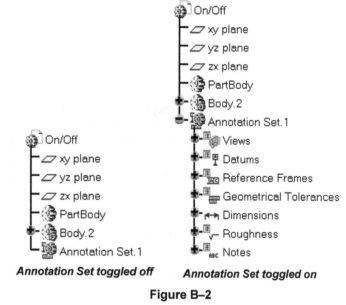

Annotation Set toggled off   **Annotation Set toggled on**

Figure B–2

B.2 Drawing Creation

Using the FT&A workbench simplifies the creation of drawing views. In the same way that drawing views can be extracted directly from the model, annotated views can also be taken directly from the model into the 2D drawing. This ability ensures that all engineering information is stored and extracted directly from the 3D model. It also enables the design and manufacturing process to minimize its reliance on the drawing for output.

General Steps

Use the following general steps to create a drawing using an annotated model:

1. Create a new drawing.
2. Extract a view from the 3D model.
3. Align the drawing views.

Step 1 - Create a new drawing.

With the annotated model open, create a new drawing. The tolerance standard and drawing standard must be the same to display an annotated view from a model.

Step 2 - Extract a view from the 3D model.

Before creating any drawing views, tile the windows (recommended) so that selections can easily be made between the model and drawing. Select **Window>Tile Horizontally**.

Click (View from 3D) in the Projections toolbar in the Drafting workbench. Expand the specification tree for the annotated model and select an annotation plane in the Views branch. The system previews the annotated view in the drawing window. Position and orient the view using the drawing compass and select anywhere in the drawing background to generate the view.

A drawing with multiple annotated views displays as shown in Figure B–3.

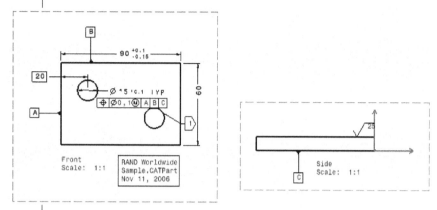

Figure B–3

Step 3 - Align the drawing views.

By default, drawing views added from the model are not aligned correctly.

How To: Align the Views

1. Right-click on the border of the drawing view that is going to move into an aligned position and select **View Positioning>Align Views Using Elements**.
2. Select an element from each view that is going to be aligned. For example, two edges are selected from the drawing views, as shown in Figure B–4.

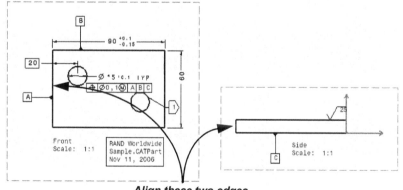

Align these two edges

Figure B–4

The aligned views display as shown in Figure B–5.

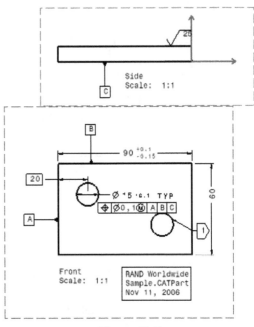

Figure B–5

Practice B1

Extracting FT&A Views

Practice Objectives

- Review an annotated model.
- Activate a view.
- Create a note.
- Create annotated drawing views from a 3D model.

In this practice, you will review a model that contains a variety of tolerances and annotations. The intent of this practice is to become familiar with a model containing 3D annotations.

After reviewing the model, you will create a new drawing file and extract annotated views from the 3D geometry. The intent is to reinforce the concept that all engineering information must be stored and extracted directly from the 3D model. This enables the design and manufacturing process to minimize its reliance on the drawing for output.

The model and completed drawing display as shown in Figure B–6.

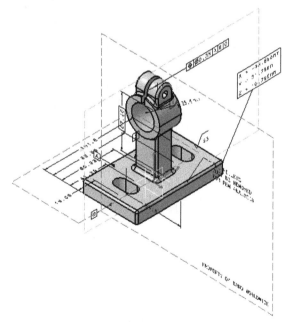

Figure B–6

Task 1 - Open a part model.

1. Open **FlangeLock.CATPart**. The model displays as shown in Figure B–7.

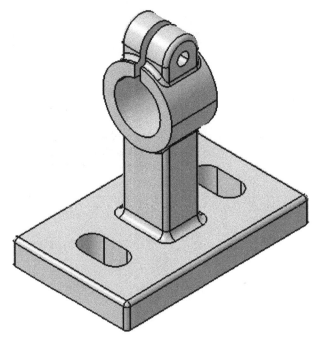

Figure B–7

Task 2 - Review the annotations.

The presence of FT&A annotations in the model can be detected by the **Annotation Set** branch in the specification tree. You can toggle the display of annotations on and off to simplify the display of the model. Currently, the display of annotations is toggled off.

1. In the specification tree, right-click on **Annotation Set.1** and select **Annotation Set Switch On/Switch Off**. Annotations display on the model, as shown in Figure B–8.

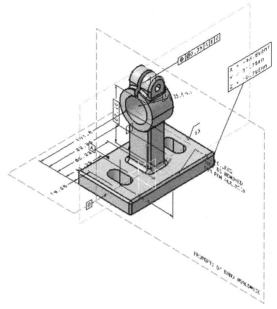

Figure B–8

Task 3 - Create a drawing.

1. Select **Start>Mechanical Design>Drafting**.

Design Considerations

The standard used to create the part and drawing must be the same for the system to display drawing views using the annotation set. Since the annotation set uses an ANSI standard, this must also be the standard used when creating the drawing.

2. Create the drawing using the following parameters:

   • *Automatic Layout:* **Empty sheet**
   • *Standard:* **ANSI**
   • *Sheet Style:* **C ANSI**

3. Select **Window>Tile Horizontally** to display the model and drawing at the same time.

4. In the Views toolbar, expand the Projections flyout and click

    (View from 3D).

5. In the specification tree, in the **Annotation Set.1>Views** branch, select **Front View.1** for the FlangeLock.CATPart window. The system displays this view and all of its associated annotations, as shown in Figure B–9.

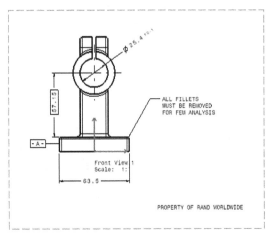

Figure B–9

6. Select anywhere in the background of the drawing window to complete the view creation.

7. Create two more views using the **View from 3D** icon, selecting **Front View.2** and **Front View.3**. Position the drawing views as shown in Figure B–10.

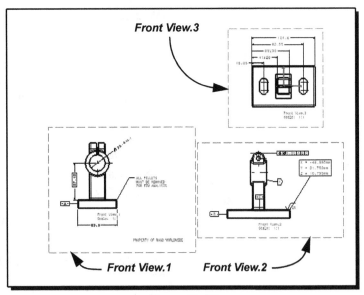

Figure B–10

You can also correct this issue by recreating the dimensions in the 3D model using geometry that is displayed in the drawing view.

Two of the dimensions in **Front View.3** display red x's. This is because their leaders are linked to geometry that is hidden in the current view. To correct this issue, you will display hidden lines in the drawing view.

8. Right-click on the border of **Front View.3** and select **Properties**.

9. In the Properties dialog box, in the *View* tab, select **Hidden Lines**, as shown in Figure B–11.

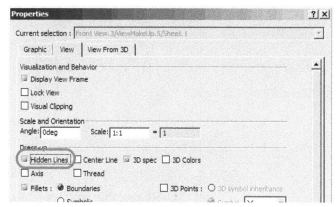

Figure B–11

10. Click **OK** to close the Properties dialog box. The view is updated and the x's are no longer displayed.

Task 4 - Align the drawing views.

1. Right-click on **Front View.3** and select **View Positioning>Align Views Using Elements**.

---

2. Select the entities from **Front View.2** and **Front View.3**, as shown in Figure B–12.

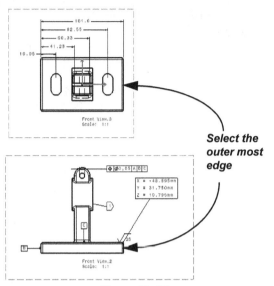

Figure B–12

3. Repeat this process to align **Front View.1** and **Front View.2**. The drawing displays as shown in Figure B–13.

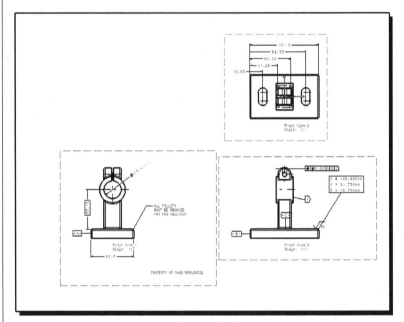

Figure B–13

4. Save the model and drawing and close all of the windows.

www.ingramcontent.com/pod-product-compliance
Lightning Source LLC
Chambersburg PA
CBHW080141060326
40689CB00018B/3809